The Plain Truth of Things

The Plain Truth of Things

A TREASURY

The Role of Values in a Complex World

COLIN GREER and HERBERT KOHL

HarperCollins*Publishers*

THE PLAIN TRUTH OF THINGS. Copyright © 1997 by Colin Greer and Herbert Kohl. All rights reserved. Printed in the United States of America. No part of this book may be used or reproduced in any manner whatsoever without written permission except in the case of brief quotations embodied in critical articles and reviews. For information address HarperCollins Publishers, Inc., 10 East 53rd Street, New York, NY 10022.

HarperCollins books may be purchased for educational, business, or sales promotional use. For information please write: Special Markets Department, HarperCollins Publishers, Inc., 10 East 53rd Street, New York, NY 10022.

FIRST EDITION

Designed by Joseph Rutt

Library of Congress Cataloging-in-Publication Data
The plain truth of things : a treasury / [compiled by] Colin Greer and Herbert
  Kohl. —1st ed.
     p.   cm.
  Includes index.
  ISBN 0-06-017481-1
    1. Values—Literary collections.   2. Literature—Collections I. Greer,
  Colin. II. Kohl, Herbert R. III. Title: Role of values in a complex world
  PN6014.P57   1997
  808.8'038—dc21   96-53352

97 98 99 00 01 ❖/RRD 10 9 8 7 6 5 4 3 2 1

To the writers whose work made this book possible
C.G.
H.K.

CONTENTS

❦ 7 To Hear the Heartbeat of Others: Compassion

Part III   If Not Now, When?: The Call to Action

Acknowledgments

In *The Plain Truth of Things*, we are, as with *A Call to Character*, indebted to each other for new learning about moral thought and creative and caring cooperation.

We are again also indebted to Leon Chazanow for his industry and good spirits in the difficult job of preparing the manuscript for the publisher. Judith Kohl did the thankless work of securing permissions, and we are grateful for her patience, persistence, and humor. Antonia Kohl scanned and copyedited the text in the book and was a wonderful source of advice and assistance throughout the entire project. Erica Kohl, Lorraine Ruddick, Wendy Ruddick, and Gabriela West also helped in various ways, including finding and checking selections, and we gratefully acknowledge their assistance. We are also grateful for many good leads and ideas from Greer and Kohl family and friends.

Our editors, Hugh van Dusen and Kate Ekrem, have been wonderfully patient and helpful all along. It has been a pleasure working with them.

And a final note about the construction of the book: All of the selections were read and agreed upon by both of us and we worked closely together on the commentary. Herbert Kohl took primary responsibility for Part I and Colin Greer was primarily responsible for Part II. We took equal responsibility in completing Part III. Once again, it has been a pleasure and an education for us to read widely and explore ideas and values as we made this book.

The Plain Truth
of Things

Come Build in the Empty House of the Stare

As adults we all struggle with moral questions. These are the questions we have to ask ourselves if we are to be morally literate, for example: "What should I do to look out for myself—and what are the limits of that?" "What's my responsibility to other people, and how much should I sacrifice for them?"

These moral dilemmas not only define how we live, but directly affect other people's lives too. The plain truth of things is that moral decisions are difficult and often involve risk and daring; they can lead to discomfort, just as they can lead to the deepest kind of comfort when you feel that you're an upright person, a person of integrity.

Sometimes these decisions involve particular dilemmas, such as whether to spend more time at home or at work, to walk past a homeless person or give them a quarter, to muster the courage to oppose someone who makes a sexist, racist, or homophobic comment or keep silent. Other times, these decisions are larger and involve environmental and social issues or issues of human rights. Still, even the larger issues demand particular decisions in concrete circumstances with specific consequences.

Moral life is a constant backdrop in our personal and social lives. Its imperatives may call us to comply with or defy cultural norms. It is in the imminent challenges of our everyday lives that our moral living takes place. Moral life is lived in the particular.

All of these decisions can call upon personal qualities such as courage, responsibility, empathy, humor, integrity, and generosity, which themselves are tested and grow through moral action. Though one can have a general set of guiding moral principles, the practical application of these principles throughout life is not served well by an overly simplistic, black-and-white approach to morality. Rather, being good and doing the right thing requires a well-developed imagination guided by love.

Turning to writers (of fiction and nonfiction) is a way for us to reflect on the moral issues we face. The human struggle to build personal and social life on a foundation of strong values is a longstanding one—and it is a perennial focus of literature.

We live in a time when moral questions are being raised with a sense of urgency. We still have far to go in achieving moral integrity as a society and as citizens in it. The tough human struggle between self-interest and human interest is forever inspired by the imaginations of artists and by our own imaginations. When our imaginations are occupied by fear and blame, the results can be devastating. When informed by a love that, whether rooted in religious or secular ideas, embraces reverence for all living things, our imaginations are the driving force of moral action.

William Butler Yeats wrote "Meditations in Time of Civil War" while reflecting on the horrors of the civil war in Ireland and the need for healing in morally uncertain times such as those we are currently experiencing:

The bees build in the crevices
Of loosening masonry, and there
The mother birds bring grubs and flies.
My wall is loosening; honey-bees,
Come build in the empty house of the stare.

We are closed in, and the key is turned
On our uncertainty; somewhere
A man is killed, or a house burned,
Yet no clear fact to be discerned:
Come build in the empty house of the stare.

A barricade of stone or of wood;
Some fourteen days of civil war;
Last night they trundled down the road
That dead young soldier in his blood:
Come build in the empty house of the stare.

We had fed the heart on fantasies,
The heart's grown brutal from the fare;
More substance in our enmities
Than in our love; O honey-bees,
Come build in the empty house of the stare.

Commenting on this poem in his Nobel Prize speech, the Irish poet Seamus Heaney says: "Yeats's work does what the necessary poetry always does, which is to touch the base of our sympathetic nature while taking in at the same time the unsympathetic reality of the world to which that nature is constantly exposed. . . . to remind us that we are hunters and gatherers of values, that our very solitudes and distresses are creditable, in so far as they too are an earnest of our veritable human being."

Today the deepest and most personal moral concerns coincide with a period of intense moral reassessment in our society. Our society is in conflict nowadays about what it expects of our young and our old, what it expects of employers and employees, how it assesses rights and responsibilities, and how it values the lives of the poor and the otherwise needy. Surely it is a "moral failing," as Bruce Springsteen says in a 1997 *New York Times* interview, when in such a wealthy country so many scramble for more while so many millions of people are without the basics necessary to have a job, to support a family, or to create a home. It is these and other morally challenging issues that the selections in this book, most of which are drawn from contemporary sources, address. Clearly, we are tearing ourselves up, blaming each other at great cost to our sense of community. And yet at the same time we feel quite uncertain how and who must take the first steps out of the quagmire of self-interest and suffering which we seem to be floundering in.

When it comes to moral decision making, many voices call on us: the voice of our own conscience and the voices of those we admire—especially those of our great artists, who bring us face to face with our highest ideals.

The Task Being to Reassemble What Has Been Scattered

In his autobiography, *The Story of My Experiments with Truth*, Mohandas Gandhi felt that the most he could say of his life was that he was steadfast in his commitment to understand truth and help make it manifest in the world. He didn't claim to have had more than a glimpse of this "Truth-Force," but he was sure that he was right in devoting his life to pursuing it. For him, moral living is not about being right, but about being awake—awake to suffering in the world and aiming to reduce it, not add to it. Hence, forgiveness was preferred to revenge, the impulse to make amends favored over willful pride, and the temptation to blame someone else for a sorrow you bring on yourself was irresponsible. In his efforts, Gandhi sought truth by engaging the world as he found it.

The search for moral truth is identified with moral relativity by some people who feel that they have certain answers to all possible moral challenges. But for most of us, there is and always will be much to understand about balancing the nature and consequences of moral action. The complexity of contemporary life does not yield itself to simplistic formulaic solutions.

In every area of life, we confront new challenges that tax both our moral reason and imagination. As we look at the dilemmas of our own time, we see all too clearly how some of the conventions of the past were not only wrong but damaging to people and the planet. Ancient traditions of wisdom have provided high standards to guide us, but we have to bring those truths into our lives through the particulars of our circumstances and the time into which we are born. The great Dervish poet Rumi believed that one of the reasons Mohammed was a great prophet and leader was because for him, "the way was always unfolding." This is especially so in America, where the voices of ancestors echo in many languages. It is in the challenges of our everyday lives that truths about moral living unfold.

Moral choices can be quiet ones or they can be momentous. The quiet choices are very often about dilemmas occasioned by the tension between selfishness and selflessness. On a grander scale, our challenge frequently is to deploy our outrage—at our own behavior, the behavior of others, or the horrific conditions of some people's lives—into new possibilities. The truth itself, as the poet Muriel Rukeyser said, resides in no one place, but has been and must be collected by imaginative and loving thought and action—"the task being to reassemble what has been scattered, the truths of outrage and the truths of possibility." By acknowledging the most venal and inhumane conditions other people endure, we may actually feel their pain and insecurity—and seek to change it.

William Faulkner put it this way, "Our tragedy today is a general and universal physical fear so long sustained by now that we can even bear it." For him the problems of the human heart in conflict were key to the understanding of tragedy and the glory of the human spirit. For him literature was the source of the inexhaustible voice of that spirit, capable of compassion, sacrifice, and endurance.

In conversation with Bill Moyers, three poets echo Faulkner as they relate their work in poetry to their lives in the world. These poets could also have been speaking about literature in general.

Sandra McPherson put it this way, "You're trying to understand what you're living through by using the tools of words and images and the beautiful inner structure of language."

For Adrienne Rich, "Poetry can bring together those parts of us which exist in dread and those which have the surviving sense of a possible happiness, collectivity, community, and a loss of isolation."

David Mura cautioned that, "If poetry gets too far towards the realm of the esthetic . . . and doesn't acknowledge the other side of existence—the history that we live in, the changes and the darkness of history—then the life goes out of poetry and it becomes escape."

We live a great deal in our imaginations. The ideas we conjure can free or imprison us. The moral truth is that how we approach these ideas and how we act because of them define who we are and what kind of society we live in.

In this anthology we draw from writers of many genres to help us and our readers as we try to engage the world morally. We've organized *The Plain Truth of Things* in three parts in order to frame the critical relationship we see between Imagination, Love, and Action; between ideas, feelings, and engagement in the formation of a moral world view and a moral life.

Part I centers on the role of the imagination in moral life. Its four sections deal with the playfulness of imaginative life, the way in which the imagination contributes to the development of the self, the role of the imagination in developing and nurturing idealism and creating visions of the good life, and finally the birth of hope through the exercise of the imagination.

Part II is focused on the many ways in which love underpins moral life. Its four sections present literature that deals with integrity, empathy, compassion, and spirituality.

Part III emphasizes the importance of action in the moral realm and focuses on key qualities that support active moral commitments: courage, responsibility, respect, and justice.

PART I

The Eight Corners of the Universe

Imagination, Creativity, and Identity

Beginning

Eyes closed, he hears an inner music; he is lost in thoughts and
    questions—
His spirit rides to the eight corners of the universe, his mind a
    thousand miles away.
And then the inner voice grows clearer as objects become defined.
And he pours forth the essence of words, savoring their sweetness.
He drifts in a heavenly lake, he dives to the depths of seas.
And he brings up living words like fishes hooked in their gills,
    leaping from the deep;
And beauty is brought down like a bird on an arrowstring shot from
    passing clouds.
He gathers his words & images from those unused by previous
    generations; his music comes from melodies unplayed for a
    thousand years or more.
The morning blossoms bloom; soon the night buds will unfold.
He sees past and present commingle; he sees the whole Four Seas in
    the single blink of an eye.

              —Lu Chi, *Wen Fu, The Art of Writing*

    Imagination is that special human faculty that makes it possible for us
to entertain the idea that things might be different than they are in our
experience. It works in personal and modest ways in artistic, spiritual, and
moral dimensions. It can conceive of eternal life, the ideal of a good and just
society, winged horses, home runs hit a thousand miles, and winning lottery
tickets. Imagination can also lead to the creation of larger social visions of
utopia or hell and enables people to conceive of themselves as kinder and
better than they are in their everyday lives. It is a major component in the
development of moral identity as it provides tools for the construction of a
moral stance toward the world.

This love poem by Ghada Al-Samman provides, beginning with the title itself, example upon delightful example of the reach and play of the imagination:

Imprisonment of a Question Mark

O stranger,
where do the songs go
after we hear them?

and after we live them,
where are the words of love?

Where is the flame of the candle
after the candle melts?

And the caresses
after your hand lifts?

Where does the lightning go
after it is extinguished?
and the storms of the forests when they abate?
and the meteors when they burn out?

Tell me where:
I shall await you there, my love.

Imagination makes it possible for us to live beyond ourselves. It opens up the possibility that we might become better than we currently are and live in new and more challenging ways. It is the creative force that makes it possible for any of us, no matter what our circumstances, to draw images, thoughts, and dreams from "the eight corners of the universe," take them into ourselves, and remake them. The critic George Steiner even speculates that "hypotheticals, 'imaginaries,' conditionals, *the syntax of counter-factuality and contingency* may well be the generative centers of human speech." Language is the main instrument of man's refusal to accept the world as it is. Ours is the ability, the need, to gainsay or un-say the world, to image and speak it otherwise."

Even in its simplest manifestations, the act of imagination is creative, which led the philosopher C. S. Peirce to comment, "Mere imagination would be mere trifling; only no imagination is *mere*." Children's play and adult daydreams equally transport us into imaginative worlds and enlarge our sense of the possible. It is perhaps even possible to claim that the free play of the imagination is what fundamentally distinguishes people from even the most sophisticated computers imaginable. They do not dream of being other than they are.

However, the imagination per se does not have a moral bias. It has led to the mad fantasies of the Marquis de Sade and the dreams of racial purification that were at the base of the Holocaust, as well as to dreams of democracy and eternal love. As the poet Wallace Stevens (in *The Necessary Angel: Essays on Reality and the Imagination*) has commented,

> It does not seem possible to say of the imagination that it has a certain single characteristic which of itself gives it a certain single value as, for example, good or evil. To say such a thing would be the same thing as to say that the reason is good or evil or, for that matter, that human nature is good or evil.

Though morally neutral, the imagination is a major force in the development of character, which extends from our earliest moral experiences in childhood through the rest of our lives. It is constantly called upon as people dream of the kind of human being they want to be and the kind of world in which they want to live. It can be impoverished through excessive exposure to a narrow range of stories and models of the sort most television presents, and it can be enriched through broad acquaintance with stories, tales, and biographies from diverse voices. Yet even extreme efforts to limit the range of the imagination and control the development of character are frequently resisted. The imagination sustains hope and a sense of decency under pressure. The central character in John Guare's *Six Degrees of Separation* describes these nurturing and transforming aspects of imagination.

> The imagination. That's our out. Our imagination teaches us our limits and then how to grow beyond those limits. The imagination says,

"Listen to me. I am your darkest voice. I am your 4 A.M. voice. I am the voice that wakes you up and says, 'This is what I'm afraid of. Do not listen to me at your peril.' The imagination is the noon voice that sees clearly and says, 'Yes, this is what I want for my life.' It's there to sort out your nightmare, to show you the exits from the maze of your nightmare, to transform the nightmare into dreams to become your bedrock. . . . The imagination is not our escape. On the contrary, the imagination is the place we are all trying to get to."

This is echoed by Wallace Stevens when he describes the imagination as a "necessary angel" and asks: "Of what value is anything to the solitary and those that live in misery and terror, except the imagination?"

The imagination is not merely of succor to individuals. It is what provides a vision of community and leads to the compassionate binding of people to each other. The social imagination can be seen as the center of the development of coherent and nurturing community. This vision, expressed by the educator and philosopher Maxine Greene, *in Releasing the Imagination*, can be a driving force in developing and nurturing the idealism that is needed to sustain efforts to construct a working democracy:

Again, it may be the recovery of imagination that lessens the social paralysis we see around us and restores the sense that something can be done in the name of what is decent and humane. I am reaching toward an idea of imagination that brings an ethical concern to the fore, a concern that, again, has to do with the community that ought to be in the making and the values that give it color and significance. My attention turns back to the importance of wide-awakeness, of awareness of what it is to be in the world. I am moved to recall the existential experience shared by so many and the associated longing to overcome somnolence and apathy in order to choose, to reach beyond.

The poetry, literature, and essays in this part of *The Plain Truth of Things* will explore the roles that social and moral imagination play in the development of character. It is divided into four sections that are intended to illustrate the multiple roles that imagination can play. Its first section will concentrate on the free play of the imagination that is manifested in stories, tales, jokes, and dreams. This play, which provides material for the exploration of possible lives, is essential to the growth of personality and the development of the kind of flexibility needed to deal with complex moral and social challenges.

The second section will then consider how people imagine the selves they would like to become and develop and sustain their characters through their most intimate and sensitive imaginings.

The third section examines the development of idealism and social and moral vision through the imagination. This will lead to the fourth section, on hope and its relationship to the power of imagining.

I

Taste and See:
The Free Play of
the Imagination

PLAYFULNESS

In *Life on the Mississippi*, Mark Twain says:

When I'm playful I use the meridians of longitude and the parallels of latitude for a seine, and drag the Atlantic Ocean for whales. I scratch my head with lightning and purr myself to sleep with thunder.

In play, we can pretend to be the person we most wish to be at one moment and the person we fear the most at another moment. We can become, for that moment, anyone or anything. We can reach beyond ourselves and let our wildest imaginations have center stage for a brief time. Play can be fun or deadly serious. Often the boundaries are blurred and reality can destroy the comfort zone that play provides for the players. Children play war games, but a war game can turn into a fight with the wrong gesture or an accidental collision. Adults are no different. A friendly game of chess can turn into a hostile battle of wills, and a simple card game can lead to unanticipated violence.

We all play with being wicked as well as good, and play is a way of testing ourselves against our dreams. It is a way of practicing life. For some people, however, the free space to play without pressure is a privilege. Their lives are hedged in by violence and there is no time-out from "real life." Yet even they often steal time for play for its own sake as a way of affirming their right to an imaginative life that affirms the dignity of their existence.

A safe place for moral exploration, fantasy play, and the development of a community of people who can play with you all contribute to the formation and further development of character that is neither rigid nor righteous, but understanding of the complexity of maintaining a consistent decency throughout the trials of actual living.

Imaginative moral play is time set aside to experiment with values and masks. But beyond the time set aside to actually play, there is a play sensibility, a sense that with good humor and in the spirit of play one can go about solving serious issues of everyday life without needing to be brutal or aggressive. Moreover, the play sensibility makes it possible to continually renew oneself, to try new ways of thinking, moving, and relating to people. This is the kind of welcome that Denise Levertov calls us to in "Taste and See," which is also an invitation to dip into the selections in this part of the anthology.

> The world is
> not with us enough
> **O taste and see**
>
> the subway Bible poster said,
> meaning **the Lord**, meaning
> if anything all that lives
> to the imagination's tongue,
>
> grief, mercy, language,
> tangerine, weather, to
> breathe them, bite,
> savor, chew, swallow, transform
>
> into our flesh our
> deaths, crossing the street, plum, quince,
> living in the orchard and being

hungry, and plucking
the fruit

Selections

The first selections characterize the nature of play and play communities.
They also help connect the play of childhood with the continuing development of the imagination as an adult.

❦ JOHANN HUIZINGA, *Homo Ludens*

Here, then, we have the first main characteristic of play; that it is free,
is in fact freedom. A second characteristic is that play is not "ordinary"
or "real" life. It is rather a stepping out of "real" life into a temporary
sphere of activity with a disposition all of its own. Nevertheless, the
consciousness of play being "only pretense" does not by any means prevent it from proceeding with the utmost seriousness, with an absorp-
tion, a devotion that passes into rapture.

❦ STEPHEN NACHMANOVITCH, *Childhood's End*

At the age of four, a child I knew drew extraordinarily vibrant,
imaginative trees. Crayon, chalk, colored pens, and Silly Putty were
all useful. These trees were remarkable in how clearly they showed
the bulbous lobes and branchy veins of individual leaves in a kind of
cubist, all-the-way-around view that would have delighted Picasso.
Meticulous observation of real trees, and a certain daring that is characteristic of four-year-olds, combined to produce these striking art-
works.

By the age of six, this child had gone through a year of first grade
and had begun drawing lollipop trees just like the other kids. Lollipop
trees consist of a single blob of green, representing the general mass of

leaves with details obliterated, stuck up on top of a brown stick, representing the tree trunk. Not the sort of place real frogs would live.

Another child, age eight, complained of the day her third-grade teacher pretended that negative numbers don't exist. While the class was doing subtraction tables, a boy asked, "What's 3 take away 5?" and the teacher insisted that there is no such thing. The girl objected, "But everyone knows it's minus 2!" The schoolteacher said, "This is the third grade and you're not supposed to know about those things!"

I later asked this girl, "What does a minus number mean to you?" She said without hesitating, "It's like looking at your reflection in a pool of water. It goes as far down as you go up." This is original mind in action, the purest form of Zen.

This clear, deep voice is latent in us from earliest childhood, but it is latent only. The adventures, difficulties, and even suffering inherent in growing up can serve to develop or reduce our original voice, but more often they bury it. It may be developed or undeveloped, excited or inhibited, by the way we are raised and trained and treated in life. Because most of our institutions are built on the Lockean fantasy that the newborn person is a *tabula rasa* on which knowledge is built up like a pyramid, we tend to erase our children's innate from-the-top-down knowledge and try to fill them instead with simplistic bottoms-up knowledge. "As up I grew," wrote e. e. cummings, "down I forgot."

❧ C. G. JUNG, *Psychological Types*

Every good idea and all creative work are the offspring of the imagination, and have their source in what one is pleased to call infantile fantasy. Not the artist alone, but every creative individual whatsoever owes all that is greatest in his life to fantasy. The dynamic principle of fantasy is *play*, a characteristic also of the child, and as such it appears inconsistent with the principle of serious work. But without this playing with fantasy no creative work has ever yet come to birth. The debt we owe to the play of imagination is incalculable. It is therefore short-sighted to treat fantasy, on account of its risky or unacceptable nature, as a thing of little worth. It must not be forgotten that it is just in the imagination that a man's highest value may lie. I say "may" advisedly, because on the other hand fantasies are also valueless, since in the form of raw material they possess no realizable worth. In order to unearth the treasures they contain they must be developed a stage further. But this development is not achieved by a simple analysis of the fantasy material; a synthesis is also needed by means of a constructive method.

❦ BERNARD DE KOVEN, *The Well-Played Game*

By empowering each other to create new conventions, by establishing guidelines, we assure each other of a common intention and mutual respect for the willingness to play, for the need for safety and trust. We need to recognize that these guidelines are fragile and fictitious, despite all the legislation we went through to be certain they were mutually held. The only real assurance we have lies within the community of people with whom we are playing.

The need for this kind of community holds true whether we are players or spectators. As a spectator, I want to be able to scream for my team. If the spectator sitting next to me wants to scream for her team, and if she insists that I also scream for her team, the likelihood is that we will wind up screaming at each other. We have to spend more of our time resisting each other than enjoying the game. I want the game to be important. She wants the game to be important. But we both lose our opportunity to relish this importance when the game becomes more important to us than we are to each other.

When mother and child play together, regardless of what they are playing, they are establishing a play community in which both people operate under the convention that they take precedence over the game. When the child cries, the mother stops playing.

When children play together, in the street or the back lot, they too establish a play community. When someone gets hurt, the game stops.

When there's a little kid around, you watch out for him, you play softer when you're near him, you give the kid a break. At all times there is an acceptance of a shared responsibility for the safety of those with whom you play.

Though this is a difficult thing to maintain, I can't believe that it is any more difficult than maintaining any other convention. The point is that somehow, in the process of becoming adult, in the attempt to establish familiarity, we tend to separate the game from the play community. We develop an official body of rules so that, even though we might not be familiar with the people we're playing with, we'll all be familiar with the game. Baseball is always baseball, no matter with whom we are playing. In the enlargement of our community to embrace the national community we abandon some of the conventions that provide us with access to play. Our goal becomes not a well-played game but a game that we or our team can win.

What's so strange about this whole shift is that the search for the well-played game never stops. What stops is our awareness of how to find it—our awareness that in fact it resides not only in the game but also in the people playing.

The conventions that we tend to enforce with each other are those which are more directly related to the maintenance of a particular game than they are to the establishment of a community. Winning takes precedence over establishing trust. Winning takes precedence over providing for the safety of the players. Winning even takes precedence over the willingness to play.

The play community becomes a game community, devoted to the pursuit of a particular game, measured in terms of our success or failure as players of that game.

Thus, we meet for the sake of the game. We go bowling or play bridge. We enter leagues and evaluate our community in terms of how successful it is in prevailing over others. As a game community, we have abandoned any authority to determine whether or not the game we are playing is, in fact, the game we can play well together. That decision depends on who wins.

The nature of a play community is such that it embraces the players more than it directs us toward any particular game. Thus, it matters less to us what game we are playing, and more to us that we are willing to play together.

In fact, as our play community develops, there are particular times when we seek out games with fewer and fewer rules. We have so affirmed our ability to play well together, to be safe with each other, that rules begin to get in the way of our freedom together.

As we begin to sense our power to create our own conventions, as we discover that the authority for determining whether or not a particular game is suitable resides not in the game but in the play community, we are willing, even, to change the very conventions that unite us.

Because we have played well together, because we have played so many different kinds of games together, we have become familiar enough with each other to allow our trust to reside not in any particular agreement but in the community itself.

We can explore other conventions. We can make it our goal to have fun. Only fun. Just fun. We can abandon even the agreement to pursue the well-played game together. The trust we have established with each other is so profound that we need no longer to aim at anything.

And so we continue, pursuing this convention of having fun together, until any attempt to decide ahead of time what game we're going to play, even an attempt to decide what rules we are going to play by, becomes too much of a hassle—unnecessary, in fact contrary to our purpose, in fact impossible.

And then, maybe, we find ourselves playing follow the leader into the woods, or we find ourselves climbing trees and skipping rocks. And when everybody's running amuck so beautifully, so caringly, who's going to ask for rules?

We are having fun. We are caring. We are safe with each other. This is what we want. We are playing well together, even though we can't name what game we're playing. We are having a good time. We trust each other. There's no doubt at all about our willingness to play. So there's nothing, anymore, that needs to be established. We are who we want to be, how we want to be, where, here, now.

And then, suddenly, we find that we have done this enough. We aren't tired of having fun. We're tired of having fun this way. We aren't tired of each other. We want to change the way we're playing together. Maybe we want to do something harder. Maybe we need some challenge.

Nobody knows how this happened—this change—but somehow all this delicious ease we had with each other has become too easy, too familiar. Now we want to have fun *doing* something—have fun doing something else, maybe. Have fun working even. Building. Gardening. Making a meal. Eating.

Until even having fun isn't enough and we establish other aesthetics. We want to feel beautiful together, to experience grace together, to express harmony.

Until that too isn't enough, and all that we want to do is find another game.

But, whatever game it is that we finally find together, whatever game we are able to play well together, we are somehow assured, even then, that we will be safe in it.

Let us hypothesize that all we are trying to do at this moment is to have a good time. We're not looking to prove anything to anyone. We simply want to play something together that will be good for all of us.

I feel like playing a game of checkers. I'm tired of running around. I want to do something mostly in my mind, and I'd like to be doing it with you.

You, on the other hand, want to swing from the tree rope. You don't want to get into anything competitive. You aren't particularly interested in thinking at all. And somebody else wants to play tug-of-war.

Now the fact is that, if we really wanted to play together, we could find a game if we needed one. That, also, is most amazing. Somewhere there's a game we could all play, each of us feeling the way he's feeling, each doing what he wants to be doing. We might have to give up the things we're using. We might have to change a few rules. We might even have to make up a whole new game. Maybe we'd wind up with our tug-of-war friend holding on to a rope that you were swinging on while I counted the swings. Maybe a card game. Who knows?

When we're looking for a well-played game, we're not as concerned with the game we wind up playing as we are with having the opportunity to play it well together.

When we look often enough, with enough people, in enough different play communities, we find eventually that it really doesn't even matter whether we're being physical or mental, competitive or cooperative. Those are just games.

We'll even find that the kind of activities we get involved in don't matter that much. You might be tired, you might be feeling thoughtful, but you also might really delight in a heavy game of soccer. Because your basis for trust and safety has broadened to such an extent that it resides not in any particular game and not even in any particular play community, you're willing to play anything. Even if you start off feeling tired or lonely or bored. It doesn't matter, because you're willing to play, and you know that any game will do, that any game will get you there. You know that because you know the energy resides not in the game but in playing with people.

So it comes back to your basic willingness. But now it seems that willingness generates more willingness—that what at first we weren't willing to do we find ourselves seeking out. We become willing to do something that we didn't even feel like doing. We even suspend judgment about whether or not we'll like doing something until the time that we find ourselves doing it. We even suspend our fear and prejudice about the people we're playing with. And all this started when we began looking for a game we could play well together. All this evolved when we realized that the people we are playing with are as important as the game we are playing with them—easily as important.

We have already begun our play community. We have played with each other, the two of us, and have found a way of playing well together. We have established the intention. By now we feel safe with each other—at least while we're volleying.

We are not yet willing to play *anything*. We have not as yet established a familiarity with each other deep enough to transcend the game we have found. We have found our union within a game, and we are not yet willing to risk it. We've played well, we just haven't played enough.

The following selections connect play to the creative and artistic imagination. Stanley Kunitz's poem is about magical transformations of play; Joan Miró's essay illustrates the complex and often contentious interaction between character and artistic expression. The selection from Gerald Vizenor's autobiography shows the sometimes desperately important connection between play, the imagination, and moral and personal coherence.

❧ STANLEY KUNITZ, *Chariot*

In this image of my friend's studio,
where curiosity runs the shop, and you
can almost smell the nostalgic dust
settling on the junk of lost mythologies,
the artist himself stays out of view.
Yet anyone could guess
this is the magician's place
from his collection of conical hats
and the sprawled puppets on a shelf,
the broken as well as the whole,
that have grown to resemble him,
or the other way round.
Butterflies, gameboards, and bells,
strewn jacks and alphabet blocks,
spindles, old music scores—
the litter spreads from wall to wall.
If you could dig to the bottom,
you might expect to find
a child's plush heart,
a shining agate eye.
Here everything waits to be renewed.
That horse-age wagon wheel
propped in the corner
against an empty picture-frame,
even in its state of disrepair,
minus three spokes,

looks poised for flight.
Tomorrow, maybe, at the crack of a whip
a flock of glittering birds will perch
on its rim, a burnished stranger
wearing an enigmatic mask
will mount its hub
and the great battered wheel
will start to spin.

❧ Joan Miró, *I Work Like a Gardener*

. . . I begin my paintings because something jolts me away from reality. This shock can be caused by a little thread that comes loose from the canvas, a drop of water that falls, the fingerprint my thumb leaves on the shiny surface of this table.

In any case, I need a point of departure, whether it's a fleck of dust or a burst of light. This form gives birth to a series of things, one thing leading to another.

A piece of thread, therefore, can unleash a world. I invent a world from a supposedly dead thing. And when I give it a title, it becomes even more alive.

I find my titles in the process of working, as one thing leads to another on my canvas. When I have found the title, I live in its atmosphere. The title then becomes completely real for me, in the same way that a model, a reclining woman for example, can become real for another painter. For me, the title is a very precise reality.

I work for a long time on the same painting, sometimes years. But during this period there are moments, sometimes very long moments, when I don't work on it at all.

What is important for me is that the point of departure be perceptible, the shock that provoked the painting in the first place.

If a painting that I am working on stays in my studio for years, it doesn't bother me. On the contrary, when I am surrounded by paintings whose point of departure is lively enough to produce a series of rhymes, a new life, new living things, I am happy. . . .

I think of my studio as a vegetable garden. Here, there are arti-
chokes. Over there, potatoes. The leaves have to be cut so the vegetables can grow. At a certain moment, you must prune.

I work like a gardener or a wine grower. Everything takes time. My
vocabulary of forms, for example, did not come to me all at once. It for-
mulated itself almost in spite of me.

Things follow their natural course. They grow, they ripen. You
have to graft. You have to water, as you do for lettuce. Things ripen in
my mind. In addition, I always work on a great many things at once.
And even in different areas: painting, etching, lithography, sculpture,
ceramics.

The medium and the instrument I am using dictate my technique,
which is a way of giving life to a thing.

If I attack a piece of wood with a gouge, that puts me in a certain
frame of mind. If I attack a lithographer's stone with a brush, or a copper plate with an etching needle, that puts me in another frame of
mind. The encounter between the instrument and the material pro-
duces a shock, and this is a live thing, something that I think will have
an effect on the viewer.

A burnished sheet of copper puts me in a state quite different from
the one I am in when I am looking at a piece of dull-finished wood.
Shiny and dull surfaces inspire me to create different forms.

The brightness of ceramics appeals to me: it seems to produce
sparks. And then there is the struggle with the elements—clay and fire.
As I said before, I am a fighter. You have to know how to control fire
when you do ceramics.

And it's unpredictable! That, too, is very seductive. Even when you
use the same formula, the same kiln temperature, you do not get the
same result. Unpredictability causes a shock, and that is something that
appeals to me now.

Etching also has its unpredictable aspects. The more unpredictable
it is, the more it interests me.

In my painting, when there is a small line with a large shape at the end of it—that's unpredictable, too. I am the first to be surprised.

In a painting, you should be able to discover new things each time you look at it. But you can look at a painting for a whole week and then never think about it again. You can also look at a painting for a second and think about it for the rest of your life. For me, a painting must give off sparks. It must dazzle like the beauty of a woman or a poem. It must radiate like the flints that shepherds in the Pyrenees use for lighting their pipes.

Even more important than the painting itself is what it gives off, what it projects. It doesn't matter if the painting is destroyed. Art can die, but what counts are the seeds it has spread over the earth. . . .

. . . All this business about nations is a question of bureaucracy. The important thing is not to be a bureaucrat, but to be a man. By truly becoming a man, you become capable of touching all men, an African as well as a Chinese, a person from the South as well as from the North.

But truly becoming a man means getting away from your false self. In my case, it means no longer being Miró, that is to say, a Spanish painter belonging to a society that is limited by frontiers and social and bureaucratic conventions.

In other words, you must move toward anonymity.

Anonymity has always reigned during the great periods of history. And today the need for it is greater than ever.

But, at the same time, there is a need for the absolutely individualistic gesture, something completely anarchic from the social point of view.

Why? Because a profoundly individualistic gesture is anonymous. By being anonymous, it can attain universality, I am convinced of it. The more local a thing, the more universal it is.

This accounts for the importance of folk art: there is a great unity between the whistles made in Majorca and certain Greek artifacts.

Mural painting interests me because it requires anonymity, because it reaches the masses directly and because it plays a role in architecture.

Truly successful architecture, such as the town of Ibiza, is anonymous.

This anonymity does not thwart what is human. On the contrary. In Ibiza, an architect friend showed me the white paint on the walls surrounding the windows. These areas, which formed a frame around each window, had been painted from the inside of the house by someone leaning out the window and painting the wall as far as his outstretched arm and brush could reach.

That gave a human scale to these white frames.

A house painter could not have done that. He would not have painted from the inside but from the outside, after building a scaffold. Everything would have been ruined.

This taste for anonymity leads to collective work. That is why doing ceramics with Artigas interests me so much. I do my prints with a team of master printers and assistants. They give me ideas, and I have complete confidence in them, but all this is impossible if you want to be a star.

By working in a group this way, I am not creating my own little country, or, if I am, it is a universal country.

Anonymous work must be both collective and very personal. Everyone must do what he wants; it should be as natural as breathing. But you can't be overly conscious about it or want to put your signature on your breathing.

❧ GERALD VIZENOR, *Imagining Landscapes*

Survival is imagination, a verbal noun, a wild transitive word in my mixed blood autobiographies; genealogies, the measured lines in our time, and place, are never the same in personal memories. Remembrance is a natural current that beats and breaks with the spring tides; the curious imagine a sensual undine on the wash, as the nasturtiums dress the barbed wire fences down to the wild sea.

My memories and interior landscapes are untamed. The back stoop of that tavern where I fed the squirrels while my grandfather drank in the dark, breaks into the exotic travels of Lafcadio Hearn. Tribal women in sueded shoes, and blonded hair, mince in my memories over the thresholds into the translated novels of Kawabata Yasunari, and Dazai Osamu.

Alice Beaulieu, in her sixties, married a blind man because he told her she looked beautiful; and now, in the white birch, with crows, bears, and a moist wind, their adventures in the suburbs to peddle brooms and brushes overturn the wisdom of modern families and their histories. The blind man and his old tribal stunner soothed lonesome women in those pastel suburban houses, the new tribal healers in the cities, and no one bought a broom from the blind man.

I had ordered a laminated miniature of my honorable discharge, bought a used car, a new suit, three shirts, a winter coat, and drove east to visit friends. I was an army veteran with two volumes of photographs to illustrate my stories that I had driven a tank, directed theater productions, survived a typhoon, and walked with the bears in the Imperial National Forest on Hokkaido. I was pensive and nineteen. Two months later I was a college student, by chance, and inspired by the novel *Look Homeward, Angel*. My dreams to be a writer, and much later the grammars, blossomed when my stories were praised by Eda Lou Walton, my first teacher of writing at New York University.

Matsuo Basho came to mind on the mound with the squirrels that late afternoon. In the distance he heard laughter, and smelled cigarette smoke; a hunter in a duck blind in a march behind the mound. Silent crows were on the trees, their eyes pinched the wind, and I squeezed the side of my nose, gathered the oil with my thumb nail and rubbed it into the dark grain of the rifle stock. I remembered laughter on a porch, through an open window, at the river, and snickers deep in the weeds behind the cabins at Silver Lake, a Salvation Army camp for welfare mothers. I taught their children how to paddle a canoe that summer, how to cook on an open fire without foil, and how to name seven birds in flight.

"I walked into the woods alone and found a place in the sun against a tree. The animals and birds were waiting in silence for me to pass.

. . . When I opened my eyes, after a short rest, the birds were singing and the squirrels were eating without fear and jumping from tree to tree. I was jumping with them but against them as the hunter," I wrote in *Growing Up in Minnesota*.

I pretend in the last sentence to be an arboreal animal, a romantic weakness. I was neither hunter nor a tribal witness to the survival hunt. I was there as a crossblood writer and hunter in a transitive confessional, in my imaginative autobiographies. I have never lived from the hunt, but I have been hunted, and cornered in wild dreams. I have shot squirrels and feasted on their bitter thighs, but I have never had to track an animal to the end, as I would to the last pronouns in my stories, to feed my families and friends.

I understand the instincts of the survival hunter, enough to mimic their movements; my compassion for animals arises from imagination and literature. My endurance has never been measured in heart muscles, livers, hides, horns, shared on the trail. My survival is mythic, an imaginative transition, an intellectual predation, deconstructed as masks and metaphors at the water holes in autobiographies.

The following poems are examples of play at work on serious questions of the role of the moral imagination in the shaping of people's lives and the development of their character.

❧ WILLIAM SHAKESPEARE, *A Midsummer Night's Dream*

The lunatic, the lover, and the poet,
Are of imagination all compact:
One sees more devils than vast hell can hold,
That is, the madman; the lover, all as frantic,
Sees Helen's beauty in a brow of Egypt:
The poet's eye, in a fine frenzy rolling,
Doth glance from heaven to earth, from earth to heaven;
And, as imagination bodies forth

The forms of things unknown, the poet's pen
Turns them to shapes, and gives to airy nothing
A local habitation and a name.
Such tricks hath strong imagination,
That, if it would but apprehend some joy,
It comprehends some bringer of that joy;
Or in the night, imagining some fear,
How easy is a bush suppos'd a bear!

❦ SEAMUS HEANEY, *Saint Francis and the Birds*

When Francis preached love to the birds,
They listened, fluttered, throttled up
Into the blue like a flock of words

Released for fun from his holy lips.
Then wheeled back, whirred about his head,
Pirouetted on brothers' capes,

Danced on the wing, for sheer joy played
And sang, like images took flight.
Which was the best poem Francis made,

His argument true, his tone light.

❦ AIDA TSUNAO, *Wild Duck*

Did the wild duck say,
"Don't ever become a wild duck,"
at that time?

No.

We plucked the bird,
burned off its hair,

broiled its meat and devoured it,
and, licking our lips,
we began to leave the edge of the marsh
where an evening mist was hanging,
when we heard a voice:

"You could still chew
on my bones."

We looked back
and saw the laughter of the wild duck
and its backbone gleaming.

❧ JOHN CADDY, *Learning Ketchup*

Dinnertime, digestion dependent on the man's
forbearance, the woman ready to be accepted
or be flayed, children wan and seated,
the formal requirements of Table.

The boy sits nearest the man, in his reach.

Tonight, meatloaf and potatoes, creamed
corn, homemade bread, lettuce, dills,
the ketchup bottle, tall and narrow-necked.

Table is the place for all to learn eating
from the man, who never grasps how
they can be so blind to his correction.

!—The boy hammers the end of the bottle again, no
ketchup, !—hammers, no ketch—the man abruptly
snatches it away, shows him How, rapping
the bottle neck against the edge of his hand.

It doesn't work. Doesn't work. Doesn't! The man
lifts the stubborn open end to his eye, stares it

down while a quirky deathwish in the boy's arm
bypasses his brain and calmly reaches across plates and
openhanded almost nonchalantly pops the bottle bottom.

Table frozen, forks halfway to mouths—a sudden red
gluts the man's right eye. The boy will die. Knows it,
can't believe—but cannot hold his laugh, the woman
squeezes her mouth but explodes, brother, sister
all rocking, rocking, and finally the redeyed man himself
cannot but laugh and laugh, the boy unbelievably alive,

the man for once himself the fool, for once seeing red and laughing.

❦ PHILIP DACEY, *Form Rejection Letter*

We are sorry we cannot use the enclosed.
We are returning it to you.
We do not mean to imply anything by this.
We would prefer not to be pinned down about this matter.
But we are not keeping—cannot, will not keep—
    what you sent us.
We did receive it, though, and our returning it to you
    is a sign of that.
It was not that we minded your sending it to us
    unasked.
That is happening all the time, they
    come when we least expect them,
        when we forget we have needed or might yet need them,
    and we send them back.
We send this back.
It is not that we minded.

At another time, there is no telling . . .
But this time, it does not suit our present needs.

We wish to make it clear it was not easy receiving it.
It came so encumbered.
And we are busy here.
We did not feel
    we could take it on.
We know it would not have ended there.
It would have led to this, and that.
We know about these things.
It is why we are here.
We wait for it. We recognize it when it comes.
Regretfully, this form letter does not allow us to elaborate
    why we send it back.
It is not that we minded.

We hope this does not discourage you. But we would not
    want to encourage you falsely.
It requires delicate handling, at this end.
If we had offered it to you,
    perhaps you would understand.
But, of course, we did not.
You cannot know what your offering it
    meant to us,
And we cannot tell you:
There is a form we must adhere to.
It is better for everyone that we use this form.

As to what you do in future
    we hope we have given you signs,
      that you have read them,
      that you have not mis-read them.
We wish we could be more helpful.
But we are busy.

We are busy returning so much.
We cannot keep it.
It all comes so encumbered.
And there is no one here to help.
Our enterprise is a small one.
We are thinking of expanding.
We hope you will send something.

❧ VICTOR HERNANDEZ CRUZ, *The Man Who Came to the Last Floor*

There was a Puerto Rican man who
came to New York
He came with a whole shopping bag
full of seeds strange to the big
city
He came and it was morning
and though many people thought the
sun was out this man wondered:
"Where is it"
"Y el sol donde esta" he asked
himself
He went to one of the neighborhoods
and searched for an apartment
He found one in the large somewhere
of New York
with a window overlooking a busy avenue
It was the kind of somewhere that is
usually elevatorless
Somewhere near wall/less
stairless
But this man enjoyed the wide space
of the room with the window that
overlooked the avenue

There was plenty of space
looking out of the window
There is a direct path to heaven
he thought
A wideness in front of the living
room
It was the sixth floor so he lived
on top of everybody in the building
The last floor of the mountain
He took to staring out of his sixth
floor window
He was a familiar sight every day
From his window he saw legs that
walked all day
Short and skinny fat legs
Legs that belonged to many people
Legs that walk embraced with nylon socks
Legs that ride bareback
Legs that were swifter than others
Legs that were always hiding
Legs that always had to turn around
and look at the horizon
Legs that were just legs against
the gray of the cement
People with no legs
He saw everything hanging out
from his room
Big city anywhere and his smile
was as wide as the space in front of him

One day his dreams were invaded by spirits
People just saw him change
Change the way rice changes when it is
sitting on top of fire
All kinds of things started to happen

at the top of the mountain
apartamento number 32
All kinds of smells started to come out
of apartamento number 32
All kinds of visitors started to come
to apartamento number 32
Wild looking ladies showed up
with large earrings and bracelets
that jingled throughout the hallways
The neighborhood became rich in legend
One could write an encyclopedia if one
collected the rumors
But nothing bothered this man who was
on top of everybody's heads
He woke one day and put the shopping bag
full of seeds that he brought from the island
near the window
He said "para que aproveche el fresco"
So that it can enjoy the fresh air
He left it there for a day
Taking air
Fresh air
Gray air
Wet air
The avenue air
The blue legs air
The teen-agers who walked below
Their air
With their black hats with the red
bandanna around them full of cocaine
That air
The heroin in the young girls that
moved slowly toward their local
high school
All the air from the outside

The shopping bag stood by the window
inhaling
Police air
Bus air
Car wind
Gringo air
Big mountain city air anywhere
That day this man from Puerto Rico
had his three radios on at the same time
Music coming from anywhere
each station was different
Music from anywhere everywhere

The following day the famous
outline of the man's head once again showed
up on the sixth floor window
This day he fell into song
and his head was in motion
No one recalls exactly at what point
in the song he started flinging the
seeds of tropical fruits down to
the earth
Down to the avenue of somewhere big
city
But no one knew what he was doing
So all the folks just smiled
"El hombre esta bien loco, algo le
cogio la cabeza"
The man is really crazy
something has taken his head
He began to throw out the last of the
Mango seeds
A policeman was walking down the avenue
and all of a sudden took off his hat
A mango seed landed nicely into his
curly hair

It somehow sailed into the man's
scalp
Deep into the grease of his curls
No one saw it
And the policeman didn't feel it
He put his hat on and walked away
The man from Puerto Rico
was singing another pretty song
His eyes were closed and his head waved.

Two weeks later the policeman felt
a bump coming out of his head
"Holy shit" he woke up telling his wife
one day
"this bump is getting so big I can't
put my hat on my head"
He took a day off and went to see his
doctor about his growing bump
The doctor looked at it and said
it'll go away
The bump didn't go away
It went toward the sky
getting bigger each day
It began to take hold of his whole head
Every time he tried to comb his hair
all his hair would fall to the comb
One morning when the sun was really hot
his wife noticed a green leaf sticking
out from the tip of his bump
Another month passed and more and more
leaves started to show on this man's head
The highest leaf was now two feet above
his forehead
Surely he was going crazy he thought
He could not go to work with a mango
tree growing out of his head

It soon got to be five feet tall
and beautifully green
He had to sleep in the living room
His bedroom could no longer contain him
Weeks later a young mango showed up
hanging from a newly formed branch
"Now look at this" he told his wife
He had to drink a lot of water or he'd
get severe headaches
The more water he drank the bigger
the mango tree flourished over his head
The people of the somewhere city heard
about it in the evening news and there was
a line of thousands ringed around his
home
They all wanted to see the man who
had an exotic mango tree growing from
his skull
And there was nothing that could be done.

Everyone was surprised when they
saw the man who lived at the top of
the mountain come down with his shopping bag
and all his luggage
He told a few of his friends that
he was going back to Puerto Rico
When they asked him why he was going back
He told them that he didn't remember
ever leaving
He said that his wife and children
were there waiting for him
The other day he noticed that he was
not on his island he said
almost singing
He danced toward the famous corner

and waved down a taxi
"El Aire port" he said
He was going to the clouds
To the island
At the airport he picked up a newspaper
and was reading an article about a mango
tree
At least that's what he could make out of
the English
Que cosa he said   Wao
Why write about a Mango tree
There're so many of them
and they are everywhere
They taste goooooood
Como eh.

SUSAN GRIFFIN, *An Answer to a Man's Question, "What Can I Do About Women's Liberation?"*

Wear a dress.
Wear a dress that you made yourself, or bought in a dress store.
Wear a dress and underneath the dress wear elastic, around
your hips, and underneath your nipples.
Wear a dress and underneath the dress wear a sanitary napkin.
Wear a dress and wear sling-back, high-heeled shoes.
Wear a dress, with elastic and a sanitary napkin underneath,
and sling-back shoes on your feet, and walk down Telegraph
    Avenue.
Wear a dress, with elastic and a sanitary napkin and sling-
back shoes on Telegraph Avenue and try to run.

Find a man.
Find a nice man who you would like to ask you for a date.
Find a nice man who *will* ask you for a date.

Keep your dress on.
Ask the nice man who asks you for a date to come to dinner.
Cook the nice man a nice dinner so the dinner is ready before
he comes and your dress is nice and clean and wear a smile.
Tell the nice man you're a virgin, or you don't have
birth control, or you would like to get to know him better.
Keep your dress on.
Go to the movies by yourself.

Find a job.
Iron your dress.
Wear your ironed dress and promise the boss you won't get
pregnant (which in your case is predictable) and you like to
type, and be sincere and wear your smile.
Find a job or get on welfare.
Borrow a child and get on welfare.
Borrow a child and stay in the house all day with the child,
or go to the public park with the child, and take the child
to the welfare office and cry and say your man left you and
be humble and wear your dress and your smile, and don't talk
back, keep your dress on, cook more nice dinners, stay
away from Telegraph Avenue, and still, you won't know the
half of it, not in a million years.

2

Halfway Up a Hill, or Down: Inventing the Self Through Imagination

IMAGINING THE SELF

Toni Morrison, in this description of one of her characters, could have been talking for all of us when she said:

> She had nothing to fall back on; not maleness, not whiteness, not ladyhood, not anything. And out of the profound desolation of her reality she may well have invented herself.

We all invent ourselves, and our moral character develops through the interplay of our experience and our imaginings. We are simultaneously the emergent consequence of our backgrounds, our parents' experiences, our childhood, our daily lives, and our dreams, aspirations, and fantasies. The choices we make about the kind of people we will become and the tests we face when trying to achieve our aspirations all contribute to the making of character. Hopes are tested against reality, and often we find secret sources of strength in our imaginary lives. Throughout life we are always, as Maxine

Kumin puts it, "halfway" between the people we are and the people we want to be—sometimes pulled in different directions by competing desires and dreams, sometimes tempted by one kind of life, sometimes by another.

Halfway

As true as I was born into
my mother's bed in Germantown,
the gambrel house in which I grew
stood halfway up a hill, or down,
between a convent and a madhouse.

The nunnery was white and brown.
In summertime they said the mass
on a side porch, from rocking chairs.
The priest came early on the grass,
black in black rubbers up the stairs
or have I got it wrong? The mass
was from the madhouse and the priest
came with a black bag to his class
and ministered who loved him least.
They shrieked because his needles stung.
They sang for Christ upon his cross.
The plainsong and the bedlam hung
on the air and blew across
into the garden where I played.

I saw the sisters' linens flap
on the clothesline while they prayed,
and heard them tell their beads and slap
their injuries. But I have got
the gardens mixed. It must have been
the mad ones who cried out to blot
the frightened sinner from his sin.
The nuns were kind. They gave me cake
and told me lives of saints who died
aflame and silent at the stake
and when I saw their Christ, I cried

where I was born, where I outgrew
my mother's bed in Germantown.
All the iron truths I knew
stood halfway up a hill, or down.

Character is not set once and for all, but always in process. The question of what is the best or most decent thing to do in a given situation is often unclear. The line between self-interest and commitment to a just society is not distinct, nor is it an easy thing to develop a consistent and morally decent character. The selections in this part of the book express the dilemmas and inspirations people face in the struggle to be decent and moral. They stand in direct contrast to those moralists who think ethical decisions are clear-cut and that there are unambiguous rules for living with and judging other people's values.

Selections

The following selections are about the challenges people face when confronted with the need to construct a coherent and centered self. They are concerned with the inspirations people draw from others, from animal and plant life, and from imagined and remembered events. These are the elements out of which character is shaped and honed by the imagination.

❦ AL YOUNG, *The Curative Powers of Silence*

Suddenly
I touch upon wordlessness,
I who watch Cheryl
the blind girl who lives up the street
walking at night
when she thinks no one's looking
deliberately heading into hedges & trees
in order to hug them
& to be kissed,

thus are we each
hugged & kissed.

Wordless
I fill up
listening for nothing
for nothing at all

as when in so-called life
I am set shivering with warmth
by a vision
with the eyes closed
of the Cheryl in me
when I think no one's looking,
plopped down in a field of grass
under watchful trees

letting the pre-mind dream
of nothing at all
nothing at all
no flicker
no shadow
no voice
no cry,

not even dreaming

—being dreamed

❧ WILLIAM CARLOS WILLIAMS, *The Yellow Flower*

What shall I say, because talk I must?
That I have found a cure
for the sick?

I have found no cure
        for the sick
                but this crooked flower
which only to look upon
        all men
                    are cured. This
is that flower
        for which all men
                sing secretly their hymns
of praise. This
        is that sacred
                flower!

Can this be so?
        A flower so crooked
                and obscure? It is
a mustard flower
        and not a mustard flower,
                a single spray
topping the deformed stem
        of fleshy leaves
                in this freezing weather
under glass.

An ungainly flower and
        an unnatural one,
                in this climate; what
can be the reason
        that it has picked me out
                to hold me, openmouthed,

rooted before this window
        in the cold,
                my will

drained from me
        so that I have only eyes
        for these yellow,
twisted petals   .   ?

That the sight,
        though strange to me,
            must be a common one,
is clear: there are such flowers
        with such leaves
            native to some climate
which they can call
        their own.

But why the torture
        and the escape through
            the flower? It is
as if Michelangelo
        had conceived the subject
            of his *Slaves* from this
—or might have done so.
        And did he not make
        the marble bloom? I
am sad
        as he was sad
            in his heroic mood.

But also
        I have eyes
            that are made to see and if
they see ruin for myself
        and all that I hold
            dear, they see

also
        through the eyes
            and through the lips

and tongue the power
          to free myself
                  and speak of it, as
Michelangelo through his hands
          had the same, if greater,
              power.

Which leaves, to account for,
          the tortured bodies
              of
the slaves themselves
          and
              the tortured body of my flower
which is not a mustard flower at all
          but some unrecognized!
              and unearthly flower
for me to naturalize
   and acclimate
              and choose it for my own.

❧ JOHN CADDY, *Eating the Sting*

Caught in the snapped circle of light
on the cookshack oilcloth,
an upright deermouse holding yellow
in her fine fingers
like an ear of black-striped corn,
a wasp I'd slapped dead earlier.

She stares, belly resonating, round above
a scatter of brittle wing, bits, a carapace—
she has already eaten the stinger—
stares at me, still,
something thrumming in her eyes

beyond herself, a mouse stung
onto an edge as far from cartoons
as the venom she's chewed into food.

She cocks a fawn ear now, trembling poisonchanger,
caught in the circle of light
I've thought myself in at times,

but never sure, I ask her softly how
she does it, if I can learn this turning
of sting into such food as startles in her eyes,
learn to suck pain into every sense
and come up spitting seeds, force poison
to a tear held fierce between my lips
and whirl it into tongue which sings, but

here I've come too loud: She drops the husk,
fusses whiskers with her paws, kicks
a scrap of wing aside, and whispers
thanks for the corn,

steps backward off the table
(and so potent she is with wasp)
flips a circle through light and
lands running on her leaf-toed feet.

❦ MURIEL RUKEYSER, *Are You Born II*

A child riding the stormy mane of noon
Sang to me past the cloud of the world:
Are you born? Are you born?
The form of this hope is the law of all things,
Our foaming sun is the toy of that force.
—Touch us alive, developing light? Today,
Revealed over the mountains, every living eyes.

Child of the possible, who rides the hour
Of dream and process, lit by every fire.
Glittering blood of song,
A glint of time, showers of human meaning
Flashing upon us all:
The song of a child; the song of the cloud of the world
Born, born, born. Cloud become real,
                              and change,
The starry form of love.

❧ DAVID BERGMAN, *Urban Renewal, Baltimore*

Nothing is lost more completely than
the commonplaces of another
age. Sifting the phosphorescent loam,
archaeologists search the site where
Baltimore's first custom house once stood
for fragments which in this damp climate
resist the dark urge to decompose.

And years ago, not far away, I
saved the black Carrara glass façade
of the Anchor Bar & Restaurant,
The waterfront saloon where sailors
fought with the whores who lived upstairs
until the balls of the wrecking crew
laid everything flat for the highway.

One night Bob and Tom and I went out,
and we pried the slick sheets off the wall.
We placed the heavy panels, acid
etched with Deco letters, in a van,
then padded the sides to keep the panes
from shattering. By dawn Tom's mother
had her bare attic crammed to the eaves.

Later came accusations and lies,
the falling out of friends, the falling
in of prospects. I'm told our salvaged
front has disappeared from its hideout,
and next that Tom has died of causes
unexplained in another city,
his folks beyond our consolation.

Whatever we loosen from the past,
burns in the solvent of memory.
Stalled at the choked throat of the harbor,
I wait in rush hour traffic, wait
where the Anchor Bar & Restaurant
had been, where tourists now browse boutiques
and the gulls wipe clean the glass-smooth sky.

In these examples we see the impediments people can encounter on the road to becoming themselves.

❧ NATHANAEL WEST, *Miss Lonelyhearts*

Dear Miss Lonelyhearts—

I am sixteen years old now and I don't know what to do and would appreciate it if you could tell me what to do. When I was a little girl it was not so bad because I got used to the kids on the block making fun of me, but now I would like to have boy friends like the other girls and go out on Saturday nites, but no boy will take me because I was born without a nose—although I am a good dancer and have a nice shape and my father buys me pretty clothes.

I sit and look at myself all day and cry. I have a big hole in the middle of my face that scares people even myself so I can't blame the boys for not wanting to take me out. My mother loves me, but she cries terrible when she looks at me.

What did I do to deserve such a terrible bad fate? Even if I did do some bad things I didn't do any before I was a year old and I was born this way. I asked Papa and he says he doesn't know, but that maybe I did something in the other world before I was born or that maybe I was being punished for his sins. I don't believe that because he is a very nice man. Ought I commit suicide?

Sincerely yours, *Desperate*

JULES HENRY, *Sham*

In *The Devil and the Good Lord* Sartre says that it is impossible to do good and in *No Exit* he tells us that hell is people. In *Tiny Alice* Albee says that whoever does not learn to accept sham as reality deserves to be shot; de Sade argues that only evil succeeds and that virtue is ridiculous and will end up corrupted. Heidegger says that the way to Being is authenticity but that the way to authenticity is through our heritage, which he never defines. Kierkegaard believes that only supine resignation, aided by striving, is the way to God. President Johnson tells us that war is peace, Martin Luther King pats the Illinois National Guard on the back for their politeness while Hubert Humphrey suggests the appropriateness of Negro revolt. The officers of a famous university issue engraved invitations to a "reception opening the Conference on Poverty in America"; and those who direct anti-poverty programs are the upper-middle class, who are not in want. It is clear that our civilization is a tissue of contradictions and lies; and that therefore the main problem for psychiatry is not to cure mental illness but to define sanity and account for its occurrence. . . .

. . . In the light of these considerations sanity is nothing more than the capacity to deal with falseness, in a false world; and it can take three forms—Albee's, which is to believe sham to be the truth; to see through sham while using it; or to see through sham but fight it. These three uses constitute three stages in the future social evolution of man: we are now in the stage of believing sham to be the truth, while entering the stage of seeing through sham while using it. The third stage is under-standing sham and knowing how to fight it. The fourth stage is a world without sham.

❧ FRANZ KAFKA, *Before the Wall*

Before the Law stands a doorkeeper. To this doorkeeper there comes a man from the country who prays for admittance to the Law. But the doorkeeper says that he cannot grant admittance at the moment. The man thinks it over and then asks if he will be allowed in later. "It is possible," says the doorkeeper, "but not at the moment." Since the gate stands open, as usual, and the doorkeeper steps to one side, the man stoops to peer through the gateway into the interior. Observing that, the doorkeeper laughs and says: "If you are so drawn to it, just try to go in despite my veto. But take note: I am powerful. And I am only the least of the doorkeepers. From hall to hall there is one doorkeeper after another, each more powerful than the last. The third doorkeeper is already so terrible that even I cannot bear to look at him." These are difficulties the man from the country has not expected; the law, he thinks, should surely be accessible at all times and to every-one, but as he now takes a closer look at the doorkeeper in his fur coat, with his big sharp nose and long, thin, black Tartar beard, he decides that it is better to wait until he gets permission to enter. The door-keeper gives him a stool and lets him sit down at one side of the door. There he sits for days and years. He makes many attempts to be admit-ted, and wearies the doorkeeper by his importunity. The doorkeeper frequently has little interviews with him, asking him questions about his home and many other things, but the questions are put indiffer-ently, as great lords put them, and always finish with the statement that he cannot be let in yet. The man, who has furnished himself with many things for his journey, sacrifices all he has, however valuable, to bribe the doorkeeper. The doorkeeper accepts everything, but always with the remark: "I am only taking it to keep you from thinking you have omitted anything." During these many years the man fixes his attention almost continuously on the doorkeeper. He forgets the other doorkeepers, and this first one seems to him the sole obstacle preventing access to the Law. He curses his bad luck, in his early years boldly and loudly, later, as he grows old, he only grumbles to himself. He becomes childish, and since in his years-long contemplation of the doorkeeper, he has come to know even the fleas in his fur collar, he begs the fleas as well to help him and to change the doorkeeper's mind. At length his eyesight begins to fail, and he does not know whether the world is really darker or whether his eyes are only deceiving him. Yet in his darkness he is now aware of a radiance that streams inextinguishably from the gateway of the Law.

Now he has not very long to live. Before he dies, all his experiences in these long years gather themselves in his head to one point, a question he has not yet asked the doorkeeper. He waves him nearer, since he can no longer raise his stiffening body. The doorkeeper has to bend low towards him, for the difference in height between them has altered much to the man's disadvantage. "What do you want to know now?" asks the doorkeeper; "you are insatiable."

"Everyone strives to reach the Law," says the man, "so how does it happen that for all these many years no one but myself has ever begged for admittance?" The doorkeeper recognizes that the man has reached his end, and to let his failing senses catch the words, roars in his ear: "No one else could ever be admitted here, since this gate was made only for you. I am now going to shut it."

❦ JANICE MIRIKITANI, *Looking for America*

I searched for myself
in the pages of Time,
among the brilliant and beautiful, best sold and discovered.
I looked for myself on the screen
wooed by Gable and Brando and McQueen,
on the tube selling Colgate or Camay or Kotex or Crisco,
hunted for me on billboards or climbing the rungs
of executive ladders,
and saw myself

being shot by John Wayne,
conquered by Stallone,
out-karated by Norris, Van Damme, Carradine and Seagal.

I found myself
in a bar, dancing for a tip,
cheong sam slit to my hip,
or in a brothel, compliant and uncomplicated,
high-heeled in bed, wiping some imperialist's lips
with hot scented towels.
I see myself pound my head
on the glass of their ceiling, two rungs up
a short corporate ladder.

I meet myself pigeon toed and shuffling, tongue twisted,
chop chop/sing song/giggle/rots of ruck/bucktoothed/
cokebottle eyeglassed/cartoon camera carrying foreigner
who is invisible

on America's pages.

❧ ANNE SEXTON, *Live*

Today life opened inside me like an egg
and there inside
after considerable digging
I found the answer.
What a bargain!
There was the sun,
her yolk moving feverishly,
tumbling her prize—
and you realize that she does this daily!
I'd known she was purifier
but I hadn't thought
she was solid,
hadn't known she was an answer.

God! It's a dream,
lovers sprouting in the yard
like celery stalks
and better,
a husband straight as a redwood,
two daughters, two sea urchins,
picking roses off my hackles.
If I'm on fire they dance around it
and cook marshmallows.
And if I'm ice
they simply skate on me
in little ballet costumes.

❦ MICHELLE CLIFF, *Passing*

I
The mystery of the world is the visible,
not the invisible.

—OSCAR WILDE

Camouflage: ground lizards in the schoolyard rustle under a pile of
leaves—some are deep-green, others shiny blue: all blend in. I
fear they might be there even—when there is no sound.

To this day camouflage terrorizes me.

The pattern of skin which makes a being invisible against its habitat.

And—yes—this camouflage exists for its protection. I am not what I
seem to be.

I must make myself visible against my habitat. But there exists a
certain danger in peeling back. The diamondback without her
mottled skin loses a level of defense.

The onlooker may be startled to recognize the visible being.
The onlooker may react with disbelief: sometimes, with recognition.

II
I am remembering: women in Jamaica asking to touch my hair.

On a map from 1740 which hangs above my desk I can see the place
where my grandmother now lives. Old-woman Savannah. That is
the place which holds colors for me. The other seems a shadow-
life.

I am remembering: in the hard dirt in the bright sun between the
house and the shed which is a kitchen my mother sat—after
church—on a wooden crate. Under the box a headless chicken
flapped its wings

Quiet. Then she rose—removed the box. Plunged the carcass into
boiling water to loosen the feathers.

She passed the carcass to her mother who cut and stewed. Sunday
dinner.

I watched this all in wonder. The two women were almost silent.
III
I thought it was only the loss of the mother—
but it was also the loss of others:
who grew up to work for us
and stood at the doorway while the tv played
and stood at the doorway while we told ghost-stories
and ironed the cloths for the tea-trays—
but this division existed even then—

Passing demands a desire to become invisible. A ghost-life. An
ignorance of connections.
IV
In America: each year the day before school after summer vacations I
sat on my bed touching my notebooks, pencils, ruler—holding
the stern and sweet-smelling brown oxfords in my lap and

spreading my skirt and blouse and underwear and socks before
me. My mother would come in and always say the same thing:
"Free paper burn now."

Such words conspire to make a past.
Such words conjure a knowledge.
Such words make assimilation impossible. They stay with you for
     years.
They puzzle but you sense a significance. I need these words.
V
People call my grandmother the miracle of the loaves and the fishes.
     People used to fill the yard at dinnertime with their enamel
     bowls and utensils waiting to be fed. And she managed to feed
     them all. Whether rice or yam or green banana cooked in dried
     saltfish.

In America this food became a secret—and a link. Shopping under
     the bridge with my mother for cho-cho and cassava and
     breadfruit. And the New Home Bakery for hard-dough bread.
     Finding a woman who makes paradise plums.

My mother sees this. She says nothing.

Passing demands quiet—silence
VI
Something used by someone else carries a history with it. A piece of
     cloth a platter. a cut-glass pitcher. a recipe.
A history and a spirit. You want to know when it was used. And how.
     And what it wants from you.

Passing demands you keep that knowledge to yourself.
VII
In Jamaica we are as common as ticks.
We graft the Bombay onto the common mango. The Valencia on
     the Seville. We mix tangerines and oranges. We create mules.

Under British rule—Zora Neale Hurston writes about this—we could have ourselves declared legally white. The rationale was that it made us better servants.

This symbolic skin was carried to the United States where passing was easy.

Isolate yourself. If they find out about you it's all over. Forget about your great-grandfather with the darkest skin—until you're back "home" where they joke about how he climbed a coconut tree when he was eighty. Go to college. Go to England to study. Learn about the Italian Renaissance and forget that they kept slaves. Ignore the tears of the Indians. Black Americans don't understand us either. We are—after all—British. If anyone asks you talk about sugar plantations and the Maroons—not the landscape of downtown Kingston and children at the roadside. Be selective. Cultivate normalcy. Stress sameness. Blend in. For God's sake don't pile difference upon difference. It's not safe.

Back on the island the deep-purple skin of the ripe fruit conceals a center which holds a star-shape. Sitting in the branches one afternoon with a friend we eat ourselves into an intimacy in which we talk about our families. He is fourteen and works for my grandmother. I am twelve. He tells me his grandmother was East Indian and therefore he is not completely black. I tell him I am white—showing my sunburnt nose—explaining only white skin burns. He laughs. Then we scuffle.

It is like trying to remember a dream in which the images slip and slide. The words connect and disconnect and you wake feeling senseless.

"No strange news," my grandmother often closes her letters.

We are not exotic—or aromatic—or poignant.
We are not aberrations. We are ordinary.
All this has happened before.

Grace Paley's story, Denise Levertov's poem, and the excerpt from Ralph Ellison's Invisible Man *illustrate the power of the imagination to think beyond present constraints and handicaps. They are examples of how imaginative reflection and rumination can sometimes lead to a fuller and more comfortable definition of self that includes strong moral definition.*

❦ GRACE PALEY, *Wants*

I saw my ex-husband in the street. I was sitting on the steps of the new library.

Hello, my life, I said. We had once been married for twenty-seven years, so I felt justified.

He said, What? What life? No life of mine.

I said, O.K. I don't argue when there's real disagreement. I got up and went into the library to see how much I owed them.

The librarian said $32 even and you've owed it for eighteen years. I didn't deny anything. Because I don't understand how time passes. I have had those books. I have often thought of them. The library is only two blocks away.

My ex-husband followed me to the Books Returned desk. He interrupted the librarian, who had more to tell. In many ways, he said, as I look back, I attribute the dissolution of our marriage to the fact that you never invited the Bertrams to dinner.

That's possible, I said. But really, if you remember: first, my father was sick that Friday, then the children were born, then I had those Tuesday-night meetings, then the war began. Then we didn't seem to know them anymore. But you're right. I should have had them to dinner.

I gave the librarian a check for $32. Immediately she trusted me, put my past behind her, wiped the record clean, which is just what most other municipal and/or state bureaucracies will *not* do.

I checked out the two Edith Wharton books I had just returned because I'd read them so long ago and they are more apropos now than ever. They were *The House of Mirth* and *The Children*, which is about how life in the United States in New York changed in twenty-seven years fifty years ago.

A nice thing I do remember is breakfast, my ex-husband said. I was surprised. All we ever had was coffee. Then I remembered there was a hole in the back of the kitchen closet which opened into the apartment next door. There, they always ate sugar-cured smoked bacon. It gave us a very grand feeling about breakfast, but we never got stuffed and sluggish.

That was when we were poor, I said.

When were we ever rich? he asked.

Oh, as time went on, as our responsibilities increased, we didn't go in need. You took adequate financial care, I reminded him. The children went to camp four weeks a year and in decent ponchos with sleeping bags and boots, just like everyone else. They looked very nice. Our place was warm in winter, and we had nice red pillows and things.

I wanted a sailboat, he said. But you didn't want anything.

Don't be bitter, I said. It's never too late.

No, he said with a great deal of bitterness. I may get a sailboat. As a matter of fact I have money down on an eighteen-foot two-rigger. I'm doing well this year and can look forward to better. But as for you, it's too late. You'll always want nothing.

He had had a habit throughout the twenty-seven years of making a narrow remark which, like a plumber's snake, could work its way through the ear down the throat, halfway to my heart. He would then disappear, leaving me choking with equipment. What I mean is, I sat down on the library steps and he went away.

I looked through *The House of Mirth*, but lost interest. I felt extremely accused. Now, it's true. I'm short of requests and absolute requirements. But I do want *something*.

I want, for instance, to be a different person. I want to be the woman who brings these two books back in two weeks. I want to be the effective citizen who changes the school system and addresses The

Board of Estimate on the troubles of this dear urban center.

I *had* promised my children to end the war before they grew up.

I wanted to have been married forever to one person, my ex-husband or my present one. Either has enough character for a whole life, which as it turns out is really not such a long time. You couldn't exhaust either man's qualities or get under the rock of his reasons in one short life.

Just this morning I looked out the window to watch the street for a while and saw that the little sycamores the city had dreamily planted a couple of years before the kids were born had come that day to the prime of their lives.

Well! I decided to bring those two books back to the library. Which proves that when a person or an event comes along to jolt or appraise me I *can* take some appropriate action, although I am better known for my hospitable remarks.

❦ DENISE LEVERTOV, *To Speak*

To speak of sorrow
works upon it
    moves it from its
crouched place barring
the way to and from the soul's hall—

out in the light it
shows clear, whether
shrunken or known as
a giant wrath—
    discrete
at least, where before
its great shadow joined
the walls and roof and seemed
to uphold the hall like a beam.

❦ RALPH ELLISON, *Invisible Man*

Whence all this passion toward conformity anyway?—diversity is the word. Let man keep his many parts and you'll have no tyrant states. Why, if they follow this conformity business they'll end up by forcing me, an invisible man, to become white, which is not a color but the lack of one. Must I strive toward colorlessness? But seriously, and without snobbery, think of what the world would lose if that should happen. America is woven of many strands; I would recognize them and let it so remain. It's "winner take nothing" that is the great truth of our country or of any country. Life is to be lived, not controlled; and humanity is won by continuing to play in face of certain defeat. Our fate is to become one, and yet many—This is not prophecy, but description. Thus one of the greatest jokes in the world is the spectacle of the whites busy escaping blackness and becoming blacker every day, and the blacks striving toward whiteness, becoming quite dull and gray. None of us seems to know who he is or where he's going.

Which reminds me of something that occurred the other day in the subway. At first I saw only an old gentleman who for the moment was lost. I knew he was lost, for as I looked down the platform I saw him approach several people and turn away without speaking. He's lost, I thought, and he'll keep coming until he sees me, then he'll ask his direction. Maybe there's an embarrassment in it if he admits he's lost to a strange white man. Perhaps to lose a sense of *where* you are implies the danger of losing a sense of *who* you are. That must be it, I thought—to lose your direction is to lose your face. So here he comes to ask his direction from the lost, the invisible. Very well, I've learned to live without direction. Let him ask.

But then he was only a few feet away and I recognized him; it was Mr. Norton. The old gentleman was thinner and wrinkled now but as dapper as ever. And seeing him made all the old life live in me for an instant, and I smiled with tear-stinging eyes. Then it was over, dead, and when he asked me how to get to Centre Street, I regarded him with mixed feelings.

"Don't you know me?" I said.

"Should I?" he said.

"You see me?" I said, watching him tensely.

"Why, of course—Sir, do you know the way to Centre Street?"

"So. Last time it was the Golden Day, now it's Centre Street. You've retrenched, sir. But don't you really know who I am?"

"Young man, I'm in a hurry," he said, cupping a hand to his ear. "Why should I know you?"

"Because I'm your destiny."

"My destiny, did you say?" He gave me a puzzled stare, backing away. "Young man, are you well? Which train did you say I should take?"

"I didn't say," I said, shaking my head. "Now, aren't you ashamed?"

"Ashamed? ASHAMED!" he said indignantly.

I laughed, suddenly taken by the idea. "Because, Mr. Norton, if you don't know *where* you are, you probably don't know *who* you are. So you came to me out of shame. You are ashamed, now aren't you?"

"Young man, I've lived too long in this world to be ashamed of anything. Are you light-headed from hunger? How do you know my name?"

"But I'm your destiny, I made you. Why shouldn't I know you?" I said, walking closer and seeing him back against a pillar. He looked around like a cornered animal. He thought I was mad.

"Don't be afraid, Mr. Norton," I said. "There's a guard down the platform there. You're safe. Take any train; they all go to the Golden D—"

But now an express had rolled up and the old man was disappearing quite spryly inside one of its doors. I stood there laughing hysterically. I laughed all the way back to my hole.

But after I had laughed I was thrown back on my thoughts—how had it all happened? And I asked myself if it were only a joke and I couldn't answer. Since then I've sometimes been overcome with a passion to return into that "heart of darkness" across the Mason-Dixon line, but then I remind myself that the true darkness lies within my own mind, and the idea loses itself in the gloom. Still the passion persists. Sometimes I feel the need to reaffirm all of it, the whole unhappy territory and all the things loved and unlovable in it, for all of it is part of me. Till now, however, this is as far as I've ever gotten, for all life seen from the hole of invisibility is absurd.

So why do I write, torturing myself to put it down? Because in spite of myself I've learned some things. Without the possibility of action, all knowledge comes to one labeled "file and forget," and I can neither file nor forget. Nor will certain ideas forget me; they keep filing away at my lethargy, my complacency. Why should I be the one to dream this nightmare? Why should I be dedicated and set aside—yes, if not to at least *tell* a few people about it? There seems to be no escape. Here I've set out to throw my anger into the world's face, but now that I've tried to put it all down the old fascination with playing a role returns, and I'm drawn upward again. So that even before I finish I've failed (maybe my anger is too heavy; perhaps, being a talker, I've used too many words). But I've failed. The very act of trying to put it all down has confused me and negated some of the anger and some of the bitterness. So it is that now I denounce and defend, or feel prepared to defend. I condemn and affirm, say no and say yes, say yes and say no. I denounce because though implicated and partially responsible, I have been hurt to the point of abysmal pain, hurt to the point of invisibility. And I defend because in spite of all I find that I love. In order to get some of it down I *have* to love. I sell you no phony forgiveness, I'm a desperate man— but too much of your life will be lost, its meaning lost, unless you approach it as much through love as through hate. So I approach it through division. So I denounce and I defend and I hate and I love.

Perhaps that makes me a little bit as human as my grandfather. Once I thought my grandfather incapable of thoughts about humanity, but I was wrong. Why should an old slave use such a phrase as, "This and this or this has made me more human," as I did in my arena speech? Hell, he never had any doubts about his humanity—that was left to his "free" offspring. He accepted his humanity just as he accepted the prin- ciple. It was his, and the principle lives on in all its human and absurd diversity. So now having tried to put it down I have disarmed myself in the process. You won't believe in my invisibility and you'll fail to see how any principle that applies to you could apply to me. You'll fail to see it even though death waits for both of us if you don't. Nevertheless, the very disarmament has brought me to a decision. The hibernation is over. I must shake off the old skin and come up for breath. There's a stench in the air, which, from this distance underground, might be the smell either of death or of spring—I hope of spring. But don't let me trick you, there *is* a death in the smell of spring and in the smell of thee as in the smell of me. And if nothing more, invisibility has taught my nose to classify the stenches of death.

In going underground, I whipped it all except the mind, the *mind*. And the mind that has conceived a plan of living must never lose sight of the chaos against which that pattern was conceived. That goes for societies as well as for individuals. Thus, having tried to give pattern to the chaos which lives within the pattern of your certainties, I must come out, I must emerge. And there's still a conflict within me: With Louis Armstrong one half of me says, "Open the window and let the foul air out," while the other says, "It was good green corn before the harvest." Of course Louie was kidding, *he* wouldn't have thrown old Bad Air out, because it would have broken up the music and the dance, when it was the good music that came from the bell of old Bad Air's horn that counted. Old Bad Air is still around with his music and his dancing and his diversity, and I'll be up and around with mine. And, as I said before, a decision has been made. I'm shaking off the old skin and I'll leave it here in the hole. I'm coming out, no less invisible without it, but coming out nevertheless. And I suppose it's damn well time. Even hibernations can be overdone, come to think of it. Perhaps that's my greatest social crime, I've overstayed my hibernation, since there's a possibility that even an invisible man has a socially responsible role to play.

"Ah," I can hear you say, "so it was all a build-up to bore us with his buggy jiving. He only wanted us to listen to him rave!" But only partially true: Being invisible and without substance, a disembodied voice, as it were, what else could I do? What else but try to tell you what was really happening when your eyes were looking through? And it is this which frightens me:

Who knows but that, on the lower frequencies, I speak for you?

3
Such Stuff as Dreams Are Made On

IDEALISM AND VISION

Prospero's farewell to the audience near the end of *The Tempest* refers directly to the players and the play, but by plausible extension to all of our lives:

> We are such stuff
> As dreams are made on, and our little life
> is rounded with a sleep.

These sentiments reflect those expressed in these pre-Socratic fragments attributed to Heracleitus:

> History is a child building a sand-castle by the
> sea, and that child is the whole majesty of
> man's power in the world.

and:

> Awake, we see a dying world; asleep, dreams.

There are many kinds of dreams, but those central in sustaining moral character are those of a world worth living in. They are big dreams spawning ideas such as "democracy," "compassion," "honesty," "integrity," "liberty," and "equality." Sometimes such dreams are laid aside or crushed by harsh realities; sometimes they perk underground keeping hope alive. On rare occasions they become strong enough to govern social life.

Idealism consists of holding on to such dreams, savoring the promise of kindness and plenty and the diminution of greed and self-obsession. It has often been fashionable for cynical and ambitious people to ridicule idealism and spurn compassionate and democratic visions as defective and dangerous subversion. At such times, it is not uncommon for idealists and visionaries to become silenced, marginalized, and scared for their lives. But even then, some people have stood their ground, growing in strength, keeping on.

Being powerful in the service of one's vision and daring to imagine a better world are sources of personal nurturance as well as healing within communities. The selections in this part of the book are about personal and community visions and about the impediments to keeping such visions alive.

Selections

This poem by Muriel Rukeyser, and the two excerpts, one from Pablo Neruda's Nobel Prize acceptance speech and the other from Ben Okri's novel *The Famished Road*, describe personal visions and the idealism they kindle. They tie vision to family and love, to the wishes people have for their children and the inspiration they get from their parents, their culture, and their ancestors.

❦ MURIEL RUKEYSER, *Waiting for Icarus*

He said he would be back and we'd drink wine together
He said that everything would be better than before
He said we were on the edge of a new relation

He said he would never again cringe before his father
He said that he was going to invent full-time
He said he loved me that going into me
He said was going into the world and the sky
He said all the buckles were very firm
He said the wax was the best wax
He said Wait for me here on the beach
He said Just don't cry

I remember the gulls and the waves
I remember the islands going dark on the sea
I remember the girls laughing
I remember they said he only wanted to get away from me
I remember mother saying: Inventors are like poets,
                                              a trashy lot
I remember she told me those who try out inventions are
    worse
I remember she added: Women who love such are the worst
    of all
I have been waiting all day, or perhaps longer.
I would have liked to try those wings myself,
It would have been better than this.

❦ PABLO NERUDA, *Toward the Splendid City*

As far as we in particular are concerned, we writers within the
tremendously far-flung American region, we listen unceasingly to the
call to fill this mighty void with beings of flesh and blood. We are conscious of our duty as fulfillers—at the same time we are faced with the
unavoidable task of critical communication within a world which is
empty but which is no less full of injustices, punishments, and sufferings because it is empty—and we feel also the responsibility for reawak-
ening the old dreams which sleep in statues of stone in the ruined
ancient monuments, in the wide-stretching silence in planetary plains,

in dense primeval forests, in rivers which roar like thunder. We must fill with words the most distant places in a dumb continent and we are intoxicated by this task of making fables and giving names. This is perhaps what is decisive in my own humble case, and if so, my exaggerations or my abundance or my rhetoric would not be anything other than the simplest of events in the daily work of an American. Each and every one of my verses has chosen to take its place as a tangible object, each and every one of my poems has claimed to be a useful working instrument, each and every one of my songs has endeavored to serve as a sign in space for a meeting between paths which cross one another, or as a piece of stone or wood on which someone, some others, those who follow after, will be able to carve new signs.

By extending to these extreme consequences the poet's duty, in truth or in error, I determined that my posture within the community and before life should be that of in a humble way taking sides. I decided this when I saw so many honorable misfortunes, lone victories, splendid defeats. In the midst of the arena of America's struggles I saw that my human task was none other than to join the extensive forces of the organized masses of the people, to join with life and soul, with suffering and hope, because it is only from this great popular stream that the necessary changes can arise for writers and for nations. And even if my attitude gave and still gives rise to bitter or friendly objections, the truth is that I can find no other way for a writer in our far-flung and cruel countries, if we want the darkness to blossom, if we are concerned that the millions of people who have learned neither to read us nor to read at all, who still cannot write or write to us, are to feel at home in the dignity without which it is impossible for them to be complete human beings.

We have inherited this damaged life of peoples dragging behind them the burden of the condemnation of centuries, the most paradisal of peoples, the purest, those who with stones and metals made marvelous towers, jewels of dazzling brilliance—peoples who were suddenly despoiled and silenced in the fearful epochs of colonialism which still linger on.

Our original guiding stars are struggle and hope. But there is no such thing as a lone struggle, no such thing as a lone hope. In every human being are combined the most distant epochs, passivity, mistakes, sufferings, the pressing urgencies of our own time, the pace of history. But what would have become of me if, for example, I had contributed in some way to the maintenance of the feudal past of the great American continent? How should I then have been able to raise my brow, illuminated by the honor which Sweden has conferred on me, if I had not been able to feel some pride in having taken part, even to a small extent, in the change which has now come over my country? It is necessary to look at the map of America, to place oneself before its splendid multiplicity, before the cosmic generosity of the wide places which surround us, in order to understand why many writers refuse to share the dishonor and plundering of the past, of all that which dark gods have taken away from the American peoples.

I chose the difficult way of divided responsibility, and rather than repeat the worship of the individual as the sun and center of the system, I have preferred to offer my services in all modesty to an honorable army which may from time to time commit mistakes but which moves forward unceasingly and struggles daily against the anachronism of the refractory and the impatience of the opinionated. For I believe that my duties as a poet involve friendship not only with the rose and with symmetry, with exalted love and endless longing, but also with unrelenting human occupations which I have incorporated into my poetry.

It is today, exactly one hundred years since an unhappy and brilliant poet, the most awesome of all despairing souls, wrote down this prophecy: "*A l'aurore, armés d'une ardente patience, nous entrerons aux splendides Villes.*" "In the dawn, armed with a burning patience, we shall enter the splendid Cities."

I believe in this prophecy of Rimbaud, the Visionary. I come from a dark region, from a land separated from all others by the steep contours of its geography. I was the most forlorn of poets and my poetry was provincial, oppressed, and rainy. But always I put my trust in man. I never lost hope. It is perhaps because of this that I have reached as far as I have with my poetry, and also with my banner.

Lastly, I wish to say to the people of good will, to the workers, to the poets, that the whole future has been expressed in this line by

Rimbaud: only with a *burning patience* can we conquer the splendid City which will give light, justice, and dignity to all mankind.

In this way the song will not have been sung in vain.

❦ BEN OKRI, *The Famished Road*

But Dad's spirit was restless for justice and more life and genuine revolution and he kept ranging farther out into other worlds where the promises of power were made before birth. And Dad travelled the spheres, seeking the restoration of our race, and the restoration of all oppressed peoples. It was as I followed Dad that I learnt that other spheres of higher energies have their justice beyond our understanding. And our sphere too. The forces of balance are turning every day. The rain lashes the bloated and the weak, the powerful and the silenced. The wind exposes the hungry, the overfed, the ill, the dying, and those who feed on the unseen suffering of others. But the restorations are slow because our perception of time is long. Time and truth always come round; those who seem to hold sway and try to prevent the turning of justice only bring it quicker; and Dad wanted the turning now. He wanted justice now. He wanted truth now. He wanted world balance now. He raised the storms of demands in his dreams. He raised impenetrable questions. He kept asking: WHY? After eons he asked: WHAT MUST WE DO? And then he asked: HOW DO WE BRING IT ABOUT? Pressing on, he wanted to know: WHEN? Relentlessly, twisting and turning, he demanded: WHAT IS THE BEST WAY? And with a bit more serenity, not drawing back from the inevitable self-confrontation, he asked: WHAT IS THE FIRST STEP? His body grew. Flowers fell on our rooftop. My grandfather appeared to me briefly, waving me on. A child was born and didn't get to its body. Was I being reborn in my father? In his journeys Dad found that all nations are children; it shocked him that ours too was an abiku nation, a spirit-child nation, one that keeps being reborn and after each birth come blood and betrayals, and the child of our will refuses to stay till we have made propitious sacrifice and displayed our serious intent to bear the weight of a unique destiny.

Each life flows to all the spheres; and as Dad slept he lived out a whole lifetime in another continent, while we listened to the rumours of Madame Koto's meetings with powerful women in her bar, meetings in which they planned the numerous arrangements for the rally and the responsibilities of organising votes for their party. It didn't surprise us that she had recovered so quickly from the death of the prostitute. It didn't surprise us either that she had been allocated vast sums of money to organise the women from our part of the city. Her bad foot grew larger as if the road had impregnated it; her stomach bloated with its abiku trinity. She was initiated into another secret society that was famous for its manufacturing of reality. She talked about turning her bar into a hotel. She bought great plots of land. Her driver went up and down our road in her car, knocking over goats and killing chickens, multiplying her enemies.

Madame Koto grew more powerful with the rainy season. She developed a walk of imposing and languid dignity. Her fatness became her. She wore clothes that made the beggars ill. She talked of leaving the wretched area; she was scornful of everyone. We listened to her berating passers-by. She grew more powerful and she grew more beautiful as well. The rainy season swelled her frame. She incarnated all her legends into her new spirit, joined with her myths. She became all the things we whispered she was and she became more. At night, when she slept, she stole the people's energies. (She was not the only one: they were legion.) The night became her ally. While Dad ranged the spheres crying for justice, Madame Koto sucked in the powers of our area. Her dreams gave the children nightmares. Her colossal form took wings at night and flew over the city, drawing power from our sleeping bodies. She expanded over the air of our existence. Her dreams were livid rashes of parties and orgies, of squander and sprees, of corruption and disintegration, of innocent women and weak men. Her snoring altered the geography of our destinies. Slowly, while the people of the area grew weaker, more accepting, more afraid, she grew stronger. That was when I understood that conflicting forces were fighting for the future of our country in the air, at night, in our dreams, riding invisible white horses and whipping us, sapping our will while we slept.

The political parties waged their battles in the spirit spaces, beyond the realm of our earthly worries. They fought and hurled counter-mythologies at one another. Herbalists, sorcerers, wizards and witches took sides and as the trucks fought for votes in the streets they fought for supremacy in the world of spirits. They called on djinns and chimeras, succubi, incubi and apparitions; they enlisted the ghosts of old warriors and politicians and strategists; they hired expatriate spirits. The Party of the Rich drew support from the spirits of the Western world. At night, over our dreams, pacts were made, contracts drawn up in that realm of nightspace, and our futures were mortgaged, our destinies delayed. In that realm the sorcerers of party politics unleashed thunder, rain flooded those below; counter-thunder, lightning and hail were returned. On and on it went, in every village, every city of the country, and all over the continent and the whole world too. Our dreams grew smaller as they waged their wars of political supremacy. Sorcerers, taking the form of spirits and omens, whispered to us of dread. We grew more afraid. Suspicion made it easier for us to be silent. Silence made it easier for us to be more powerless. The forms of dominance grew more colossal in the nightspaces. And those of us who were poor, who had no great powers on our side, and who didn't see the power of our own hunger, a power that would frighten even the gods, found that our dreams became locked out of the freedom of the air. Our yearnings became blocked out of the realms of manifestation. The battles for our destiny raged and we could no longer fly to the moon or accompany the aeroplanes on their journeys through rarefied spaces or imagine how our lives could be different and better. So we had bad dreams about one another while Madame Koto, dressed in red, her hair covered with a white kerchief, three green umbrellas in her hand, extended her powers over the ghetto and sent her secret emissaries into our bodies. Our fantasies fed her. Many of us dreamt of her as a future spirit bride to heads of state and presidents. She became known as the Queen of the Ghetto Night. Anyone who wanted help went to her. She received only a few callers. Because she expanded so much at night, she suffered untold agonies in her body during the day. She showed no signs of pain. But the sweat on her forehead widened her wrinkles. Her prostitutes deserted her; they couldn't forgive her for so quickly forgetting the girl's death. When they left, the emptiness of her bar and the magnetism of her new powers drew a greater flock.

One night she appeared to me in my sleep and begged me to give her some of my youth.

"Why?" I asked.

And she replied:

"I am two hundred years old and unless I get your young blood I will die soon."

Her enormous spirit lowered over me. Her spirit was about to swallow me up completely, when a great lion roared from above, quaking the house, and driving her spirit away. Then I realised that new forces were being born to match the demands of the age. Leopards and lions of the spirit world, dragons of justice, winged tigers of truth, fierce animals of the divine, forces that swirl in the midst of inexorable hurricanes, they too restore balances and feed on the chimeras and vile intentions of the open air; and with every monstrous breath exhaled, for every blast of wind from evil wings, and for every power on the sides of those that feed on the earth's blood, a fabulous angel is born; and I saw an angel flying over our roof on the third day of Dad's sleep. It went past and the wind quietened and strange trees cracked in the forest and in the morning the rain stopped, the floods of water sank mysteriously into the secrets of the absorbent earth. Mum went up and down the streets hawking and sold off all her provisions and she kept finding pound notes floating on the dazzling waters and it seemed that the air had been cleared. But that morning I saw the first intimations; they were not intimations of a new season of calm, but of a cycle coming to an end. And how was I to know that it would be the beggars who would represent the first sign, with their expectancy, their air of people awaiting the word of a Messiah's birth, when in fact all they were waiting for was an omen to inform them that the time for their departure had arrived.

For in the evenings, as Mum prepared food, the fevers of the rally and its whispers of a long curfew were gathering. Then one evening, under the spell of incense and prayers and mosquito-coil smoke, under the holes of our roof, with the multiplied bugs on the floor, and with the room invaded by the green moths that understood the transformative properties of fire, offering themselves as willing sacrificial victims, Dad woke suddenly, he awoke powerfully, he rose from the bed as from death. His wounds had healed, his spirit had sharpened, his despair was deeper, he was a bigger man with a bigger madness. He got up and sat on his chair. And while the candles fluttered and burned brighter for the air that his sleep no longer deprived them of, Dad with his new deep sad voice began to speak to us. He spoke as if he hadn't been away. He spoke as if he hadn't made great journeys in spirit. And he spoke with the great enthusiastic innocence of a recuperating man.

"My wife and my son, listen to me. In my sleep I saw many wonderful things. Our ancestors taught me many philosophies. My father, Priest of Roads, appeared to me and said I should keep my door open. My heart must be open. My life must be open. Our road must be open. A road that is open is never hungry. Strange times are coming. "

"What about thieves?" I asked.

"Shut up, Azaro. We are protected, you hear. We are fortified against invaders and wicked people. Nothing evil will enter our lives."

He paused, creaked his bones, and continued.

"A single thought of ours could change the universe. We human beings are small things. Life is a great thing. As I am talking now they are holding elections in heaven and under the sea. We have entered a new age. We must be prepared. There are strange bombs in the world. Great powers in space are fighting to control our destiny. Machines and poisons and selfish dreams will eat us up. I entered a space ship and found myself on another planet. People who look like human beings are not human beings. Strange people are amongst us. We must be careful. Our lives are changing. Our gods are silent. Our ancestors are silent. A great something is going to come from the sky and change the face of the earth. We must take an interest in politics. We must become spies on behalf of justice. Human beings are dreaming of wiping out their fellow human beings from this earth. Rats and frogs understand their destiny. Why not man, eh? My wife, my son, where are we going? There is no rest for the soul. God is hungry for us to grow. When you look around and you see empty spaces, beware. In those spaces are cities, invisible civilisations, future histories, everything is HERE. We must look at the world with new eyes. We must look at ourselves differently. We are freer than we think. We haven't begun to live yet. The man whose light has come on in his head, in his dormant sun, can never be kept down or defeated. We can redream this world and make the dream real. Human beings are gods hidden from themselves. My son, our hunger can change the world, make it better, sweeter. People who use only their eyes do not SEE. People who use only their ears do not HEAR. It is more difficult to love than to die. It is not death that human beings are most afraid of, it is love. The heart is bigger than a mountain. One human life is deeper than the ocean. Strange fishes and sea-monsters and mighty plants live in the rock-bed of our spirits. The whole of human history is an undiscovered continent deep in our souls. There are dolphins, plants that dream, magic birds inside us. The sky is inside us. The earth is in us. The trees of the forest, the animals of the bushes, tortoises, birds, and flowers know our future. The world that we see and the world that is there are two different things. Wars are not fought on battlegrounds but in a space smaller than the head of a needle. We need a new language to talk to one another. Inside a cat there are many histories, many books. When you look into the eyes of dogs strange fishes swim in your mind. All roads lead to death, but some roads lead to things which can never be finished. Wonderful things. There are human beings who are small but if you can SEE you will notice that their spirits are ten thousand feet wide. In my dream I met a child sitting on a cloud and his spirit covered half the earth. Angels and demons are amongst us; they take many forms. They can enter us and dwell there for one second or half a lifetime. Sometimes both of them dwell in us together. Before everything was born there was first the spirit. It is the spirit which invites things in, good things, or bad. Invite only good things, my son. Listen to the spirit of things. To your own spirit. Follow it. Master it. So long as we are alive, so long as we feel, so long as we love, everything in us is an energy we can use. There is a stillness which makes you travel faster. There is a silence which makes you fly. If your heart is a friend of Time nothing can destroy you. Death has taught me the religion of living—I am converted—I am blinded—I am beginning to see—I am drunk on sleep—My words are the words of a stranger—Wear a smile on your faces—Pour me some wine and buy me some cigarettes, my son, for your father has returned to his true home."

There was a long silence as we swam around in the strange currents of Dad's words. After a long while Mum gave me some money and I rushed out to buy him the ogogoro and cigarettes. The beggars followed me half-way back on my return journey. There were spaces full of green moths in the air. The lights over our lives had changed. A deeper tint of indigo had coloured the clouds. I passed through a floating island of sepia midges. When I got to our room a lizard with a lavender tail scurried in after me. I was about to chase it out when Dad said:

"All creatures must be treated with respect from now on. If you want the lizard out command it to go and it will go. We must use our powers wisely. We must not become tyrants, you hear?"

I nodded. Then Dad got up from his chair and in a high-pitched, almost comical, voice, he said:

"Mr. Lizard, where are you? Out! Leave this room and go somewhere else. Now."

We watched the floor. There was no movement. Mum sighed. Dad didn't repeat his order. He sat back down on the chair. We sat in silence. Then, after a while, the lizard came out from under the cupboard, nodded three times, and fled from the room. There was a very long silence. Dad did not acknowledge the event. He reached out his hands and I gave him the cigarettes and the bottle of ogogoro, transparent with its bubbling acrid dreams. Dad drank in peace. He smoked quietly. We watched him in silent wonderment, as if an alien had entered his body.

"Many people reside in us," Dad said, as if he were reading our thoughts, "many past lives, many future lives. If you listen carefully the air is full of laughter. Human beings are a great mystery."

A long time passed in the silence that followed. Then Mum got up and laid out for Dad what food there was. He ate ravenously and when he finished he turned the plates over and looked at their undersides as if he were searching for more food.

"There's not much money in the house," Mum said. "You haven't been working."

Dad drank what seemed like a gallon of water. Then he wore his only pair of socks, which were full of holes; he wore his smelling boots, and began to pace up and down, his fearful energies swirling about him, disturbing the invisible residents of the room.

Mum turned the mattress over, dressed the bed, cleared the table, and spread out my mat.

"My husband," she said, "we have been worried about you. For three nights we have wrestled to bring your spirit back. We have been hungry and full of fear. Get some more sleep now. In the morning resume work. Resume your struggles. Be what you are. We are happy that you are well again."

Dad came over and embraced Mum tenderly for the first time in months. Then he lit a mosquito coil, left the door slightly ajar, took off his boots and socks, and lay down on the protesting bed. In the darkness I heard Mum say:

"You have become heavier, my husband."

Dad didn't say anything. His spirit was gentle through the night. The air in the room was calm. There were no turbulences. His presence protected our nightspace. There were no forms invading our air, pressing down on our roof, walking through the objects. The air was clear and wide. In my sleep I found open spaces where I floated without fear. The sky was serene. A good breeze blew over our road, cleaning away the strange excesses in the air. It was so silent and peaceful that after some time I was a bit worried. I was not used to such a gift of quietude. The deeper it was, the deeper was my fear. I kept expecting eerie songs to break into my mind. I kept expecting to see spirit-lovers entwined in blades of sunlight. Nothing happened. The sweetness dissolved my fears. I was not afraid of Time.

And then it was another morning. The room was empty. Mum and Dad were gone. And the good breeze hadn't lasted for ever.

A dream can be the highest point of a life.

These two selections move from the personal vision to the social vision. They are statements by people who are proud of their idealism and commitment to the substance of democratic living. In different genres and styles, they have the common purpose of articulating a perspective on life in which the communal is as central as the personal and in which the joy of being alive is expressed as much in the company of others as it is in the development of the self.

❦ MAXINE GREENE, *Releasing the Imagination*

If we can link imagination to our sense of possibility and our ability to respond to other human beings, can we link it to the making of community as well? Can we encourage the ability of young persons to interpret their experiences in a world they come together to name? G. B. Madison, writing about the centrality of the imagination, says that "it is through imagination, the realm of pure possibility that we freely make ourselves to be who or what we are, that we creatively and imaginatively become who we are, while in the process preserving the freedom and possibility to be yet otherwise than what we have become and merely are." I believe that the kind of becoming Madison describes is in a large degree dependent on membership in a community of regard. Those who are labeled as deficient, fixed in that category as firmly as flies in amber, have little chance to feel they can be yet otherwise than what they have become. Marginalized, they are left to the experience of powerlessness unless (usually with support) they are enabled to explain their "shocks" and reach beyond.

How are we to comprehend the kind of community that offers the opportunity to be otherwise? Democracy, we realize, means a community that is always in the making. Marked by an emerging solidarity, a sharing of certain beliefs, and a dialogue about others, it must remain open to newcomers, those too long thrust aside. This can happen even in the local spaces of classrooms, particularly when students are encouraged to find their voices and their images. Hannah Arendt once wrote about the importance of diverse persons speaking to one another as "who" and not "what" they are and, in so doing, creating an "in-between" among themselves.

❧ TONY KUSHNER, *American Things*

Summer is the season for celebrating freedom, summer is the time when we can almost believe it is possible to be free. American education conditions us for this expectation: School's out! The climate shift seductively whispers emancipation. Warmth opens up the body and envelops it. The body in summer is most easily at home in the world. This is true even when the summer is torrid. I have lived half my life in Louisiana and half in New York City. I know from torrid summers.

On my seventh birthday, midsummer 1963, my mother deco-rated my cake with sparklers she'd saved from the Fourth of July. This, I thought, was extraordinary, fantastic, sparklers spitting and smoking, dangerous and beautiful atop my birthday cake. In one indelible, ecstatic instant my mother completed a circuit of identifi-cation for me, melding two iconographies, of self and of liberty: of birthday cake, delicious confectionery emblem of maternal enthusi-asm about my existence, which enthusiasm I shared; and of the night-time fireworks of pyroromantic Americana, fireworks-liberty-light which slashed across the evening sky, light which thrilled the heart, light which exclaimed loudly in the thick summer air, light which occasionally tore off fingers and burned houses, the fiery fierce explo-sive risky light of Independence, of Freedom.

Stonewall, the festival day of lesbian and gay liberation, is followed closely by the Fourth of July; they are exactly one summer week apart. The contiguity of these two festivals of freedom is important, at least to me. Each adds piquancy and meaning to the other. In the years follow-ing my seventh birthday I had lost some of my enthusiasm for my own existence, as most queer kids growing up in a hostile world will do. I'd certainly begun to realize how unenthusiastic others, even my parents, would be if they knew I was gay. Such joy in being alive as I can now lay claim to has been returned to me largely because of the successes of the political movement which began, more or less officially, twenty-five years ago on that June night in the Village. I've learned how absolutely essential to life freedom is.

Lesbian and gay freedom is the same freedom celebrated annually on the Fourth of July. Of this I have no doubt; my mother told me so, back in 1963, by putting sparklers on that cake. She couldn't have made her point more powerfully if she'd planted them on my head. Hers was a gesture we both understood, though at the time neither could have articulated it: "This fantastic fire is yours." Mothers and fathers should do that for their kids: give them fire, and link them proudly and durably to the world in which they live.

One of the paths down which my political instruction came was our family Seder. Passover, too, is a celebration of Freedom in sultry, intoxicating heat. (Passover actually comes in the spring, but in Louisiana the distinction between spring and summer was as never clear.) Our family read from Haggadahs written by a New Deal Reform rabbinate which was unafraid to draw connections between Pharaonic and modern capitalist exploitations; between the exodus of Jews from Goshen and the journey towards civil rights for African-Americans; unafraid to make of the yearning which Jews have repeated for thousands of years a democratic dream of freedom for all peoples. It was impressed upon us, as we sang "America the Beautiful" at the Seder's conclusion, that the dream of millennia was due to find its ultimate realization not in Jerusalem but in this country.

The American political tradition to which my parents made me an heir is mostly an immigrant appropriation of certain features and promises of our Constitution, and of the idea of democracy and federalism. This appropriation marries freedom—up-for-grabs, morally and ideologically indeterminate freedom—to the more strenuous, grave and specific mandates of justice. It is the aggressive, unapologetic, progressive liberalism of the thirties and forties, a liberalism strongly spiced with socialism, trade unionism and the ethos of internationalism and solidarity.

This liberalism at its best held that citizenship was bestowable on everyone, and sooner or later it would be bestowed. Based first and foremost on reason, and then secondarily on protecting certain articles of faith such as the Bill of Rights, democratic process would eventually perform the action of shifting power from the mighty to the many, in whose hands, democratically and morally speaking, it belongs. Over the course of two hundred years, brave, visionary activists and ordinary, moral people had carved out a space, a large sheltering room from which many were now excluded, but which was clearly intended to be capable of multitudes. Within the space of American Freedom there was room for any possibility. American Freedom would become the birthplace of social and economic Justice.

Jews who came to America had gained entrance into this grand salon, as had other immigrant groups: Italians, Irish. Black people, Chicanos and Latinos, Asian-Americans would soon make their own ways, I was told, as would women, as would the working class and the poor—it could only be a matter of time and struggle.

People who desired sex with people of their own gender, transgender people, fags and dykes, drag kings and drag queens, queers, deviants from heterosexual normality were not discussed. There was identity, and then there was illness.

I am nearly thirty-eight, and anyone who's lived thirty-eight years should have made generational improvements on the politics of his or her parents. For any gay man or lesbian since Stonewall, the politics of homosexual enfranchisement is part of what is to be added to the fund of human experience and understanding, to the cosmologies, described and assumed, that we pass on to the next generation—upon which we hope improvements will be made.

The true motion of freedom is to expand outward. To say that lesbian and gay freedom is the same freedom celebrated annually on the Fourth of July is simply to say that queer and other American freedoms have changed historically, generally in a healthy direction (with allowances for some costly periods of faltering, including recently), and must continue to change if they are to remain meaningful. No freedom that fails to grow will last.

Lesbians and gay men of this generation have added homophobia to the consensus list of social evils: poverty, racism, sexism, exploitation, the ravaging of the environment, censorship, imperialism, war. To be a progressive person is to believe that there are ways to actively intervene against these evils. To be a progressive person is to resist Balkanization, tribalism, separatism, is to resist the temptation to hunker down; to be progressive is to seek out connection. I am homosexual, and this ought to make me consider how my experience of the world, as someone who is not always welcome, resembles that of others, however unlike me, who have had similar experiences. I demand to be accorded my rights by others; and so I must be prepared to accord to others their rights. The truest characteristic of freedom is generosity, the basic gesture of freedom is to include, not to exclude.

That there would be a reasonably successful movement for lesbian and gay civil rights was scarcely conceivable a generation ago. In spite of these gains, much of the social progress, which to my parents seemed a foregone conclusion has not yet been made, and much ground has been lost. Will racism prove to be more intractable, finally, than homophobia? Will the hatred of women, gay and straight, continue to find new and more violent forms of expression, and will gay men and women of color remain doubly, or triply oppressed, while white gay men find greater measures of acceptance, simply because they are white men?

Along with the principle of freedom, much that is gory and disgraceful is celebrated on the Fourth of July, much that is brutal and oppressive. American history is the source for some people of a belief in the inevitable triumph of justice; for others it is the source of a sense of absolute power and ownership which obviates the need to be concerned about justice; while for still others American history is a source of despair that anything like justice will ever come. The can-do liberalism of an earlier day may be faulted for having failed to consider the awesome weight of the crimes of the past, the propensity for tragedy in history, the river of spilled blood that precedes us into the future.

The tensions that have defined American history and American political consciousness have most often been those existing between the margin and the center, the many and the few, the individual and society, the dispossessed and the possessors. It is a peculiar feature of our political life that some of these tensions are frequently discussed and easily grasped, such as those existing between the states and the federal government, or between the rights of individuals and any claim society might make upon them; while other tensions, especially those which are occasioned by the claims of minorities, of marginalized peoples, are regarded with suspicion and fear. Listing the full catalogue of the complaints of the disenfranchised is sure to raise howls decrying "victimology" and "political correctness" from those who need desperately to believe that democracy is a simple thing.

Democracy isn't simple and it doesn't mean that majorities tyrannize minorities. We learned this a long time ago, from, among others, the demi-Moses of that Jewish American Book of Exodus, Louis Dembitz Brandeis, or in more recent times from Thurgood Marshall. In these days of demographic shifts, when majorities are disappearing, this knowledge is particularly useful, and it needs to be expanded. There are in this country political traditions congenial to the idea that democracy is multicolor and multicultural and also multigendered, that democracy is about returning to individuals the fullest range of their freedoms, but also about the sharing of power, about the rediscovery of collective responsibility. There are in this country political traditions— from organized labor, from the civil rights and black power movements, from feminist and homosexual liberation movements, from movements for economic reform—which postulate democracy as an ongoing project, as a dynamic process. These traditions exist in opposition to those which make fixed fetishes of democracy and freedom, talismans for Reaction.

These traditions, which constitute the history of progressive and radical America, have been shunted to the side, covered over in an attempt at revisionism that began during the McCarthy era. Over the course of American history since the Second World War, the terms of the national debate have subtly, insidiously shifted. What used to be called liberal is now called radical; what used to be called radical is now called insane. What used to be called reactionary is now called moderate, and what used to be called insane is now called solid conservative thinking.

The recovery of antecedents is immensely important work. Historians are reconstructing the lost history of homosexual America, along with all the other lost histories. Freedom, I think, is finally being at home in the world, it is a returning—to an enlargement of the best particulars of the home you came from, or the arrival, after a lengthy and arduous journey, at the home you never had, which your dreams and desires have described for you.

I have a guilty confession to make. When I am depressed, when nerve or inspiration or energy flags, I put Dvořák's Ninth Symphony, *From the New World*, on the CD player; I get teary listening to the Largo. It's become classical Muzak, one of the all-time most shopworn musical clichés, which I think is regrettable. My father, who is a symphony conductor, told me that Dvořák wrote it in Spillville, Iowa. The National Conservatory of Music brought him to America to start a nationalist school of American composers. Dvořák contributed all the money from the *New World Symphony*'s premiere to a school for former slaves. But then his daughter fell in love with a Native American from the Spillville reservation and Dvořák freaked and took the whole family back to Bohemia.

Like many Americans, I'm looking for home. Home is an absence, it is a loss that impels us. I want this home to be like the Largo from the *New World Symphony*. But life most frequently resembles something by Schoenberg, the last quartet, the one he wrote after his first heart attack and they had to stick a five-inch needle into his heart to revive him. Life these days is played out to the tune of that soundtrack. Or something atonal, anyway, something derivative of Schoenberg, some piece written by one of his less talented pupils, something else.

The only politics that can survive an encounter with this world, and still speak convincingly of freedom and justice and democracy, is a politics that can encompass both the harmonics and the dissonance. The frazzle, the rubbed raw, the unresolved, the fragile and the fiery and the dangerous: These are American things. This jangle is our movement forward, if we are to move forward; it is our survival, if we are to survive.

Idealism and concern for all of humanity can be seen as a calling and an obligation. Czeslaw Milosz's poem talks about angels, inspiration, and obligation. Simone Weil's essay is a universal plea for people to assume obligations toward each other. It represents a common theme in idealism—the idea that what is due one human being should also be due the rest of humanity.

❦ Czeslaw Milosz, *On Angels*

All was taken away from you: white dresses,
wings, even existence.
Yet I believe you,
messengers.

There, where the world is turned inside out,
a heavy fabric embroidered with stars and beasts,
you stroll, inspecting the trustworthy seams.

Short is your stay here:
now and then at a matinal hour, if the sky is clear,
in a melody repeated by a bird,
or in the smell of apples at close of day
when the light makes the orchards magic.

They say somebody has invented you
but to me this does not sound convincing
for the humans invented themselves as well.

The voice—no doubt it is a valid proof,
as it can belong only to radiant creatures,
weightless and winged (after all, why not?),
girdled with the lightning

I have heard that voice many a time when asleep
and, what is strange, I understood more or less
an order or an appeal in an unearthly tongue:

day draws near
another one
do what you can

❦ SIMONE WEIL, *Draft for a Statement of Human Obligations, 1943: Profession of Faith*

There is a reality outside the world, that is to say, outside space and time, outside man's mental universe, outside any sphere whatsoever that is accessible to human faculties.

Corresponding to this reality, at the centre of the human heart, is the longing for an absolute good, a longing which is always there and is never appeased by any object in this world.

Another terrestrial manifestation of this reality lies in the absurd and insoluble contradictions which are always the terminus of human thought when it moves exclusively in this world.

Just as the reality of this world is the sole foundation of facts, so that other reality is the sole foundation of good.

That reality is the unique source of all the good that can exist in this world: that is to say, all beauty, all truth, all justice, all legitimacy, all order, and all human behaviour that is mindful of obligations.

Those minds whose attention and love are turned towards that reality are the sole intermediary through which good can descend from there and come among men.

Although it is beyond the reach of any human faculties, man has the power of turning his attention and love towards it.

Nothing can ever justify the assumption that any man, whoever he may be, has been deprived of this power.

It is a power which is only real in this world in so far as it is exercised. The sole condition for exercising it is consent.

This act of consent may be expressed, or it may not be, even tacitly; it may not be clearly conscious, although it has really taken place in the soul. Very often it is verbally expressed although it has not in fact taken place. But whether expressed or not, the one condition suffices: that it shall in fact have taken place.

❦   ❦   ❦

To anyone who does actually consent to directing his attention and love beyond the world, towards the reality that exists outside the reach of all human faculties, it is given to succeed in doing so. In that case, sooner or later, there descends upon him a part of the good, which shines through him upon all that surrounds him.

The combination of these two facts—the longing in the depth of the heart for absolute good, and the power, though only latent, of directing attention and love to a reality beyond the world and of receiving good from it—constitutes a link which attaches every man without exception to that other reality.

Whoever recognizes that reality recognizes also that link. Because of it, he holds every human being without any exception as something sacred to which he is bound to show respect.

This is the only possible motive for universal respect towards all human beings. Whatever formulation of belief or disbelief a man may choose to make, if his heart inclines him to feel this respect, then he in fact also recognizes a reality other than this world's reality. Whoever in fact does not feel this respect is alien to that other reality also.

The reality of the world we live in is composed of variety. Unequal objects unequally solicit our attention. Certain people personally attract our attention, either through the hazard of circumstances or some chance affinity. For the lack of such circumstance or affinity other people remain unidentified. They escape our attention or, at the most, it only sees them as items of a collectivity.

If our attention is entirely confined to this world it is entirely subject to the effect of these inequalities, which it is all the less able to resist because it is unaware of it.

It is impossible to feel equal respect for things that are in fact unequal unless the respect is given to something that is identical in all of them. Men are unequal in all their relations with the things of this world, without exception. The only thing that is identical in all men is the presence of a link with the reality outside the world.

All human beings are absolutely identical in so far as they can be thought of as consisting of a centre, which is an unquenchable desire for good, surrounded by an accretion of psychical and bodily matter.

. . . Because of it, when a man's life is destroyed or damaged by some wound or privation of soul or body, which is due to other men's actions or negligence, it is not only his sensibility that suffers but also his aspiration towards the good. Therefore there has been sacrilege towards that which is sacred in him.

On the other hand, there are cases where it is only a man's sensibility that is affected; for example, where his wound or privation is solely the result of the blind working of natural forces, or where he recognizes that the people who seem to be making him suffer are far from bearing him any ill will, but are acting solely in obedience to a necessity which he also acknowledges.

The possibility of indirect expression of respect for the human being is the basis of obligation. Obligation is concerned with the needs in this world of the souls and bodies of human beings, whoever they may be. For each need there is a corresponding obligation; for each obligation a corresponding need. There is no other kind of obligation, so far as human affairs are concerned.

If there seem to be others, they are either false or else it is only by error that they have not been classed among the obligations mentioned.

Anyone whose attention and love are really directed towards the reality outside the world recognizes at the same time that he is bound, both in public and private life, by the single and permanent obligation to remedy, according to his responsibilities and to the extent of his power, all the privations of soul and body which are liable to destroy or damage the earthly life of any human being whatsoever.

This obligation cannot legitimately be held to be limited by the insufficiency of power or the nature of the responsibilities until everything possible has been done to explain the necessity of the limitation to those who will suffer by it; the explanation must be completely truthful and must be such as to make it possible for them to acknowledge the necessity.

No combination of circumstances ever cancels this obligation. If there are circumstances which seem to cancel it as regards a certain man or category of men, they impose it in fact all the more imperatively.

Statement of Obligations

. . . The human soul has need of security and also of risk. The fear of violence or of hunger or of any other extreme evil is a sickness of the soul. The boredom produced by a complete absence of risk is also a sickness of the soul.

The human soul needs above all to be rooted in several natural environments and to make contact with the universe through them.

Examples of natural human environments are: a man's country, and places where his language is spoken, and places with a culture or a historical past which he shares, and his professional milieu, and his neighbourhood.

Everything which has the effect of uprooting a man or of preventing him from becoming rooted is criminal.

Any place where the needs of human beings are satisfied can be recognized by the fact that there is a flowering of fraternity, joy, beauty, and happiness. Wherever people are lonely and turned in on themselves, wherever there is sadness or ugliness, there are privations that need remedying.

Practical Application

For this statement to become the practical inspiration of the country's life, the first condition is that it should be adopted by the people with that intention.

The second condition is that anyone who wields or desires to wield any power of any kind—political, administrative, legal, economic, technical, spiritual, or other—should have to pledge himself to adopt it as his practical rule of conduct.

In such cases the equal and universal character of the obligation is to some extent modified by the particular responsibilities attaching to a particular office. It would therefore be necessary to amplify the pledge with the words: "... paying especial attention to the needs of the human beings who are in my charge."

The violation of such a pledge, either in word or deed, should always in principle be punishable. But, in most cases, the institutions and public morals which would make such punishment possible would take several generations to create.

Assent to this Statement implies a continual effort to bring such institutions and such morals into existence as rapidly as possible.

There are internal and external impediments to sustaining idealistic visions. Sometimes personal interest or necessity makes idealism seem foolish or hopeless. Other times idealism is rooted in someone else's ideas and actions and when they fail one's own idealism can collapse. These two poems show different faces of the struggle to remain idealistic.

❦ C. P. CAVAFY, *Waiting for the Barbarians*

What are we waiting for, assembled in the forum?

    The barbarians are due here today.

Why isn't anything going on in the senate?
Why are the senators sitting there without legislating?
    Because the barbarians are coming today.
    What's the point of senators making laws now?
    Once the barbarians are here, they'll do the legislating.

Why did our emperor get up so early,
and why is he sitting enthroned at the city's main gate,
in state, wearing the crown?

    Because the barbarians are coming today
    and the emperor's waiting to receive their leader.

He's even got a scroll to give him,
loaded with titles, with imposing names.

Why have our two consuls and praetors come out today
wearing their embroidered, their scarlet togas?
Why have they put on bracelets with so many amethysts,
rings sparkling with magnificent emeralds?
Why are they carrying elegant canes
beautifully worked in silver and gold?

    Because the barbarians are coming today
    and things like that dazzle the barbarians.

Why don't our distinguished orators turn up as usual
to make their speeches, say what they have to say?

    Because the barbarians are coming today
    and they're bored by rhetoric and public speaking.

Why this sudden bewilderment, this confusion?
(How serious people's faces have become.)
Why are the streets and squares emptying so rapidly,
everyone going home lost in thought?

    Because night has fallen and the barbarians haven't come
    and some of our men just in from the border say
    there are no barbarians any longer.

Now what's going to happen to us without barbarians?
They were, those people, a kind of solution.

❦ BOB KAUFMAN, *I Have Folded My Sorrows*

I have folded my sorrows into the mantle of summer night,
Assigning each brief storm its allotted space in time,

Quietly pursuing catastrophic histories buried in my eyes.
And yes, the world is not some unplayed Cosmic Game,
And the sun is still ninety-three million miles from me,
And in the imaginary forest, the shingled hippo becomes the gay
　　unicorn.
No, my traffic is not with addled keepers of yesterday's disasters,
Seekers of manifest disembowelment on shafts of yesterday's pains.
Blues come dressed like introspective echoes of a journey.
And yes, I have searched the rooms of the moon on cold summer
　　nights.
And yes, I have refought those unfinished encounters.
　　Still, they remain unfinished.
And yes, I have at times wished myself something different.

The tragedies are sung nightly at the funerals of the poet;
The revisited soul is wrapped in the aura of familiarity.

In Wesley Brown's Darktown Strutters, *a fictional history of the persistence of idealism in the face of racism, we find a powerful and enduring vision of justice despite oppression. Here are two vignettes taken from the long and complex story of Jim Crow, dancer and entertainer extraordinaire.*

WESLEY BROWN, *Darktown Strutters*

I

　　It wasn't long before Tom Rice was thinking about ways to put what happened in Paducah into the show. But while Rice was thinking up new gimmicks to get people's attention, the government was putting on a show to settle the argument over slavery that had the whole country riled up. Blacks didn't like the idea that even though slavery was at centerstage of all the talk about the future of the country, the government only wanted to set a limit on the states where it could be taken on the road. But blacks didn't let that stop them from walking out on slavery wherever it was playing.

❧ ❧ ❧

Tom Rice's Non-Pareil Minstrel Show played to full houses wherever it went. And Jim had gotten even more popular after Paducah. All the attention bothered him because he knew people wanted to look at his face for the same reasons they came to see the other actors in black face. Everybody else could wipe their faces off at the end of the show. But like his color, the scar, growing like a worm out of the corner of his mouth, was there for good. Jim became very moody and didn't talk to anyone except Jack Diamond. He even stopped acting in skits with the other actors so he wouldn't have to be around them. Many in the show started saying among themselves that Jim had gotten as good at playing the dandy as Rice was at playing the darky.

While Rice didn't like the change in Jim, he had other things on his mind. He was still working on his skit about the attack on Jim in Paducah. But he decided not to tell anyone until it was finished. When the skit was done, Rice told everyone else before he talked with Jim. Things between them had gotten worse after Jim found out that Rice had known about his father being lynched.

On a train to Cincinnati, Rice walked into the Jim Crow car and was surprised to find Jim reading a newspaper.

"I didn't know you could read," he said.

"You know how it is, Mister Rice? Being Jim Crow means I gotta keep a lotta things to myself."

"I got a new skit I wanna run by you. I got the idea from when those rednecks cut you in Paducah. The way it goes is—we'd all be in black face on one side of our face and white on the other. When we start talkin out of both sides of our faces, you try to figure out who's on your side and who ain't. We keep the audience guessin right along with you until the end when everybody finds out who's who."

Jim tried not to laugh, but couldn't help himself and felt the usual itch in his scarred cheek.

Rice smiled.

"I was hopin you'd like it," he said.

"No you wasn't, Mister Rice. You was hopin I'd be in it. But like I told you before, I wanna do what I do by myself."

Rice shook his head.

"I'm not askin you to black up."

"I still ain't gon do it."

"I guess what everybody's been sayin bout you is true?"

"What's that?"

"That you done turned into a duded-up slave actin like some white-assed dandy!"

"I had me some good teachers."

"Jim, don't you think you carryin this act a yours a little too far?"

"Ain't that what bein a minstrel's all about?"

"You know what I'm talkin about."

"Yeah. I know. You think I don't buck in the middle enough. Well, this took all the buck out a me!" Jim said, pointing to his scar.

"I ain't sayin you have to wipe your face on nobody's ass. But you gotta understand that if you wasn't in this show and acted the way you act, you wouldn't be scarred for life. You'd be dead! One way or another, you gonna have to accept that, slave or free, white folks and maybe even some a your own people ain't gonna 'low you to act like you dance when you come offstage. . . . Even I got sense enough to know that the life I got once I come off stage ain't never gonna be more than an intermission between shows."

"Inna-mission? Is that what you call what you was doin when that man come out your dressing room?" Jim said, snapping the newspaper open in front of his face so he wouldn't have to look at Rice.

Rice smiled, turned to leave the car but stopped.

"I know you ain't had much practice yet. But lemme know what it does for you to feel like you better than me."

Rice's new skit opened in Cincinnati and was called, "WHO's WHO IN PADUCAH?" Jim didn't change his mind about not wanting to be in it. Another actor was picked for the lead role of a fugitive slave who got into town just ahead of slave-catchers and hid in a theater while a minstrel show was going on. The slave-catchers spotted the slave slipping in the back door of the theater. They followed him inside; and when they saw all the actors onstage in black face, they blackened their own faces so the escaped slave wouldn't notice them.

They found him backstage and chased him through the curtains into the middle of a scene full of actors in black face. The black-faced actors, the escaped black-faced slave, and the black-faced slave-catchers got so tangled together that everyone had a hold of something that belonged to someone else. The skit ended when the black-faced slave got lost in the mix-up of black-faced white actors and slave catchers with none of them knowing who anyone was. The theater rocked from the side-splitting laughter of the audience, and the cast closed out the show singing the title song, "Who's Who In Paducah?"

Tom Rice's Non-Pareil Minstrel Show played to standing room-only crowds for the whole five-day run in Cincinnati. It was a hit in cities and towns all along the Ohio River and made Tom Rice the most famous minstrel in the country. "WHO's WHO IN PADUCAH?" became the most loved popular entertainment in America until a book came on the scene that shook the nation up, first on the page and then on the stage. It was called UNCLE TOM's CABIN!

II

"You wanna fight for the Union Army?" Diamond asked.

"Not for the Union Army. For myself!"

"You put the man's uniform on, you fight for what he want you to fight for," Jubilee said.

"Like you said: puttin on the uniform's the same as puttin on the mask," Jim said, grinding anger between his teeth.

"Listen to you! You against blackin up but you ready to do white face in the Union Army. Ain't you somethin! Shaughnessy! Another round for everybody!"

Jubilee slapped the money down on the bar, pushed himself away from it, and headed for the door. Everyone had another drink on Jubilee and huddled up in their own thoughts. This was not the case in the streets outside The Jig as voices were heard rising up in a mist of song:

Slavery chain done broke at last!
Broke at last! Broke at last!
Slavery chain done broke at last!
Gonna praise God till I die!

That spring Jim heard that Frederick Douglass was going to speak in Philadelphia. He decided to go, not only to see the great man, but to hear Douglass's reasons for wanting blacks to fight for the Union. At the train station on the morning Jim was leaving, the conductor pointed to him.

"First car behind the engine," he said.

Jim turned around just before boarding the train but didn't see the conductor telling anyone else which car to ride in. The car was about half-filled with blacks. Jim took a seat next to a man and watched blacks continue to file into the car.

"You travel by train much?" he asked the man.

"Now and again," the man said.

"I was just wonderin cause it seem like all the colored folks ridin in this car."

"So?"

"It's just that the conductor told me to ride in this car, but he didn't say anything to the white folks behind me."

"Ain't you been on a train before?"

"Plenty times."

"Then you either funnin with me or you crazy as a jaybird."

"You sayin, we ain't allowed in the same car with white folks?"

"Well now!" the man said, smiling. "I'm glad you back from wherever you been hidin yourself!"

At the station in Philadelphia, Jim was given directions to the church where Douglass was speaking. The church was on a narrow street of frame houses that were crammed together. It was the last house on the block and seemed to be leaning off to one side.

Jim took a seat in the back of the packed church and had to strain to get a better look at the speakers seated in the front. Even from that distance, he could tell which one was Douglass from the eyes that went right through you and the thick, woolly hair rising high above his forehead. When Douglass was finally introduced, he stood up, and his body spread out from his vest-covered chest, up the sleeves of his coat, to his bull neck and out of his shirt collar to his lion's head.

Then he spoke. And his words echoed through the church like cracking timber, fresh from the cut of an ax.

"President Lincoln once said to me that a man with few vices has even fewer virtues. I responded by saying that the Negro people were well acquainted with the vices of presidents but would be patient and wait for the new President's virtuous deeds to overtake his many failings."

The applause was swift, making ear-splitting sounds in the rafters of the church.

"Our patience has been rewarded, if only in part, by Lincoln's Emancipation Proclamation!"

There was more applause but not as loud as before.

"I know you ask yourselves, what if anything do we owe a government whose crimes against us are too numerous to catalogue? But I am not here to recount our dreaded past! I am here to propose a way for us to create the future! I have here," he said, holding a stack of papers above his head, "the living present, in the form of recruitment applications! If you put your mark on this paper, you will be taking the first step toward placing your destiny in your own hands! Most of what we've done with our hands has enriched someone else's crop. Now we have an opportunity to tend our own. And it's right here!" he said, shaking the papers in his hand again. "If we take hold of the present, the future is within our grasp!"

After his speech, Douglass passed out recruitment forms. People pressed in all around him, and it was a while before Jim was able to get near enough to speak to him.

"Mister Douglass," he said, after taking one of the forms, "you really think we gonna get to fight?"

"The war cannot be won without us," Douglass said, as his eyes zeroed in on Jim. "I've seen you before. What's your name?"

"Jim Crow."

"The dancer?"

Jim nodded.

"Do you intend to enlist?"

"I'm thinkin on it."

"If you did, many of our people might follow your example."

"I don't think so, Mister Douglass. I'm not somebody colored people gonna pay much mind to, one way or the other."

The fire in Douglass's eyes simmered, making him seem more relaxed.

"To be perfectly honest, Mister Crow, I have often been puzzled by your popularity among our people and have wondered whether your dancing in minstrel shows has done our race more harm than good. But in recent years, to my surprise, I've been hearing people say the same thing about me. . . . I guess that's what happens when you're around long enough to have lived through even worse times than those younger than yourself can remember. Some people never forgive you for having survived. Maybe they're right, Mister Crow. The longer we live, the more we should have to answer for."

Jim didn't know if he understood all of what Douglass had said. But he did know that at some point while Douglass spoke, his eyes moved away from him and seemed to be looking for something far in the distance.

4
One Green Tomato

HOPEFULNESS

Nelson Mandela, in his presidential inaugural speech in 1994, reminded the world about hope and its deep reservoir in all of us if we can be free of fear:

> As we let our light shine, we unconsciously give other people permission to do the same. As we are liberated from our own fear, our presence automatically liberates others.

Hope is the quality of character that sustains belief under seemingly impossible situations—when love seems impossible or poverty inevitable or when the world seems cruel and life unbearable. People encounter sources of hope in the imagination, in the words and examples of others, and in witness to the miracle of growth in nature that calls them back to life. Hope does not extinguish suffering but sustains the belief that there can be an end to it, if not in one's own life, then after life or in the future.

The imagination in its many manifestations sustains this hope and often makes it vivid. A lively and active imagination sustains dreams, visions, and daydreams. It does not confuse life on the ground with these manifestations of hope, but it does not deny them the power to transform the world either. Hope projects alternate realities and is rooted in some deep-seated need to believe that the world can be other than it is.

Selections

This section will explore ways of understanding hope and illustrate how it enriches people's lives. It will also explore the small ways in which hope is germinated, as well as the impediments people face that can erode hope and lead to despair. It will begin with a poem that celebrates the hopeful potential of the seed in one green tomato.

❦ LOUIS JENKINS, *Green Tomato*

This morning
after the first frost,
there is a green tomato
among the kleenex
combs and loose change,
the more usual clutter
on the dresser.
That's the way it is
around here,
things picked up,
put down, lost
or forgotten.
Here is the possibility
of next year's crop,
even more,
in one green tomato.
It makes me smile
to see it there,
newly discovered
confident and
mysterious as the face
of my young son
who comes to the bedroom
early, ready to play.
There is no point in

my telling you too much
of what makes me
happy or sad.
I did not wake to find,
at this moment,
in this unlikely place,
only my own life.

Vaclav Havel sets the scene for this section with a meditation on hope. However, lest hope seem too easy an answer to the problems of life, Havel's remarks, made while the Soviet-backed government still controlled Czechoslovakia, are followed by an excerpt from Richard II *that underlines the impediments to hope and the anguish of being silenced. They provide a counterpoint to the affirmations that the other selections on hope project, though Tillie Olsen, after documenting silences, shares her journey toward speaking out.*

❧ VACLAV HAVEL, *1986 Speech*

Hope is an orientation of the spirit, an orientation of the heart; it transcends the world that is immediately experienced, and is anchored somewhere beyond its horizons. It is not the conviction that something will turn out well, but the certainty that something makes sense regardless of how it turns out. The more unpropitious the situation in which we demonstrate hope, the deeper the hope is. It is this hope, above all, which gives us the hope to live and continually try new things, even in conditions that seem as hopeless as ours do here and now.

❧ WILLIAM SHAKESPEARE, *Richard II*

O! Who can hold a fire in his hand
by thinking on the frosty Caucuses?
Or cloy the hungry edge of appetite

By bare imagination of a feast?
Or wallow naked in December snow
By thinking on fantastic summer's heat?
O, no! the apprehension of the good
Gives but the greater feeling to the worse.

❧ TILLIE OLSEN, *Silences*

As for myself, who did not publish a book until I was fifty, who raised children without household help or the help of the "technological sublime" (the atom bomb was in manufacture before the first automatic washing machine); who worked outside the house on everyday jobs as well (as nearly half of all women do now, though a woman with a paid job, except as a maid or prostitute, is still rarest of any in literature); who could not kill the essential angel (there was no one else to do her work); would not—if I could—have killed the caring part of the Woolf angel; as distant from the world of literature most of my life as literature is distant (in content too) from my world:

The years when I should have been writing, my hands and being were at other (inescapable) tasks. Now, lightened as they are, when I must do those tasks into which most of my life went, like the old mother, grandmother in my *Tell Me a Riddle* who could not make herself touch a baby, I pay a psychic cost: "the sweat beads, the long shudder begins." The habits of a lifetime when everything else had to come before writing are not easily broken, even when circumstances now often make it possible for writing to be first; habits of years—response to others, distractibility, responsibility for daily matters—stay with you, mark you, become you. The cost of "discontinuity" (that pattern still imposed on women) is such a weight of things unsaid, an accumulation of material so great, that every thing starts up something else in me; what should take weeks, takes me sometimes months to write; what should take months, takes years.

I speak of myself to bring here the sense of those others to whom this is in the process of happening (unnecessarily happening, for it need not, must not continue to be) and to remind us of those (I so nearly was one) who never come to writing at all.

We must not speak of women writers in our century (as we cannot speak of women in any area of recognized human achievement) without speaking also of the invisible, the as-innately-capable: the born to the wrong circumstances—diminished, excluded, foundered, silenced.

We who write are survivors, *"only's." One-out-of-twelve.*

Ernst Bloch provides what might be called notes toward a definition of hope. It explores the relationship of hopes, dreams, and daydreams—projections of the self into the realm of the possible. This is followed by Ursula K. Le Guin's speculations on world-making. She speaks of the creation of a world that ties the past to a hopeful future that can be called forth by first imagining it.

❧ ERNST BLOCH, *The Principle of Hope*

Who are we? Where do we come from? Where are we going? What are we waiting for? What awaits us?

Many only feel confused. The ground shakes, they do not know why and with what. Theirs is a state of anxiety; if it becomes more definite, then it is fear.

Once a man travelled far and wide to learn fear. In the time that has just passed, it came easier and closer, the art was mastered in a terrible fashion. But now that the creators of fear have been dealt with, a feeling that suits us better is overdue.

It is a question of learning hope. Its work does not renounce, it is in love with success rather than failure. Hope, superior to fear, is neither passive like the latter, nor locked into nothingness. The emotion of hope goes out of itself, makes people broad instead of confining them, cannot know nearly enough of what it is that makes them inwardly aimed, of what may be allied to them outwardly. The work of this emotion requires people who throw themselves actively into what is becoming, to which they themselves belong. It will not tolerate a dog's life which feels itself only passively thrown into What Is, which is not seen through, even wretchedly recognized.

The work against anxiety about life and the machinations of fear is that against its creators, who are for the most part easy to identify, and it looks in the world itself for what can help the world; this can be found. How richly people have always dreamed of this, dreamed of the better life that might be possible. Everybody's life is pervaded by daydreams: one part of this is just stale, even enervating escapism, even booty for swindlers, but another part is provocative, is not content just to accept the bad which exists, does not accept renunciation. This other part has hoping at its core, and is teachable. It can be extricated from the unregulated daydream and from its sly misuse, can be activated undimmed. Nobody has ever lived without daydreams, but it is a question of knowing them deeper and deeper and in this way keeping them trained unerringly, usefully, on what is right. Let the daydreams grow even fuller, since this means they are enriching themselves around the sober glance: not in the sense of clogging, but of becoming clear. Not in the sense of merely contemplative reason which takes things as they are and as they stand, but of participating reason which takes them as they go, and therefore also as they could go better. Then let the daydreams grow really fuller, that is, clearer, less random, more familiar, more clearly understood and more mediated with the course of things. So that the wheat which is trying to ripen can be encouraged to grow and be harvested.

❦ Ursula K. Le Guin, *World-Making*

I was invited to participate in a symposium called Lost Worlds and Future Worlds at Stanford University in 1981. The text of my short contribution follows.

We're supposed to be talking about world-making. The idea of making makes me think of making new. Making a new world; a different world: Middle Earth, say, or the planets of science fiction. That's the work of the fantastic imagination. Or there's making the world new: making the world different: a utopia or dystopia, the work of the political imagination.

But what about making the world, this world, the old one? That seems to be the province of the religious imagination, or of the will to survive (they may be the same thing). The old world is made new at the birth of every baby, and every New Year's Day, and every morning, and the Buddhist says at every instant.

That, in every practical sense, we make the world we inhabit is pretty well beyond question, but I leave it to the philosophers to decide whether we make it all from scratch—mmmm! tastes like a scratch world! but it's Bishop Berkeley's Cosmo-Mix!—or whether we patch it together by a more or less judicious selection of what strikes us as useful or entertaining in the inexhaustible chaos of the real.

In either case, what artists do is make a particularly skillful selection of fragments of cosmos, unusually useful and entertaining bits chosen and arranged to give an illusion of coherence and duration amidst the uncontrollable streaming of events. An artist makes the world her world. An artist makes her world the world. For a little while. For as long as it takes to look at or listen to or watch or read the work of art. Like a crystal, the work of art seems to contain the whole, and to imply eternity. And yet all it is is an explorer's sketch-map. A chart of shorelines on a foggy coast.

To make something is to invent it, to discover it, to uncover it, like Michelangelo cutting away the marble that hid the statue. Perhaps we think less often of the proposition reversed, thus: To discover something is to make it. As Julius Caesar said, "The existence of Britain was uncertain, until I went there." We can safely assume that the ancient Britons were perfectly certain of the existence of Britain, down to such details as where to go for the best wood. But, as Einstein said, it all depends on how you look at it, and as far as Rome, not Britain, is concerned, Caesar invented (*invenire*, "to come into, to come upon") Britain. He made it be, for the rest of the world.

Alexander the Great sat down and cried, somewhere in the middle of India, I think, because there were no more new worlds to conquer.

What a silly man he was. There he sits sniveling, halfway to China! A conqueror. Conquistadores, always running into new worlds, and quickly running out of them. Conquest is not finding, and it is not making. Our culture, which conquered what is called the New World, and which sees the world of nature as an adversary to be conquered: look at us now. Running out of everything.

The name of our meeting is Lost Worlds and Future Worlds. Whether our ancestors came seeking gold, or freedom, or as slaves, we are the conquerors, we who live here now, in possession, in the New World. We are the inhabitants of a Lost World. It is utterly lost. Even the names are lost. The people who lived here, in this place, on these hills, for tens of thousands of years, are remembered (when they are remembered at all) in the language of the conquistadores: the "Costanos," the "Santa Claras," the "San Franciscos," names taken from foreign demigods. Sixty-three years ago, in the *Handbook of the Indians of California*, my father wrote:

> The Costanoan group is extinct so far as all practical purposes are concerned. A few scattered individuals survive.... The larger part of a century has passed since the missions were abolished, and nearly a century and a half since they commenced to be founded. These periods have sufficed to efface even traditional recollections of the forefathers' habits, except for occasional fragments.

Here is one such fragment, a song; they sang it here, under the live oaks, but there weren't any wild oaks here then, only the Californian bunch-grasses. The people sang:

I dream of you,
I dream of you jumping,
Rabbit, jackrabbit, and quail.
And one line is left of a dancing song:
Dancing on the brink of the world.

With such fragments I might have shored my ruin, but I didn't know how. Only knowing that we must have a past to make a future

with, I took what I could from the European-based culture of my own
forefathers and mothers. I learned, like most of us, to use whatever I
could, to filch an idea from China and steal a god from India, and so
patch together a world as best I could. But still there is a mystery. This
place where I was born and grew up and love beyond all other, my
world, my California, still needs to be made. To make a new world you
start with an old one, certainly. To find a world, maybe you have to
have lost one. Maybe you have to be lost. The dance of renewal, the
dance that made the world, was always danced here at the edge of
things, on the brink, on the foggy coast.

*W.E.B. DuBois, Myles Horton, and Janice Mirikitani, in different cultural
and personal circumstances, reflect upon the way in which hope can sustain one over
the long haul—through oppression and apparent defeat. Hope is not a simple feeling or emotion, but a long-range, life-sustaining state of mind that characterizes
the will to live and love and thrive. It is a refusal to give up on the best in people
and in particular in oneself and the people one loves.*

❧ W.E.B. DuBois, *Of the Faith of the Fathers*

It was out in the country, far from home, far from my foster home,
on a dark Sunday night. The road wandered from our rambling log-
house up the stony bed of a creek, past wheat and corn, until we could
hear dimly across the fields a rhythmic cadence of song—soft, thrilling,
powerful, that swelled and died sorrowfully in our ears. I was a country
school-teacher then, fresh from the East, and had never seen a Southern
Negro revival. To be sure, we in Berkshire were not perhaps as stiff and
formal as they in Suffolk of olden time; yet we were very quiet and sub-
dued, and I know not what would have happened those clear Sabbath
mornings had some one punctuated the sermon with a wild scream or
interrupted the long prayer with a loud Amen! And so most striking to
me, as I approached the village and the little plain church perched aloft,
was the air of intense excitement that possessed that mass of black folk.
A sort of suppressed terror hung in the air and seemed to seize us,—a
pythian madness, a demoniac possession, that lent terrible reality to

song and word. The black and massive form of the preacher swayed and quivered as the words crowded to his lips and flew at us in singular eloquence. The people moaned and fluttered, and then the gaunt-cheeked brown woman beside me suddenly leaped straight into the air and shrieked like a lost soul, while round about came wail and groan and outcry, and a scene of human passion such as I had never conceived before.

Those who have not thus witnessed the frenzy of a Negro revival in the untouched backwoods of the South can but dimly realize the religious feeling of the slave; as described, such scenes appear grotesque and funny, but as seen they are awful. Three things characterized this religion of the slave,—the Preacher, the Music, and the Frenzy. The Preacher is the most unique personality developed by the Negro on American soil . A leader, a politician, an orator, a "boss," an intriguer, an idealist,—all these he is, and ever, too, the centre of a group of men, now twenty, now a thousand in number. The combination of a certain adroitness with deep-seated earnestness, of tact with consummate ability, gave him his preeminence, and helps him maintain it. The type, of course, varies according to time and place, from the West Indies in the sixteenth century to New England in the nineteenth, and from the Mississippi bottoms to cities like New Orleans or New York.

The Music of Negro religion is that plaintive rhythmic melody, with its touching minor cadences, which, despite caricature and defilement, still remains the most original and beautiful expression of human life and longing yet born on American soil. Sprung from the African forests, where its counterpart can still be heard, it was adapted, changed, and intensified by the tragic soul-life of the slave, until, under the stress of law and whip, it became the one true expression of people's sorrow, despair, and hope.

❧ MYLES HORTON, *The Long Haul: An Autobiography*

The Future

When I speak about a social goal, the goal for society, and for myself, I don't say, "This is exactly what it's going to be like." I don't have a blueprint in mind. I'm thinking more of a vision, I'm thinking of direction and I'm thinking of steps. I'm thinking more in terms of signs pointing in the right direction than I am of the shape of future society, because I don't know what that shape is going to be—I don't know of anybody who has predicted correctly. Marx, for example, who has probably been the most help to me analyzing problems, wasn't a prophet or a seer. When he speculated about what society would be, and how it would happen, he was frequently wrong. He was certainly wrong about where the revolution would first occur: It has taken place in countries where he said it wouldn't, and it's not taken place in countries where he said it would. The world has changed since he made his original analysis.

I think it's important to understand that the quality of the process you use to get to a place determines the ends, so when you want to build a democratic society, you have to act democratically in every way. If you want love and brotherhood, you've got to incorporate them as you go along, because you can't just expect them to occur in the future without experiencing them before you get there. I agree with Che Guevara: the true revolutionary is guided by great feelings of love. If that love isn't built in, you'll end up with a fascist society.

A long-range goal to me is a direction that grows out of loving people, and caring for people, and believing in people's capacity to govern themselves. The way to know they have these capabilities is to see something work well on a small scale. I've seen it in the labor movement, I've seen it in the civil rights movement, I've seen it in the antiwar movement. Since I know those things can happen on a small scale, I assume that if we ever get wise enough and involve enough people, it could happen on a bigger scale. If you have that hope, when you work with people and try to help them learn—and not teach them, because that gets into techniques and gimmicks—and you believe in them, then you inspire them by your belief. You can't help people grow if you don't think they can, because you are going to find ways to help prevent them from growing. I think your belief in people's capabilities is tied in with your belief in a goal that involves people being free and being able to govern themselves.

It is important to distinguish between this goal of freedom and self-governance and the goals of people who want only to "Save the whales" or to "Desegregate the South" or to organize a labor union. Those aren't necessarily long-range social goals. I don't mean they're antisocial, but the goal I'm talking about is one that can never be reached. It's a direction, a concept of society that grows as you go along. You could go out of business if you were only for saving the whales: you'd save them, then you'd be out of work. That would be the end of it. It's not that I'm against saving the whales. I'm all for it, but the reason for saving whales is that they are a part of life, and you want to save life. You must make your goal a part of something larger. If it's an end-all, then it has severe limitations. A long-range goal has to be something for everybody. It can't be a goal that helps some people but hurts others.

Goals are unattainable in the sense that they always grow. My goal for the tree I planted in front of my house is for it to get big enough to shade the house, but that tree is not going to stop growing once it shades my house. It's going to keep on growing bigger regardless of whether I want it to or not. The nature of my visions are to keep on growing beyond my conception. That is why I say it's never completed. I think there always needs to be struggle. In any situation there will always be something that's worse, and there will always be something that's better, so you continually strive to make it better. That will always be so, and that's good, because there ought to be growth. You die when you stop growing.

Your vision will grow, but you will never be able to achieve your goals as you envision them. My vision cannot be achieved by me. You may save the whales, but the dream must push beyond that. It's a dream which I can't even dream. Other people will pick it up and go beyond. To put it in a simpler way, I once said that I was going to start out on a life's work. It had to be big enough to last all my life. And since I didn't want to have to rethink and start over again, I needed to have a goal that would at least take my lifetime. After making that decision, I never thought of doing anything else, because I knew that I could just hack away on it, and what little I could do would take my lifetime. And even if we had a revolution, the quality of that revolution wouldn't necessarily be satisfactory, so I'd have to try to make it better.

❧ JANICE MIRIKITANI, *We, the Dangerous*

I swore
it would not devour me
I swore
it would not humble me
I swore
it would not break me.

    And they commanded we dwell in the desert
    Our children be spawn of barbed wire and barracks

We, closer to the earth,
squat, short thighed,
knowing the dust better.

    And they would have us make the garden
    Rake the grass to soothe their feet

We, akin to the jungle,
plotting with the snake,
tails shedding in civilized America.

    And they would have us skin their fish
    deft hands like blades/sliding back flesh/bloodless

We, who awake in the river
Ocean's child
Whale eater.

    And they would have us strange scented women,
    Round shouldered/strong and yellow/like the moon
    to pull the thread to the cloth
    to loosen their backs massaged in myth

We, who fill the secret bed,
the sweat shops
the laundries.

    And they would dress us in napalm,
    Skin shred to clothe the earth,
    Bodies filling pock marked fields.
    Dead fish bloating our harbors.

We, the dangerous,
Dwelling in the ocean.
Akin to the jungle.
Close to the earth.

    Hiroshima
    Vietnam
    Tule Lake

And yet we were not devoured.
And yet we were not humbled.
And yet we are not broken.

The poems by Lu Chi and William Carlos Williams, the scene from Athol Fugard's play The Road to Mecca, *and the two excerpts from Ralph Ellison's essay* "The Little Man at Chehaw Station" *all illustrate the way in which hope arises from an imaginative engagement with the possible. Often it emerges through love for the magic contained in the ordinary, in the miracle of life itself. Equally, it arises from the unexpected intelligence that the most ordinary of us manifest and express in our love of the beautiful. The selections are about encounters with life that overwhelm us with a sense of how wonderful things can be when positive change erases the unnecessary pain and trials people often encounter.*

❦ Lu Chi, *Shadow and Echo and Jade*

Perhaps only a single blossom of the whole bouquet will bloom;
    perhaps a single cornstalk rises in the field.
Shadows cannot be held. Echoes cannot be harnessed.

Poor work is an eyesore, & always obvious; it cannot be woven into
    music.
When the mind is caged & separate, the spirit wanders, and nothing
    is controlled.
When the vein of jade is revealed in the rock, the mountain glistens;
    the images must shine like pearls in water.
The thorn-bush, left unpruned, opens its arms to glory.
A common song sung to a great melody is another way to find
    beauty.

❧ WILLIAM CARLOS WILLIAMS, *The Descent*

The descent beckons
        as the ascent beckoned.
                Memory is a kind
of accomplishment,
        a sort of renewal
            even
an initiation, since the spaces it opens are new places
        inhabited by hordes
            heretofore unrealized,
of new kinds—
        since their movements
            are toward new objectives
(even though formerly they were abandoned).

No defeat is made up entirely of defeat—since
the world it opens is always a place
        formerly
            unsuspected. A
world lost,
        a world unsuspected,
            beckons to new places
and no whiteness (lost) is so white as the memory
of whiteness

With evening, love wakens
        though its shadows
                which are alive by reason
of the sun shining—
        grow sleepy now and drop away
            from desire
Love without shadows stirs now
        beginning to awaken
           as night
advances.

The descent
        made up of despairs
           and without accomplishment
realizes a new awakening:
           which is a reversal
of despair.
        For what we cannot accomplish, what
is denied to love,
        what we have lost in the anticipation—
           a descent follows,
endless and indestructible.

❧ ATHOL FUGARD, *The Road to Mecca*

MARIUS: . . . Helen, may I sit down for a moment?

HELEN: Of course, Marius. Forgive me, I'm forgetting my manners.

MARIUS: (Hangs up hat and scarf in the hallway and then joins Helen at the table.) I won't stay long. I must put down a few thoughts for tomorrow's sermon. And thanks to you I know what I want to say.

HELEN: Me?

MARIUS: Yes, you. (Teasing her.) You are responsible . . .

HELEN: Oh dear!

MARIUS: (A little laugh.) Relax, Helen. I only said thanks to you because it came to me this afternoon while I was digging up your vegetables. I spent a lot of time while I was out in the garden doing that, just leaning on my spade. My back is giving me a bit of trouble again and to tell you the truth, I also felt lazy. I wasn't thinking about anything in particular . . . just looking, you know, the way an old man does, looking around, recognizing once again and saying the names. Spitskop in the distance! Aasvoelkrans down at the other end of the valley. The poplars with their autumn foliage standing around as yellow and bright as that candle flame! And a lot of remembering. As you know, Helen, I had deep and very painful wounds in my soul when I first came here. Wounds I thought would never heal. This was going to be where I finally escaped from life, turned my back on it and justified what was left of my existence by ministering to you people's simple needs. I was very wrong. I didn't escape from life here, I discovered it, what it really means, the fullness and goodness of it. It's a deep and lasting regret that Aletta wasn't alive to share that discovery with me. Anyway, all of this was going on in my head when I realized I was hearing a small little voice, and the small little voice was saying "thank you." With every spade-full of earth that I turned, when I went down on my knees to lift the potatoes out of the soil, there it was: Thank you. It was mine! I was muttering away to myself the way we old folks are inclined to do when nobody is around. It was me saying "thank you." That is what I want to do tomorrow, Helen. Give thanks, but in a way that I've never done before. I know I've stood there in the pulpit many times telling all of you to do exactly that, but oh dear me! the cleverness and conceit in the soul of Marius Byleveld when he was doing that. I had an actor's vanity up there, Helen. I'm not saying I was a total hypocrite, but believe me in those thanksgivings I was listening to my Dominee's voice and its hoped-for eloquence every bit as much as to the true little voice inside my heart . . . the voice I heard so clearly this afternoon. That's the voice that must speak tomorrow! And to do that I must find words as simple as the sky I was standing under or the earth I was turning over with my spade. They have got no vanities or conceits. They are just "there." And if the Almighty takes pity on us, the one gives us rain so that the other can in turn . . . give us this day our daily potato. (A smile at this gentle little joke.) Am I making any sense, Helen? Answer me truthfully.

HELEN: Yes, you are, Marius. And if all you do tomorrow is say what you have just said to me, it will be very moving and beautiful.

MARIUS: (Sincerely.) Truly, Helen? Do you really mean that?

HELEN: Every word of it.

MARIUS: Then I will try. (Rests his hand on HELEN's. THEY both withdraw. A pause.) My twentieth anniversary comes up next month. Yes, that is how long I've been here. Twenty-one years ago, May the sixteenth, the Good Lord called my Aletta to his side and just over a year later, June the eleventh, I gave my first sermon in New Bethesda. (A little laugh at the memory.) What an occasion that was! I don't know if I showed it, Helen, but let me confess now that I was more than just a little nervous when I went up into the pulpit and looked down at the stern and formidable array of faces. A very different proposition to the town and city congregations I had been preaching to up until then. When Miss de Klerk played the first bars of the hymn at the end of it, I heaved a very deep sigh of relief. None of you had fallen asleep! (HELEN is shaking her head.) What's the matter, Helen?

HELEN: Young Miss de Klerk came later. Mrs. Retief was still our organist when you gave your first service.

MARIUS: Are you sure?

HELEN: Yes. Mrs. Retief also played at the reception we gave you afterwards in Mr. van Heerden's house. She played the piano and Sterling Retief sang.

MARIUS: You know something, I do believe you're right! Good heavens, Helen, your memory is better than mine.

HELEN: And you had no cause to be nervous, Marius. You were very impressive.

MARIUS: (A small pause as HE remembers something else.) Yes, of course. You were in that congregation. Stefanus was at your side as he was going to be every Sunday after that for . . . how long?

HELEN: Five years.

MARIUS: Another five years. That was all a long time ago.

HELEN: More than a long time, Marius. It feels like another life. (ELSA returns with a tray of tea and sandwiches.)

MARIUS: Ah, here comes your supper. I must be running along.

ELSA: Just a sandwich, Dominee. Neither of us is very hungry.

MARIUS: I'll drop by tomorrow night after the service if that is alright with you, Helen. (Collects his hat and scarf.)

ELSA: Won't you have a cup of tea with us? It's the least we can offer in return for all those lovely vegetables.

MARIUS: Why, Helen? Why? I will take that question with me to my grave. What possessed you to abandon the life you had, your faith?

HELEN: What life, Marius? What faith? The one that brought me to Church every Sunday? (Shaking her head.) No. You were much too late if you only started worrying about that . . . on that first Sunday I wasn't there in my place. The worst had happened long, long before that. All those years when, as Elsa said, I sat there so obediently next to Stefanus, it was a terrible, terrible lie. I tried hard, Marius, but your sermons, the prayers, the hymns, they had all become just words. Do you know what the word "God" looks like when you've lost your faith? It looks like a little stone, a cold round little stone. "Heaven" is another one, but it's got an awkward, useless shape, while "Hell" is flat and smooth. All of them . . . damnation, grace, salvation . . . a handful of stones.

MARIUS: (Sits next to Miss Helen.) Why didn't you come to me, Helen! If only you had trusted me enough to tell me, and we had faced it together, I would have broken my soul to help you win back that faith.

HELEN: It was too late. I'd accepted it. Nothing more was going to happen to me except time and the emptiness inside and I had got used to that . . . until the night in here after Stefanus' funeral. (Pause. MISS HELEN makes a decision.) Do you remember it, Marius? You brought me home from the cemetery and after we had got inside the house and you had helped me off with my coat, you put on the kettle for a pot of tea and then . . . ever so thoughtfully! . . . pulled the curtains and closed the shutters. Such a small little thing, and I know you meant well by it, that you didn't want people to stare in at me and my grief . . . but in doing that it felt as if you were putting away my life as surely as the undertaker had done to Stefanus a little earlier when he closed the coffin lid. There was even an odor of death in here with us, wasn't there, sitting in the gloom and talking, both of us in black, our Bibles on our laps. Your words of comfort didn't help. But that wasn't your fault. You didn't know I wasn't mourning Stefanus' death. He was a good man, and it's very sad that he had died so young, but I never loved him. My black widowhood was really for my own life, Marius.

While Stefanus was alive there had at least been some pretense at it . . . of a life I hadn't lived, but with him gone . . . ! You had a little girl in here with you, Marius, who had used up all the prayers she knew and was dreading the moment when her mother would bend down, blow out the candle and leave her in the dark. You lit one for me before you left . . . there was a lot of darkness in this room! . . . and after you had gone I sat here with it. Such a sad little light, with its little tears of wax running down the side! I had none, neither for Stefanus nor myself. That little candle did all the crying in here that night, and it burnt down very low while doing that. I don't know how much time had passed while I just sat here staring into its flame . . . I had already surrendered myself to what was going to happen when it went out . . . but instead of it doing the same, allowing the darkness to defeat it, that small uncertain little light seemed to find its courage again. It started to get brighter and brighter, leading me, Marius. . . . a strange feeling it was leading me to a place I had never been before. (Looks around the room and then speaks with quiet authority.) Light the candles, Elsa. That one first. (Indicating a candelabra that has been set up very prominently on an old trunk. Using a taper ELSA lights the candles on the trunk candelabra then gracefully continues around the room lighting the candles on the window sill, the Shaker table and the top of the sideboard.) . . . and you know why, Marius? That is the East. Go out there into the yard and you'll see that all my Wise Men and their camels are traveling in that direction. Follow that candle on and one day you'll come to Mecca. Oh yes, Marius, it's true! I've done it. That is where I went that night and it was the candle you lit that led me there. (Radiantly alive with her vision.)

A city, Marius! A city of light and color more splendid than anything I had ever imagined. There were palaces and beautiful buildings everywhere, with dazzling white walls and glittering minarets. Strange statues filled the courtyards. The streets were crowded with camels and turbaned men speaking in a language I didn't understand, but that didn't matter because I knew, oh, I just knew it was Mecca! And I was on my way to the grand temple. In the center of Mecca there is a temple, Marius, and in the center of the temple is a vast room with hundreds of mirrors on the walls and hanging lamps and that is where the Wise Men of the East study the celestial geometry of light and color. I became an apprentice that night. Light them all, Elsa, so that I can show Marius what I've learnt. (ELSA does so, continuing around the lounge, bedroom alcove and the backrooms. For the first time we see the full magic and splendor of the room. MISS HELEN laughs ecstatically as SHE lights a taper and holds it up to Marius.) Look, Marius! Look! Light. Don't be nervous. It's harmless. It only wants to play. That is what I do in here. We play with it like children with a magical toy that never ceases to delight and amuse. Light just one little candle in here, let in the light from just one little star and the dancing starts. (Lights the oil lamp on the post.)

I've even taught it how to skip around corners. Yes I have. When I'm in the dark and look in that mirror I can see that mirror, and in that one the full moon when it rises over the Sneeuberg behind my back! (Triumphantly taking in the whole room. ELSA is sitting on the chaise.) This is my world and I have banished darkness from it. It is not madness, Marius. They say mad people can't tell the difference between what is real and what is not. I can. I know my little Mecca out there, and this room, for what they really are. I had to learn how to bend rusty wire into the right shape and mix sand into cement to make my Wise Men and their camels, how to grind down beer bottles in a coffee mill to put glitter on my walls. My hands will never let me forget. They'll keep me sane. It's the best I could do, as near as I could get to the real Mecca. My journey is over now. This is as far as I can go. (Hands back the application form to Marius.) I won't be using this. I can't reduce my world to a few ornaments in a small room in an old-age home. (MARIUS takes the form. When HE speaks again we sense a defeated man, an acceptance of the inevitable behind the quiet attempt to maintain his dignity.)

MARIUS: Mecca! So that's where you went. I'll look for it in my atlas of the world when I get home tonight. That's a long way away, Helen! I didn't realize you had traveled that far from me. So to find you I must light a candle and follow it to the East! (A helpless gesture.) No. I think I'm too old now for that journey . . . and I have a feeling that you will never come back.

HELEN: I'm also too old for another journey, Marius. It's taken me my whole life to get here. I know I've disappointed you . . . most probably bitterly so . . . please believe me that it wasn't intentional. I had as little choice over all that has happened as I did over the day I was born.

MARIUS: You know something, Helen? I think I do believe you . . . which only makes it all the harder to accept. All these years it always felt as if I could reach you. It seemed so inevitable that I would . . . so right! That we should find each other again and be together for what time was left to us in the same world. It seems wrong . . . terribly wrong . . . that we won't. Aletta's death was wrong in the same way.

(Pause. MARIUS tries to collect his spectacles and pens but falters.)

HELEN: Marius?

MARIUS: I am trying to go. It's not easy . . . trying to find the first moment in a life that must be lived out in the shadow of something that is terribly wrong.

HELEN: We're trying to say good-bye to each other, aren't we, Marius?

MARIUS: Yes, I suppose it has come to that. I never thought that was going to happen tonight but I suppose there is nothing else left to say. (Collects his things, puts on his hat and scarf.) Make sure all the candles are out when you go to bed, Helen. (Pauses at the door.) I've never seen you as happy as that! There was more light in you than in all your candles put together. (MARIUS leaves. A silence follows his departure; MISS HELEN puts out the oil lamp. ELSA eventually makes a move and starts blowing out the candles on the window sill and the shaker table.)

HELEN: No, don't! I must do it.

❦ RALPH ELLISON, *The Little Man at Chehaw Station*

I

It was at Tuskegee Institute during the mid-1930s that I was made aware of the little man behind the stove. At the time I was a trumpeter majoring in music, and had aspirations of becoming a classical composer. As such, shortly before the little man came to my attention, I had outraged the faculty members who judged my monthly student's recital by substituting a certain skill of lips and fingers for the intelligent and artistic structuring of emotion that was demanded in performing the music assigned to me. Afterward, still dressed in my hired tuxedo, my ears burning from the harsh negatives of their criticism, I had sought solace in the basement studio of Hazel Harrison, a highly respected concert pianist and teacher. Miss Harrison had been one of Ferruccio Busoni's prize pupils, had lived (until the rise of Hitler had driven her back to a U.S.A. that was not yet ready to recognize her talents) in Busoni's home in Berlin, and was a friend of such masters as Egon Petri, Percy Grainger and Sergei Prokofiev. It was not the first time that I had appealed to Miss Harrison's generosity of spirit, but today her reaction to my rather adolescent complaint was less than sympathetic.

"But, baby," she said, "in this country you must always prepare yourself to play your very best wherever you are, and on all occasions."

"But everybody tells you that," I said.

"Yes," she said, "but there's more to it than you're usually told. Of course you've always been taught to *do* your best, *look* your best, *be* your best. You've been told such things all your life. But now you're becoming a musician, an artist, and when it comes to performing the classics in this country, there's something more involved."

Watching me closely, she paused. "Are you ready to listen?"

"Yes, ma'am."

"All right," she said, "you must *always* play your best, even if it's only in the waiting room at Chehaw Station, because in this country there'll always be a little man hidden behind the stove."

"A *what?*"

She nodded. "That's right," she said. "There'll always be the little man whom you don't expect, and he'll know the *music*, and the *tradition*, and the standards of *musicianship* required for whatever you set out to perform!"

Speechless, I stared at her. After the working-over I'd just received from the faculty, I was in no mood for joking. But no, Miss Harrison's face was quite serious. So what did she mean? Chehaw Station was a lonely whistle-stop where swift north- or southbound trains paused with haughty impatience to drop off or take on passengers; the point where, on homecoming weekends, special coaches crowded with festive visitors were cut loose, coupled to a waiting switch engine, and hauled to Tuskegee's railroad siding. I knew it well, and as I stood beside Miss Harrison's piano, visualizing the station, I told myself, *She has* got *to be kidding!* For in my view, the atmosphere of Chehaw's claustrophobic little waiting room was enough to discourage even a blind street musician from picking out blues on his guitar, no matter how tedious his wait for a train. Biased toward disaster by bruised feelings, my imagination pictured the vibrations set in motion by the winding of a trumpet within that drab, utilitarian structure: first shattering, then bringing its walls "a-tumbling down"—like Jericho's at the sounding of Joshua's priest-blown ram horns.

True, Tuskegee possessed a rich musical tradition, both classical and folk, and many music lovers and musicians lived or moved through its environs, but—and my regard for Miss Harrison not withstanding— Chehaw Station was the last place in the area where I would expect to encounter a connoisseur lying in wait to pounce upon some rash, unsuspecting musician. Sure, a connoisseur might hear the haunting, blues-echoing, train-whistle rhapsodies blared by fast express trains as they thundered past, but the classics? not a chance!

So as Miss Harrison watched to see the effect of her words, I said with a shrug, "Yes, ma'am."

She smiled, her prominent eyes a-twinkle. "I hope so," she said. "But if you don't just now, you will by the time you become an artist. So remember the little man behind the stove."

With that, seating herself at her piano, she began thumbing through a sheaf of scores, a signal that our discussion was ended.

So, I thought, *you ask for sympathy and you get a riddle.*

II

Three years later, having abandoned my hope of becoming a musician, I had just about forgotten Miss Harrison's mythical little man behind the stove. Then, in faraway New York, concrete evidence of his actual existence arose and blasted me like the heat from an internally combusted ton of coal.

As a member of the Federal Writers' Project, I was spending a clammy late-fall afternoon of freedom circulating a petition in support of some now long-forgotten social issue that I regarded as indispensable to the public good. I found myself inside a tenement building in San Juan Hill, a Negro district that disappeared with the coming of Lincoln Center. Starting on the top floor of the building, I had collected an acceptable number of signatures, and having descended from the ground floor to the basement level, was moving along the dimly lit hallway toward a door through which I could hear loud voices. They were male Afro-American voices, raised in violent argument. The language was profane, the style of speech a Southern idiomatic vernacular such as was spoken by formally uneducated Afro-American workingmen. Reaching the door, I paused, sounding out the lay of the land before knocking to present my petition.

But my delay led to indecision. Not, however, because of the loud, unmistakable anger sounding within; being myself a slum dweller, I knew that voices in slums are often raised in anger, but that the *rhetoric* of anger, itself cathartic, is not necessarily a prelude to physical violence. Rather, it is frequently a form of symbolic action, a verbal equivalent of fisticuffs. No, I hesitated because I realized that behind the door a mystery was unfolding. A mystery so incongruous, outrageous, and surreal that it struck me as a threat to my sense of rational order. It was as though a bizarre practical joke had been staged and its perpetrators were waiting for me, its designated but unknowing scapegoat, to arrive: a joke designed to assault my knowledge of American culture and its hierarchical dispersal. At the very least, it appeared that my pride in my knowledge of my own people was under attack.

For the angry voices behind the door were proclaiming an intimate familiarity with a subject of which, by all the logic of their linguistically projected social status, they should have been oblivious. The subject of their contention confounded all my assumptions regarding the correlation between educational levels, class, race and the possession of conscious culture. Impossible as it seemed, these foul-mouthed black workingmen were locked in verbal combat over which of two celebrated Metropolitan Opera divas was the superior soprano!

I myself attended the opera only when I could raise the funds, and I knew full well that opera-going was far from the usual cultural pursuit of men identified with the linguistic style of such voices. Yet, confounding such facile logic, they were voicing (and loudly) a familiarity with the Met far greater than my own. In their graphic, irreverent, and vehement criticism they were describing not only the two sopranos' acting abilities, but were ridiculing the gestures with which each gave animation to her roles, and they shouted strong opinions as to the ranges of the divas' vocal equipment. Thus, with such a distortion of perspective being imposed upon me, I was challenged either to solve the mystery of their knowledge by entering into their midst or to leave the building with my sense of logic reduced forever to a level of college-trained absurdity.

So challenged, I knocked. I knocked out of curiosity, I knocked out of outrage. I knocked in fear and trembling. I knocked in anticipation of whatever insights—malicious or transcendent, I no longer cared which—I would discover beyond the door.

For a moment there was an abrupt and portentous silence; then came the sound of chair legs thumping dully upon the floor, followed by further silence. I knocked again, loudly, with an authority fired by an impatient and anxious urgency.

Again silence, until a gravel voice boomed an annoyed "Come in!"

Opening the door with an unsteady hand, I looked inside, and was even less prepared for the scene that met my eyes than for the content of their loudmouthed contention.

In a small, rank-smelling, lamplit room, four huge black men sat sprawled around a circular dining-room table, looking toward me with undisguised hostility. The sooty-chimneyed lamp glowed in the center of the bare oak table, casting its yellow light upon four water tumblers and a half-empty pint of whiskey. As the men straightened in their chairs I became aware of a fireplace with a coal fire glowing in its grate, and leaning against the ornate marble facing of its mantelpiece, I saw four enormous coal scoops.

"All right," one of the men said, rising to his feet. "What the hell can we do *for you?*"

"And we ain't buying nothing, buddy," one of the seated men added, his palm slapping the table.

Closing the door, I moved forward, holding my petition like a flag of truce before me, noting that the men wore faded blue overalls and jumper jackets, and becoming aware that while all were of dark complexion, their blackness was accentuated in the dim lamplight by the dust and grime of their profession.

"Come on, man, speak up," the man who had arisen said. "We ain't got all day."

"I'm sorry to interrupt," I said, "but I thought you might be interested in supporting my petition," and began hurriedly to explain.

"Say," one of the men said, "you look like one of them relief investigators. You're not out to jive us, are you?"

"Oh, no, sir," I said. "I happen to work on the Writers' Project . . ."

The standing man leaned toward me. "You on the Writers' Project?" he said, looking me up and down.

"That's right," I said. "I'm a writer."

"Now is that right?" he said. "How long you been writing?"

I hesitated. "About a year," I said.

He grinned, looking at the others. "Y'all hear that? Ol' Home boy here has done up and jumped on the *gravy* train! Now that's pretty good. Pretty damn good! So what did you do before that?" he said.

"I studied music," I said, "at Tuskegee."

"Hey, now!" the standing man said. "They got a damn good choir down there. Y'all remember back when they opened Radio City? They had that fellow William L. Dawson for a director. Son, let's see that paper."

Relieved, I handed him the petition, watching him stretch it between his hardened hands. After a moment of soundlessly mouthing the words of its appeal, he gave me a skeptical look and turned to the others.

"What the hell," he said, "signing this piece of paper won't do no good, but since Home here's a musician, it won't do us no harm to help him out. Let's go along with him."

Fishing a blunt-pointed pencil from the bib of his overalls, he wrote his name and passed the petition to his friends, who followed suit.

This took some time, and as I watched the petition move from hand to hand, I could barely contain myself or control my need to unravel the mystery that had now become far more important than just getting their signatures on my petition.

"There you go," the last one said, extending the petition toward me. "Having our names on there don't mean a thing, but you got 'em."

"Thank you," I said. "Thank you very much."

They watched me with amused eyes, expecting me to leave, but, clearing my throat nervously, I stood in my tracks, too intrigued to leave and suddenly too embarrassed to ask my question.

"So what're you waiting for?" one of them said. "You got what you came for. What else do you want?"

And then I blurted it out. "I'd like to ask you just one question," I said.

"Like what?" the standing one said.

"Like where on earth did you gentlemen learn so much about grand opera?"

For a moment he stared at me with parted lips; then, pounding the mantelpiece with his palm, he collapsed with a roar of laughter. As the laughter of the others erupted like a string of giant firecrackers, I looked on with growing feelings of embarrassment and insult, trying to grasp the handle of what appeared to be an unfriendly joke. Finally, wiping coal-dust-stained tears from his cheeks, he interrupted his laughter long enough to initiate me into the mystery.

"Hell, son," he laughed, "we learn it down at the Met, that's where . . ."

"You learned it *where?*"

"At the Metropolitan Opera, just like I told you. Strip us fellows down and give us some costumes and we make about the finest damn bunch of Egyptians you ever seen. Hell, we been down there wearing leopard skins and carrying spears or waving things like palm leafs and ostrich-tail fans for *years!*"

Now, purged by the revelation, and with Hazel Harrison's voice echoing in my ears, it was my turn to roar with laughter. With a shock of recognition I joined them in appreciation of the hilarious American joke that centered on the incongruities of race, economic status and culture. My sense of order restored, my appreciation of the arcane ways of American cultural possibility was vastly extended. The men were products of both past *and* present; were both coal heavers *and* Met extras; were both workingmen *and* opera buffs. Seen in the clear, pluralistic, melting-pot light of American cultural possibility, there was no contradiction. The joke, the apparent contradiction, sprang from my attempting to see them by the light of social concepts that cast less illumination than an inert lump of coal. I was delighted, because during a moment when I least expected to encounter the little man behind the stove (Miss Harrison's vernacular music critic, as it were), I had stumbled upon four such men. Not behind the stove, it is true, but even more wondrously, they had materialized at an even more unexpected location: at the depth of the American social hierarchy and, of all possible hiding places, behind a coal pile. Where there's a melting pot there's smoke, and where there's smoke it is not simply optimistic to expect fire, it's imperative to watch for the phoenix's vernacular, but transcendent, rising.

Many traditional stories and praise songs are celebrations of strength and hope. They embrace the world despite all of the troubles people encounter as they try to be good and sustain decency. This section ends with two praises, hallelujahs, affirmations. Hope is a way of standing up to what cynical people call "reality" or "the real world." Hope points to a path, through the imagination, to the realization of our deepest and most compassionate dreams.

❧ JOHN EDGAR WIDEMAN, *One Day*

One day neither in the past nor in the future, and not at this moment, either, all the people gathered on a high ridge that overlooked the rolling plain of earth, its forests, deserts, rivers unscrolling below them like a painting on parchment. Then the people began speaking, one by one, telling the story of a life—everything seen, heard, and felt by each soul. As the voices dreamed, a vast, bluish mist enveloped the land and the seas below. Nothing was visible. It was as if the solid earth had evaporated. Now there was nothing but the voices and the stories and the mist; and the people were afraid to stop the storytelling and afraid not to stop, because no one knew where the earth had gone.

Finally, when only a few storytellers remained to take a turn, someone shouted: Stop! Enough, enough of this talk! Enough of us have spoken! We must find the earth again!

Suddenly, the mist cleared. Below the people, the earth had changed. It had grown into the shape of the stories they'd told—a shape as wondrous and new and real as the words they'd spoken. But it was also a world unfinished, because not all the stories had been told.

Some say that death and evil entered the world because some of the people had no chance to speak. Some say that the world would be worse than it is if all the stories had been told. Some say that there are no more stories to tell. Some believe that untold stories are the only ones of value and we are lost when they are lost. Some are certain that the storytelling never stops; and this is one more story, and the earth always lies under its blanket of mist being born.

❧ MAYA ANGELOU, *Praise Poem*

Here on the pulse of this new day
You may have the grace to look up and out
And into your sister's eyes,
And into your brother's face,
Your country,
And say simply
Very simply
With hope—
Good morning.

PART II

Kissing Joy As It Flies

Love and the Completeness of Being

The capacity for a loving connection with others is what makes the promise of a deeply fulfilled life conceivable and believable. Falling in love, being in love, and staying in love are all parts of stages in the love cycle. Falling in love and being in love can bless us with a sense of wonder, reopening us to the beauty in things, rolling back the cover of convention from our eyes. Staying in love, sharing oneself over time, allows love to grow greater. To love in a full, deep, and openhearted way means, at times, great imaginative leaps—of faith, trust, and kindness.

Love is what leads us to open our souls to others and humanity. When we love, we are able to move beyond our expectations and fears—in William Blake's words:

He binds for himself a joy
Does the wingèd life destroy;
But he who kisses the joy as it flies
Lives in eternity's sunrise.

The ability to love fully without reservation nourishes and sustains the growth of other values. When the rational and spiritual intelligence merge in love, we express the fullest sense of ourselves and the greatest appreciation for others and the world we share.

Love mediates the imagination. Through love in its myriad dimensions we convert imagination into ideals of right living. Without love, our imaginations can take us to hellish places—at times driven by fear and paranoia, at times by longing and despair. As an expression of the necessity of sharing and community, love is also the foundation of our vision for a better world. But when love is smothered by fear or wounded by humiliation and rejection, our longing for love can turn to hate and loathing. We can end up hurting those close to us and disparaging those who are needy—because they remind us of our own pain and threaten the brittle security we have won. And in so doing, we can also hurt ourselves quite badly.

When the great longing to give and receive love is paved with substitutes for love, like gifts or rewards or medals, we've damaged ourselves deeply. The substitutes are only fragile replacements that put our whole selves at risk, in part because we lose our freedom to explore, discover, and be deeply a part of life with others.

Lao-tzu, in summing up the dilemma, gives good advice:

> What means more to you
> You or your renown?
> What brings you more
> You or what you own?
> What would you miss more if it were gone?
> The niggard pays
> The miser loses,
> The least ashamed of men
> Goes back if he chooses
> He knows both ways
> He starts again.

Yet, love of one's self—understood as self-acceptance—and receiving the acceptance of others is not always easy, as Fleur Adcock reminds us in her poem *Epitaph*:

> I wish to apologize for being mangled.
> It was the romantic temperament
> that did for me. I could stand rejection—
> so grand, "the stone the builders rejected . . ."
> but not acceptance.
> "Alas," I said
> (a word I use), "alas, I am taken up, or in, or out of myself:
> the up, or in, or out of myself:
> shall I never be solitary?"
> Acceptance follows me like a sand bag.
> My bones crack. It squelches out of them.
> Ah, acceptance! Leave me under this stone.

◆ ◆ ◆

The deep bonds between friends, relatives, and romantic couples, together with ideals and concerns for humanity, are all—including sexual love—expressions of the capacity we humans have to be open and connected with one another. This kind of loving feeling is the generative connection that brings people together to live, work, worship, and build a future together. It is the foundation of deep trust and an abiding sense of security.

But love has to operate in the real world. That means it must have operational tools for it to be nurtured and sustained. Those tools are to be found in some of the basic values through which we actually express our love—for ourselves, for others, for humanity. These values include:

Integrity: aiming for a high level of consistency between what we do and what we value, and being prepared to risk something for the ideals and people we cherish.

Empathy: understanding and appreciating someone else's feelings and experiences almost as if they were your own.

Compassion: feeling sympathy for the pain and struggle of others, and to be willing to reach out to help them.

Spirituality: awaking to our lives instead of going on "automatic," permitting us a deep sense of connection with the diversity and unity of humanity and the more than human natural world.

The selections that follow in this section are organized according to these values.

5
Trumpet in the Morning

INTEGRITY

Shakespeare liked to remind his audiences of the celestial simplicity of integrity—grounding it both in restraint and self-reliance, as well as in caring connection with others. Corin, the shepherd in *As You Like It*, wisely concludes:

> Sir, I am a true laborer: I earn that I eat, get that I wear; owe no man hate, envy no man's happiness; glad of other men's good, content with my harm; and the greatest of my pride is to see my ewes graze and my lambs suck.

We have a duty to be true to ourselves—and this rock-bottom integrity may mean at times being ready to fall out of love with habits, conventions, and comforts that lull us into false quietude. To be sure, narrow self-assuredness is a conceit, but it is also a self-deception to forget that integrity is an ultimate consolation and savior of ourselves, our families, and our friends.

The direct link between self-love, self-esteem, and integrity is captured well by Eleanor Roosevelt:

> "Before we make friends with anyone else, we must first make friends with ourselves."

How easy it is for integrity to be overwhelmed by the distorting and self-justifying impact of our own wishes, fears, and biases. Each of us can act narrowly and delusionally, as D. H. Lawrence whimsically reminds us:

Yes, and if oxen or lions had hands, and could paint with their hands, and produce works of art as men do, horses would paint the forms of the gods like horses, and oxen like oxen, and make their bodies in the image of their several kinds.

Albert Camus went so far as to think of intelligence as a form of personal integrity in his 1945 Defense of Intelligence:

Our poison hearts must be cured. And the most difficult battle to be won against the enemy in the future must be fought within ourselves, with an exceptional effort that will transform our appetite for hatred into a desire for justice. Not giving in to hatred, not making any concessions to violence, not allowing our passions to become blind—these are the things we can still do for friendship and against Hitlerism. . . .

Even now, intelligence is ill-treated. This proves simply that the enemy is not yet conquered. If you merely make an effort to understand without preconceptions, if you merely talk of objectivity, you will be accused of sophistry and criticized for having pretensions. No, we can't have that! That is what must be reformed. For I know as well as anyone the excesses of intelligence, and I know as well as anyone that the intellectual is a dangerous animal, ever ready to betray. But that is not the right kind of intelligence. We are speaking of the kind that is backed by courage, the kind that for four years paid whatever was necessary to have the right to respect.

Selections

Vaclav Havel and Sharon Olds write about the internal fears and external forces that affect who we are. In *The Man Without Qualities*, Robert Musil writes of self-deception.

❧ VACLAV HAVEL, *The Power of the Powerless*

The manager of a fruit and vegetable shop places in his window, among the onions and carrots, the slogan: "Workers of the world, unite!" Why does he do it? What is he trying to communicate to the world? Is he genuinely enthusiastic about the idea of unity among the workers of the world? Is his enthusiasm so great that he feels an irrepressible impulse to acquaint the public with his ideals? Has he really given more than a moment's thought to how such a unification might occur and what it would mean?

I think it can safely be assumed that the overwhelming majority of shopkeepers never think about the slogans they put in their windows, nor do they use them to express their real opinions. That poster was delivered to our greengrocer from the enterprise headquarters along with the onions and carrots. He put them all into the window simply because it has been done that way for years, because everyone does it, and because that is the way it has to be. If he were to refuse, there could be trouble. He could be reproached for not having the proper "decoration" in his window; someone might even accuse him of disloyalty. He does it because these things must be done if one is to get along in life. It is one of the thousands of details that guarantee him a relatively tranquil life "in harmony with society," as they say.

Obviously the greengrocer is indifferent to the semantic content of the slogan on exhibit; he does not put the slogan in his window from any personal desire to acquaint the public with the ideal it expresses. This, of course, does not mean that his action has no motive or significance at all, or that the slogan communicates nothing to anyone. The slogan is really a *sign*, and as such it contains a subliminal but very definite message. Verbally, it might be expressed this way: "I, the greengrocer XY, live here and I know what I must do. I behave in the manner expected of me. I can be depended upon and am beyond reproach. I am obedient and therefore I have the right to be left in peace." This message, of course, has an addressee: it is directed above, to the greengrocer's superior, and at the same time it is a shield that protects the greengrocer from potential informers. The slogan's real meaning, therefore, is rooted firmly in the greengrocer's existence. It reflects his vital interests. But what are those vital interests?

Let us take note: if the greengrocer had been instructed to display the slogan "I am afraid and therefore unquestioningly obedient," he would not be nearly as indifferent to its semantics, even though the statement would reflect the truth. The greengrocer would be embarrassed and ashamed to put such an unequivocal statement of his own degradation in the shop window, and quite naturally so, for he is a human being and thus has a sense of his own dignity. To overcome this complication, his expression of loyalty must take the form of a sign which, at least on its textual surface, indicates a level of disinterested conviction. It must allow the greengrocer to say, "What's wrong with the workers of the world uniting?" Thus the sign helps the greengrocer to conceal from himself the low foundations of his obedience, at the same time concealing the low foundations of power. It hides them behind the facade of something high. And that something is *ideology*.

Ideology is a specious way of relating to the world. It offers human beings the illusion of an identity, of dignity, and of morality while making it easier for them to *part* with them. As the repository of something "supra-personal" and objective, it enables people to deceive their conscience and conceal their true position and their inglorious *modus vivendi*, both from the world and from themselves. It is a very pragmatic, but at the same time an apparently dignified, way of legitimizing what is above, below, and on either side. It is directed towards people and towards God. It is a veil behind which human beings can hide their own "fallen existence," their trivialization, and their adaptation to the status quo. It is an excuse that everyone can use, from the greengrocer, who conceals his fear of losing his job behind an alleged interest in the unification of the workers of the world, to the highest functionary, whose interest in staying in power can be cloaked in phrases about service to the working class. The primary excusatory function of ideology, therefore, is to provide people, both as victims and pillars of the post-totalitarian system, with the illusion that the system is in harmony with the human order and the order of the universe.

The smaller a dictatorship and the less stratified by modernization the society under it, the more directly the will of the dictator can be exercised. In other words, the dictator can employ more or less naked discipline, avoiding the complex processes of relating to the world and of self-justification which ideology involves. But the more complex the mechanisms of power become, the larger and more stratified the society they embrace, and the longer they have operated historically, the more individuals must be connected to them from outside, and the greater the importance attached to the ideological excuse. It acts as a kind of bridge between the regime and the people, across which the regime approaches the people and the people approach the regime. This explains why ideology plays such an important role in the post-totalitarian system: that complex machinery of units, hierarchies, transmission belts, and indirect instruments of manipulation which ensure in countless ways the integrity of the regime, leaving nothing to chance, would be quite simply unthinkable without ideology acting as its all-embracing excuse and as the excuse for each of its parts.

❦ SHARON OLDS, *Greed and Aggression*

Someone in Quaker meeting talks about greed and aggression
and I think of the way I lay the massive
weight of my body down on you
like a tiger lying down in gluttony and pleasure on the
elegant heavy body of the eland it eats,
the spiral horn pointing to the sky like heaven.
Ecstasy has been given to the tiger,
forced into its nature the way the
forcemeat is cranked down the throat of the held goose,
it cannot help it, hunger and the glory of
eating packed at the center of each
tiger cell, for the life of the tiger and the
making of new tigers, so there will
always be tigers on the earth, their stripes like

stripes of night and stripes of fire-light—
so if they had a God it would be striped,
burnt-gold and black, the way if
I had a God it would renew itself the
way you live and live while I take you as if
consuming you while you take me as if
consuming me, it would be a God of
love as complete satiety,
greed and fullness, aggression and fullness, the
way we once drank at the body of an animal
until we were so happy we could only
faint, our mouths running, into sleep.

❧ ROBERT MUSIL, *The Man Without Qualities*

When the Man Without Qualities returned from abroad some time earlier, it was only out of whimsicality and a detestation of the usual kind of apartment that he rented this little chateau, which had once been a summer residence outside the city gates, losing its meaning when the city grew out and round it, amounting in the end to nothing more than a neglected piece of real estate waiting for a rise in the price of land, and in the meantime untenanted. The rent was correspondingly low, but all the rest—getting the place into a state of good repair and bringing it into line with modern ideas of comfort—had cost an unexpectedly large amount of money. It had become an adventure that finally forced him to turn to his father for help, which was by no means agreeable; for his independence was precious to him. He was thirty-two years of age, and his father was sixty-nine.

The old gentleman was aghast—not, actually, at being descended on in this way (although it was partly on that account too, since he detested imprudence) and not at the contribution levied on him, for at bottom he approved of his son's manifesting a need for domesticity and a proper establishment of his own. What affronted his feelings was the taking over of a building that one had no choice but to call a chateau, even though it were only in the diminutive; it was the ill-omened pre-sumption of it that upset him.

He himself had begun as a tutor in houses of the high nobility when he was a student and had continued in that capacity when a junior lawyer—though not from necessity, for his father before him had been comfortably off. Later, when he became a university lecturer and then professor, he felt the benefit of it all, for the careful nursing of these connections brought it about that he gradually rose to be legal adviser to almost all the old aristocratic families in the country, although he was by then even less in need of a professional side-line than formerly. Indeed, long after the fortune thus accumulated could very well stand comparison with the dowry provided by a Rhineland industrialist fam-ily for his early deceased wife, the mother of his son, these connections, established in his youth and strengthened in his prime, still did not lapse. Although the savant, who had attained to honours, now retired from legal practice proper, only on occasion giving counsel's opinion for an exalted fee, every event that concerned the circle of his former patrons was still meticulously entered up in special records, which were very precisely carried forward from the fathers to the sons and grand-sons; and no official honour, no marriage, birthday or fete-day passed without a letter in which the recipient was congratulated in a delicate blend of veneration and shared reminiscence. Each time, with equal punctilio, short letters came in reply, expressing thanks to the old fam-ily friend, the esteemed scholar. So his son was from boyhood well acquainted with the aristocracy's talent for condescension, which unconsciously yet so accurately weighed and measured out the exact quantity of affability required; and he had always been irritated by this subservience—of one who did, after all, belong to the intellectual elite—towards the possessors of horses, lands and traditions. It was, however, not calculated servility that made the father insensitive on this score. It was quite instinctively that he had made a great career in this manner, not only becoming a professor and a member of academies, sitting on many learned and official committees, but also being made Knight, then Commander, and even Grand-Cross of high orders, finally being elevated by His Majesty into the ranks of the hereditary nobility, subsequent to having been appointed a member of the Upper House. Once there, the man so distinguished attached himself to the liberal bourgeois wing, which was sometimes in opposition to the high nobility. But, characteristically enough, none of his noble patrons bore him any ill-will for it or felt even the slightest surprise; they had never regarded him as anything but a personification of the rising third estate. The old gentleman took an assiduous part in the expert work of legislation, and even when a controversial division found him on the bourgeois side, the opposite side bore him no grudge, conscious as they were that he had not been invited to act otherwise. In politics he did nothing but what it had formerly always been his function to do, namely combine his superior and sometimes gently emendatory knowledge with the suggestion that his personal loyalty could nevertheless be depended upon; and so he had risen without essential change, as his son declared, from being a tutor to the upper classes to being a tutor to the Upper House.

When the matter of the chateau came to his notice, it struck him as a violation of a boundary-line that had to be respected all the more punctiliously because it was not legally defined; and he took his son to task in terms even more bitter than the many reproaches he had heaped upon him in the course of time, making it all positively sound like a prophecy that this would turn out to be the beginning to the bad end to which he was bound to come. It was an affront to the old man's feelings about life. As with many men who have achieved something of note, these feelings, far from being selfish, sprang from a deep love of what might be called the generally and suprapersonally useful, in other words, from a sincere veneration for what advances one's own interests—and this not for the sake of advancing them, but in harmony with that advancement and simultaneously with it, and also on general grounds. This is of great importance: even a pedigree dog seeks its place under the dining table, undisturbed by kicks, and not out of doggish abjection, but from affection and fidelity. And indeed the most coldly calculating people do not have half the success in life that comes to those rightly blended personalities who are capable of feeling a really deep attachment to such persons and conditions as will advance their own interests.

In "A Trumpet in the Morning," Arthur Brown revels gloriously in himself. Erica Hunt and Edmond Jabès tell of keeping heart and soul together in intimate encounters with another.

❧ ARTHUR BROWN, *A Trumpet in the Morning*

you can bury me in the east you can
bury me in the west
i'm gonna rise up be a trumpet
in the morning cause
i been bent in the forge been struck
by the hammer been scorched by fire so
be a trumpet this morning
(o dont touch my shoes
o let 'em shine let 'em shine)
i been all night
in the dew
john-revelated in the marshy bottoms
lazarused in the crook of a willow whittled
a gospel-boat from a simple reed
launched that skiff in the spittle
of a mule's jaw
gouged a skysong from the black giant's thigh
and shackled it to a cotton flower
o i freighted all my sorrows (o these is florsheim shoes
all bright with dew) and i feels like noah
riding these ankle-boats on god's stony waters
and i feels like doves in my ear-lobes fetching freedom-sound
in a single green leaf from dry land
feels like glory walking in the blues
tenfingers ten centipedal toes
trebling jubilee from an acoustic crotch

steel and catgut i say i feels
unstrung
like a broken guitar but
be a trumpet soon this morning (o dont touch my clothes
i'm gonna sit on a rainbow seat) o my wings is sprouted out
wings is sprouted
and i feels like mating bird's mother this morning
in the middle of the air
o i been over matched by salvation done broke the rock
of living waters done founded a home in that water shed
done looped the promise-harness round my shoulders
(o dont touch my clothes
cause i'm a sin-bright-standing-pat-jb-stetson-hat-initials-
carved-in-the-back-of-my-shirt-umbrellaed-in-hallelujahs-man
and jackodiamond-hard-to-play
got one eye to see and one to believe
a hellhound on my breath
a crossroad in my breast
stone in my passway
i'm accelerating
and i feels like whiskey talkin rye) o i feels like blowing
my lonesome horn this morning
cause i woke up this morning
more than something on my mind
holy ghost shining down
i aint nothing but love nothing but love
o i feels so injected this morning so strung-out
justa justa whole saharas of loving
is what i'm talking bout
like a flaming desert flower feels like
i'm sipping in the sand
(now tell me did you ever ever ever see
a possum at rehearsal
or a raccoon steal away now watch me

steal
away)
o i got a feeling down deep i
be a trumpet soon-in-the-morning
be a trumpet soon-in-the-morning

❦ ERICA HUNT, Correspondence Theory

Dear Dear

I read looks. While passing a store today I noticed sawdust leaking
from a dummy in the display. The figure moved abruptly every
few moments as part of its musculature seeped out of its burlap
skin.

This is a distillation of your letters, zeroes between the words. All
the phrases engaged or apologetic no one could blame you. But
finally, this is what I have left of you, a stooping silhouette. I'm
asking you to step into the picture, make a guest appearance.

It doesn't improve it but it sure beats reading the impression left in a
round-shouldered jacket as you wag your shoulders in imitation
of a serene coastal day on the mesa where we were last August
and leaving a pair of shoes on the rocks that complicated the
walk back.

I snap the album shut but you're still here in one of the photographs
tentatively dipping your foot in the surf wearing as usual your
spectator tee shirt.

If we're not who we were then who are we now? Characters multiply
as the dubbing editor loses interest. Imagination is not a jinni to
slight; often we are forced to consent to the supposition that we
are as continuous as others imagine us to be. When you change
your mind though you make me an accessory to a peculiar kind
of treason.

In lighter moments I recall what I liked about you at a safe distance:
the way you carry yourself like a Central African ancestor figure,
stomach relaxed, legs bent and parted, and your back curved in a
delicate S with no hurry at all.

Secondly you seemed unafraid to call a relic a wreck, a belief a
symptom, a skirmish a fool's errand. What some call domestic
others call privileged torpor. What some call security from
another angle resembles only the knack of imprisoning oneself
with as many objects as can be dreamt of.

Similarly I am willing to admit that I often arrange for dramas to be
performed with the unwilling assistance of whoever happens to
be standing around. That is why I am surprised that you revert
to using the descriptions of things to create a war of no practical
advantage.

In lighter moments, as I was saying, I'm struck by the coincidence. I
got tired of waking up in a lake. You were eating out of your
hand and not liking it. It's impossible to have a more mutual
subject.

❦ EDMOND JABÈS, *Book of Resemblances*

Perhaps the time has come to strip off your first
name. Long, arduous task. You must reach your
death without identity, naked, again a virgin.

The man you were, was he like you? You doubt it
now. And yet you took advantage of the likeness.

You were never more than the distance at which
you kept yourself.
. . . yourself, that is, the inadmissible emptiness
you rival.
Availability remains salvation.

Emptier than emptiness, for having been its insane
likeness.

Forbidden, the fruit of Knowledge, put on the index for stimulating sweetness.

*Fernando Pessoa writes of rich moments of purposelessness and solitude. Walt
Whitman warns against feelings of separation and superiority. Rumi and Primo
Levi remind how easy it is to fall asleep on yourself, to lose yourself.*

❧ FERNANDO PESSOA, *The Startling Reality of Things*

The startling reality of things
Is my discovery every single day.
Every thing is what it is,
And it's hard to explain to anyone how much this delights me
And suffices me.

To be whole, it is enough simply to exist.

I've written a good many poems.
I shall write many more, naturally.
Each of my poems speaks of this,
And yet all my poems are different,
Because each thing that exists is one way of saying this.

Sometimes I start looking at a stone.
I don't start thinking, Does it have feeling?
don't fuss about calling it my sister.
But I get pleasure out of its being a stone,
Enjoying it because it feels nothing,
Enjoying it because it's not at all related to me.

Occasionally I hear the wind blow,
And I find that just hearing the wind blow makes it worth having
been born.

I don't know what others reading this will think;
But I find it must be good since it's what I think without effort,
With no idea that other people are listening to me think;
Because I think it without thoughts,
Because I say it as my words say it.

I was once called a materialist poet
And I was surprised, because I didn't imagine
I could be called anything at all.
I'm not even a poet: I see.
If what I write has any merit, it's not in me;
The merit is there, in my verses.
All this is absolutely independent of my will.

❧ WALT WHITMAN, *Song of Myself*

My tread scares the wood-drake and the wood-duck, on my distant
    and day-long ramble;
They rise together—they slowly circle around.

I believe in the wing'd purposes,
And acknowledge red, yellow, white, playing with me,
And consider green and violet and the tufted crown intentional;
And do not call the tortoise unworthy because she is not something
    else;
And the jay in the woods never studied the gamut, yet trills pretty
    well to me;
And the look of the bay mare shames silliness out of me.

❧ RUMI, *The Servant Who Loved His Prayers*

When prayers were over, and the priest and all the worshippers
had left, still Sunqur remained inside. The master waited
and waited. Finally, he yelled into the mosque,

"Sunqur,
why don't you come out?"
                                        "I can't. This clever one
won't let me. Have a little more patience.
I hear you out there."
                                        Seven times the master waited,
and then shouted. Sunqur's reply was always the same,
"Not yet. He won't let me come out yet."
                                        "But there's no one
in there but you. Everyone else has left.
Who makes you sit still so long?"

"The one who keeps me in here is the one
who keeps you out there.
The same who will not let you in or not let me out."

❧ RUMI, *Praise to Early-Waking Grievers*

. . . . I was sleeping, and being comforted
by a cool breeze, when suddenly a gray dove
from a thicket sang and sobbed with longing,
and reminded me of my own passion.

I had been away from my own soul so long,
so late-sleeping, but that dove's crying
woke me and made me cry. *Praise*
to all early-waking grievers!

❧ PRIMO LEVI, *After R. M. Rilke*

Lord, it's time; the wine is already fermenting.
The time has come to have a home,
Or to remain for a long time without one.

The time has come not to be alone,
Or else we will stay alone for a long time.
We will consume the hours over books,
Or in writing letters to distant places,
Long letters from our solitude.
And we will go back and forth through the streets,
Restless, while the leaves fall.

As David Hume long ago understood and Emma Thompson discovered much more recently, obligatory routines of convention can easily control us.

❦ DAVID HUME, *Treatise on Human Nature*

In every system of morality which I have hitherto met with, I have always remarked that the author proceeds for some time in the ordinary way of reasoning, and establishes the being of a God, or makes observations concerning human affairs; whereon of a sudden, I am surprised to find, that instead of the usual copulations of proposition, "is" and "is not," I meet with no proposition that is not connected with an "ought" or "ought not."

The change is imperceptible; but, however, of the last consequence. For this "ought" or "ought not" expresses some new relation or affirmation, it is necessary that it should be observed or explained; and at the same time, a reason should be given for what seems altogether inconceivable, how this new relation can be a deduction from others, which are entirely different from it.

❦ EMMA THOMPSON, *Vanity Fair* Interview

I did a very interesting course in Paris . . . with Philippe Gaulier . . . his notion was of the Tragedians' play to the gods. The Buffoons were sort of subhumans who were brought in to amuse *la jeunesse dorée* who had nothing to lose and, therefore, their gift was parody.

Then there were clowns. Clowns are between the two. They play to the heart . . .

We don't really do the grotesque anymore, the sort of freak shows. It's very ancient, but it's still a part of our nature. Maybe it's rock and roll. Maybe it's the tabloid press. Maybe it's daytime talk shows. Maybe that's what it is, but there is something necessary about it. The middle ground—Clowning—is very interesting. The really good clown comes on and fails miserably. But by coming on, a clown makes people laugh, because you're saying, "I shouldn't be here at all. I can't do this." It's about failing. It's wonderful because laughter is a celebration of all our failings—that recognition that we are not gods, that we are human. That's what clowns are for. That's why they are so important. And that's definitely what I am.

Robert Francis's "Waxwings" pushes us from the usual questions "why am I" and "who am I" to perhaps the more demanding question of "who can—and how can—I become." Tennessee Williams and Audre Lorde each teach that the challenge of becoming is the challenge of not being frozen as a person.

❧ ROBERT FRANCIS, *Waxwings*

Four tao philosophers as cedar waxwings
chat on a February berrybush
in sun, and I am one.

Such merriment and such sobriety—
the small wild fruit on the tall stalk—
was this not always my true style?

Above an elegance of snow, beneath
a silk-blue sky a brotherhood of four
birds. Can you mistake us?

To sun, to feast, and to converse
and all together—for this I have abandoned all my other
    lives.

❧ Tennessee Williams, *After the Boston Opening*

It was in the minds of others, certainly this suspicion was never com-
municated to me. Was I totally amoral? Was I too innocent or too
evil—that I remained unprepared for what the audiences, censors and
magistracy of Boston were going to find in my play? I knew, of course,
that I had written a play that touched upon human longings, about the
sometimes conflicting desires of the flesh and the spirit. This struggle
was thematic; implicit in the title of the play. Why had I never dreamed
that such struggles could strike many as filthy and seem to them unfit
for articulation? The very experience of writing it was like taking a bath
in snow. Its purity seemed beyond question.

❧ Tennessee Williams, *Battle of Angels*

    (Young Man proposes that he and Dorothy meet that night and
take a ride to the cemetery at Cypress Hill)

DOROTHY: Why there?

YOUNG MAN: Because dead people give the best advice.

DOROTHY: Advice on what?

YOUNG MAN: The problems of the living.

DOROTHY: What advice do they give?

YOUNG MAN: Just one word: live!

DOROTHY: Live?

YOUNG MAN: Yes, live, live, live! It's all they know, it's the
only word left in their vocabulary.

❦ AUDRE LORDE, *Movement Song*

I have studied the tight curls on the back of your neck
moving away from me
beyond anger or failure
your face in the evening schools of longing
through mornings of wish and ripen
we were always saying goodbye
in the blood in the bone over coffee
before dashing for elevators going
in opposite directions
without goodbyes.

Do not remember me as a bridge nor a roof
as the maker of legends
nor as a trap
door to that world
where black and white clericals
hang on the edge of beauty in five o'clock elevators
twitching their shoulders to avoid other flesh
and now
there is someone to speak for them

moving away from me into tomorrows
morning of wish and ripen
your goodbye is a promise of lightning
in the last angels hand
unwelcome and warning
the sands have run out against us
we were rewarded by journeys

away from each other
into desire
into mornings alone
where excuse and endurance mingle
conceiving decision.

Do not remember me
as disaster
nor as the keeper of secrets
I am the fellow rider in the cattle cars
watching
you move
slowly out of my bed
saying we cannot waste time
only ourselves.

Fleur Adcock, Nellie Wong, D. H. Lawrence, and Diane Glancy all recognize how important it is to connect intimately with others, to resist building fences after hurt, and to know that healing a hurt self means reconnecting with love again.

❧ FLEUR ADCOCK, *Outwood*

Milkmaids, buttercups, ox-eye daisies,
white and yellow in the tall grass:
I fought my way to school through flowers—
bird's-foot trefoil, clover, vetch—
my sandals all smudged with pollen,
seedy grass-heads caught in my socks.

At school I used to read, mostly,
and hide in the shed at dinnertime,
writing poems in my notebook.
'Little fairies dancing,' I wrote,
and 'Peter and I, we watch the birds fly,
high in the sky, in the evening.'

Then home across the warm common
to tease my little sister again:
'I suppose you thought I'd been to school:
I've been to work in a bicycle shop.'
Mummy went to a real job
every day, on a real bicycle;

Doris used to look after us.
She took us for a walk with a soldier,
through the damp ferns in the wood
into a clearing like a garden,
rosy-pink with beds of campion,
herb-robert, lady's smock.

The blackberry briars were pale with blossom.
I snagged my tussore dress on a thorn;
Doris didn't even notice.
She and the soldier lay on the grass;
he leaned over her pink blouse
and their voices went soft and round, like petals.

❧ NELLIE WONG, *Picnic*

Each Sunday I climb the mountain to picnic
with my mother and father in their twin coats,
breathing air
that only the mountains can give,
air as fresh as carp swimming upstream.

These Sundays my mother and father and I talk.
Oh, how we talk and talk!
Of apples and lace and cloth bound books,
of sour plums that make our mouths water,
changing expressions on our putty faces.

Although we talk together, we three,
we promise each other nothing. Not trees,

not oranges, not fish
for it is not our time to be fenced in,
not when spring promises its own
flowering quince.

I hold my mother's and father's hands tightly,
drinking the pools of their eyes.
It is strange we communicate now,
this way,
where there are no phones.

Together we celebrate the Tiger's Year.
We feast on chicken, mushrooms and the monk's fish,
pregnant with its cellophane noodles and fine black hair.
Our laughter is perfumed with incense
that the spirits drink.

❧ D. H. Lawrence, *Healing*

I am not a mechanism, an assembly of various sections.
And it is not because the mechanism is working wrongly, that I am ill.
I am ill because of wounds to the soul, to the deep emotional self
and the wounds to the soul take a long, long time, only time can help
and patience, and a certain difficult repentance,
long, difficult repentance, realization of life's mistake, and the
    freeing one's self
from the endless repetition of the mistake
which mankind at large has chosen to sanctify.

❧ Diane Glancy, *Tonta*

It's now you look
into yourself
& feel one hill touch
the other

all your life
land separated
from itself
leaving months
of isolation
but after the hurt
a box of tenderness
a joining that lets the
flat prairie bend
& somewhere out of it
in the long run
you may learn something
the memory
you set aside
the desire to be first
on the aisle
but you accept the slight
bouquet of flowers
knowing you pave
a road
not for generations
but just now starting
out from your soul.

The people Kai Erickson meets in Buffalo Creek know themselves best by how they are with one another and by what they share. In All God's Dangers, *Nate Shaw is certain that what he's done and what he's prepared to do for his beliefs and values make him who he is.*

◆ KAI ERICKSON, *Everything in Its Path*

When one asks the residents of the hollow what community they belong to, they normally respond with the name of the village in which they happen to live; this is their post office address, after all, and the site of a good many of their everyday activities. But it is evident that they think of Buffalo Creek in general as their real territory. This is where they come from. This is what they mean by "home."

Now sociologists have given a good deal of elaborate thought to what the term "community" does (or should) mean, and we will turn again to that subject later. For the moment, though, it should be noted that the kinds of human relationship that obtain up and down the creek reflect the spirit of *gemeinschaft* as much as anything one can expect to find anywhere in the land. Few status differentiations are made between people (although relations between black and white have a character all their own), and, in true Appalachian fashion, few people are ready to accept the responsibility of leadership. So far as a skeptical outsider can tell, the society of the hollow has become as level in respect to prestige and rank as human habits permit. This means that people are identified by the place they occupy in the larger linkages of family and community rather than by the work they do or the way they live. The assumption seems to be that everyone lives by the same values, knows the same lore, does the same tasks, is acquainted with the same people, and even shares the same thoughts. Relationships between people are thus based on a high degree of mutuality, and they emerge from a quiet agreement to look out for one another and to submerge one's separate sense of self into the larger tissues of communal life. In that sense, the sentiments that are supposed to be characteristic of families reach outward to embrace wider clusters of people—a neighborhood, a village, a whole valley—and this extension is explicitly recognized by the people of the hollow when they comment, as they regularly do, that their neighbors are "just like kin" or that Buffalo Creek in general is "just one big family." "Community," of course, comes from the same root as "communion," and the ancient meaning of the term is entirely apt here. The people of the creek feel that they are joined together in a common enterprise, even though they disagree often as to how that enterprise should be managed, and they feel that they are attached to one another by a common past, a common present, and a common future.

The residents of the hollow are attached to one another in deep and enduring ways, then, but they are also attached to the land. This tendency has roots deep in the Appalachian past and it is reinforced on the creek by the exaggerated contours of the ground. To begin with, the men earn their living by going down into the depths of the earth and delivering themselves to the uncertain mercies of nature. But in other respects, too, people do not so much live on the land as in it. Most of the terrain they see and relate to is either above them or below them, enveloping them on all sides, and the natural dangers they face, many of them connected with water, come at them from all directions. Danger lashes down on them from above in the form of rain, loosening the mounds of debris on the sides of the mountains; it reaches up from underneath in the form of swelling streams and flooding bottoms; and it pours in sideways when the mountains give way and send torrents of water and rock toward the settlements on the creek. The people of Buffalo Creek are more tuned to the rhythms of nature than a casual observer, impressed by the industrial character of their work, might imagine. The mountains are their security and their insecurity, their solace as well as their curse. They are a familiar, comforting part of the landscape, yet they can become a terrible threat with scarcely a moment's notice.

On the eve of the disaster [the Buffalo Creek Flood], then, Buffalo Creek was home for a close nucleus of people, held together by a common occupation, a common sense of the past, a common community, and a common feeling of belonging to, being a part of, a defined place.

❦ THEODORE ROSENGARTEN, *All God's Dangers*

My own dear boys don't understand why I done what I done. I have never had one of 'em walk up to me and hold me a hearty conversation in regards to this business. They don't talk with me against it, they don't talk with me in favor of it. But if they do say anything, they show me the weak spots in it. Ain't a one of 'em ever put his arm around me and said, "Papa, I'm proud of you for joinin' the union and doin' what you done." They don't see that deep in regards to their own selves.

They're scared to do it. White folks shot over 'em, messed with 'em so bad, in the fall of '32, kept 'em bluffed down, and they seed what was done to me—it put a mark on 'em. Well, I don't want no chicken-hearted boys. I want some of 'em, for God's sake, to show and prove the spit of their daddy.

They done all they could for me after I was put in prison, they stuck with their mother—all of 'em did except Calvin—but they felt ashamed of what happened. They never caught my meanin'—they never asked me. They was just scared to death and ashamed—that's the same thing.

Some of 'em that don't like the standard I proved in these union affairs tells me I talk too much. Now you take Calvin, Vernon, Garvan, that's three of my boys, my two oldest boys and my youngest boy, none of 'em have left home today, in a way of speakin'; and they don't want nothin' said about the past days of this organization. They wish, if they had their way about it, they'd blot all that out so never a word would come up about it no more as long as they live or I live. I caught 'em caucusin' about it, figurin' how can they stop their daddy from talkin' about it. And they're my children. Francis, that's my third boy, stays in Philadelphia, and Eugene, that's my fourth boy, stays in Ohio, what they call Middletown, and I've heard less said out of them about it—less said by Eugene than Francis. They lived through them times too. Garvan he's dry, don't say much—I know a person, especially if I raised him—and if he was to say somethin' he'd run to consult with Vernon and Calvin. And if I was to please them three boys today—Calvin, Vernon, Garvan—I wouldn't say another word. But if you don't like what I have done, then you are against the man I am today. I ain't goin' to take no backwater about it. If you don't like me for the way I have lived, get on off in the woods and bushes and shut your mouth and let me go for what I'm worth. And if I come out of my scrapes, all right; if I don't come out, don't let it worry you, this is me. Don't nobody try to tell me to keep quiet and undo my history. There ain't no get-back in me as far as I can reach my arm. And if anything comes up and favors me to knock down and drag out this old "ism" that's been plunderin' me and plunderin' the colored race of people ever since I got big enough to know, and before that, before that—old mothers and fathers before I come into this world was treated the same, knuckled under. Well, I'm tired of it, I don't want to bear all that. Anything tries to master me I wish to remove it. And I'm willin' to slap my shoulder to the wheel if it's ary a pound I can push. And for God's sake don't come up messin' with me. If there's any better life for me to live, any more rights that I can enjoy, get out the way and let me enjoy 'em or let me go down. And if I go down, in the name of the Lord, I'm done with it. Them all that has a mind to stop the wheel rollin' by droppin' their heads and hidin' their faces, that's them. I can't help it but it stirs me from the bottom. I'd fight this mornin' for my rights. I'd do it—and for other folks' rights if they'll push along.

I don't call for nobody to run their heads up under a gun, but if you don't rise up in defense of your portion, what good are you? Every nigger in this country that's ever heard about this organization oughta wake up and speak out for it for their own sake. And realize: any business that's transacted for the benefit of you, you ought to risk somethin', you got to risk.

I ain't got nothin' to give my children when I leave this world. I've already gived 'em—I raised 'em, and teached 'em a way of life, and I never did have nothin' but some personal property. I ain't been able to save a penny. If you find any bank in this country that has a dollar in it I deposited, you more likely to find a apple on a pear tree. I'm willin' to vow that I've never had a nickel in the bank in all the history of my life.

I left all I had in Vernon's hands when I was carried off to prison. That gived him a chance to get a foothold and come on up. And what I gived him to start off with—it was gived for the benefit of all of 'em— it was wore out or destroyed someway, but it had all produced heavy for 'em. They had full possession and it was enough in the way of personal property for none of 'em not to suffer. Left it with 'em premature— that was the moment I gived 'em whatever I had to give 'em, left it all to 'em. I'll have no chance to give 'em no more.

There's Vernon, only child I got in the world that's farmin'. Calvin ain't farmin', Francis ain't farmin', Eugene ain't farmin', Garvan ain't farmin'—Vernon farmin', makin' a success at it, too. With all of his conditions—dropped now and lost part of his health; he got sugar. Somethin' goin' to kill us all and that sugar's a bad thing—I think he's beatin' the other ones. There's all of my boys, start from Garvan, youngest boy I got. He owns a lot and I reckon he's about paid up and everything, and he's got a nice buildin' out there. Eugene, he's got a lot in Ohio. He works some but his legs has done failed him. Before he come home the last time he'd got under a doctor on account of his legs, but still he managed to come. I hadn't seen the boy in eight years. Francis, he's got a nice brick house in Philadelphia. There's Calvin, he owns two lots in Tuskegee and a nice new brick home. But a lot won't compare with a small plantation; Vernon's the top of 'em all. He only owns sixty-one acres but he got about thirty-six head of cattle—I've counted 'em myself. That's a right smart cattle for a poor fellow got nobody to see after 'em but him, and then he's farmin' too. The reason I say "poor" fellow, he ain't got nothin' above farmin' to work at for his livin' and got no way to work more land than he do now. Still and all he's a pretty heavy farmer; he never comes under thirty odd and up around forty bales of cotton. And he don't think about puttin' down less than five to seven hundred pounds of fertilize to the acre. I'm not braggin' on him cause he's my child, but he runs about as nice a farm as you will find in this country.

And he done got to where he can handle the money part of the business himself. He gets a little help from his daughters but he don't say so. They stays in Brooklyn, New York—ain't but two of 'em—and they helps him. He got three tractors and two Chevrolet trucks, one of 'em brand new, and a nice Chevrolet car. Just got 'em since this movement that's workin' today opened things up for him. Vernon didn't have all he has now before these ways and rulins started to change. The boy, he's my child, but he's very careful. He's weedin' his way through this world the best he can, and he's yet dealin' with white people. Of course, he's dealin' with moneyed men and he don't want to offend 'em.

And, as God would have it, he raised up two of his grandchildren. And out of them three grandchildren that stays with him now, one girl and two boys, any one of them boys is about as heavy as I am—one of 'em's heavier than I am, I expect. He get on the tractor he can do any-thing Vernon can do on it. Well, that's a help to him. And that other ones the least boy, jump on that tractor, break land like a bull. But that oldest boy, jump on that tractor, straddle several rows of cotton and gone, cultivatin' or breakin'.

If Vernon were to die out, the dogs dead and the hunt's up, that's all. That place will fall to his daughters' hands and just as soon as it come to them, there's nothin' doin'. No doubt if his equipment and machinery is any account, it'll be dealt off at some price—just as well to do it. No doubt they'll sell the home. They ain't comin' back here; they is devoted to the northern country. Well, if Vernon drops out of there, what'll become of the land? His wife might just go north, liable to, or go back to some of her people out here the other side of Apafalya. She's got three brothers: two of 'em stays in Florida, Davis and Charles, one of 'em's half white, and this here'n over here, the other side of Apafalya, he's colored in full.

My children today is dear in my thoughts and dear towards me. That Francis, his talk is this: he realizes I was his father; he realizes I labored for him and raised him up in the world—that's his talk—when he couldn't help hisself; and how I stood by my children as a father and by their mother as a husband. Francis—and Rachel, oldest girl in the family, she'll talk to me—I don't remember whippin' that child but twice in her life; didn't whip her then, just whisked her light. Might say I nettled her.

I don't say that the rest of my children won't talk it, but they ain't done it, they never has divulged it up to me that they realizes me as a father, by the way I treated 'em. Now there's Vernon up there, my child, I love him, with all due respect for him—

I can't say what they thinks but I knows how they acts. And they've all but Vernon lost touch with farmin' and some of 'em has lost touch with me as their father, in a way of speakin'. Now I don't expect 'em to support me, I'm not that kind of man and I don't need that, but I'm lookin' for 'em to bear me in their thoughts and feelins. I wish my children peace and good will. I wish the way will be clearer for 'em than ever in history and to know that I had a part in makin' it clear—that's the grandest of all. I'd appreciate it, if at the time I'm dead and gone, they know that I did my part for peace and pleasure and unity. And I did it for them.

I've noticed many things through the past history of my life—uneducated man that I am—that point to a plan. Time passes and the generations die. But the condition of the people that's livin' today ain't like it was for the people that's gone. And it ain't now like it's goin' to be for the people that comes after us. I can't say exactly what the future way of life will be, but I has a idea. My color, the colored race of people on earth, goin' to shed theirselves of these slavery ways. But it takes many a trip to the river to get clean.

God knows how this race has been treated. And there's a certain element that's workin' to please God and overturn this southern way of life. How many people is it today that it needs and it requires to carry out this movement? How many is it knows just what it's goin' to take? It's taken time, untold time, and more time it'll take before it's finished. Who's to do it? It's the best people of the United States to do it, in the defense of the uneducated, unacknowledged ones that's livin' here in this country. They goin' to win! They goin' to win! But it's goin' to take a great effort; we ought to realize that. It won't come easy. Somebody got to move and remove and it may take—how do I know how many it's goin' to take?—I just realize in my mind, it's goin' to take thousands and millions of words, thousands and millions of steps, to complete this business.

I'd like to live; and if the Lord see fit to able me to stay here and see it, I'd love to know that the black race had fully shed the veil from their eyes and the shackles from their feet. And I hope to God that I won't be one of the slackers that would set down and refuse to labor to that end.

6
A Wonderful
In-Between

EMPATHY

In *Night of the Iguana*, Tennessee Williams describes empathy when he defines "home":

Home is not a place, a building, a house of wood, bricks, or stone. I think of home as a thing that two people have between them in which each can nest, rest, live-in, emotionally speaking.

The overall pleasure that comes from this kind of loving contact when a person can reproduce in his or her awareness a shared inner world and meaning with someone else is nowhere better summarized than in A. A. Milne's *Winnie the Pooh*:

And then he thought that being with Christopher Robin was a very good thing to do, having Piglet was a very friendly thing to have; and so, when he had thought it all out, he said, "What I like best in the whole world is Me and Piglet going to see You, and You saying 'What about a little something?' and Me saying, 'I shouldn't mind a little something, should you, Piglet?' and it being a hummy sort of day outside and birds singing."

Being between yourself and somebody else and finding that known place there is the kind of empathetic understanding Yehuda Amichai calls "In-Between":

Where will we be when these flowers turn into fruit
In the narrow in-between, when the flower is no longer a flower
And the fruit is not yet fruit. And what a wonderful in-between did we
    make
For each other, between body and body. In-between eyes, between waking
    and sleep.
In-between twilight, not day, not night.

Empathetic understanding may come uninvited or may need to be invited. You may need to play host and invent just the right kind of readiness in yourself that will be encouraging. There are means to these ends, and Hannah Merker has beautifully described some of them in *Listening*:

The world stands still where we are. And the small piece of planet is ours alone. However, cluttered in crowds of colleagues and comrades, families, friends, we each receive the messages of earth and respond to them from our separate stance.

Sometimes the messages are unclear. Sometimes we do not receive them at all and so do not respond.

How can you know that the world around me is quiet—that I do not hear your step behind me, or hear you call my name from a distance? The silence around me is invisible. How can you know that the songs of new birds in spring, the crunch of old leaves, the soft sigh of the west wind, all subtle sounds that color the day for you, are not there for me? The whirr of a car, the pounding feet of a runner behind us as we walk, the soft slap of rain on a roof, are so elementary a part of your perception, you cannot imagine that for a person at your side they may not exist. How can you know unless I tell you?

And how can I tell you about something that is not there, if part of my mind is asleep, no longer associates sound with a particular circumstance?

So, then, we must talk to each other, listening in our own ways. Perhaps, while walking with me on the beach, or on some sandy shoreside path, you will ask yourself, what do I hear at this moment . . . ?

Perhaps you will touch my arm, so that I will look at you, and you will say, "the wind is whispering in the willow trees . . . ," or "the gulls there, are screeching over the fishing nets . . ." or "someone nearby is playing a violin . . ."

I still will not hear these things, but now I will know they are there, perhaps remember that once I knew without conscious thought that sound is connected to the swaying willow, the gull. The world becomes larger as the mind reawakens to the soaring symphony of everyday life.

And empathy is not just about two people finding each other, it is also about feeling so intensely the experience of people whose slim life chances are in fact produced by the habits, privileges, and distance of others that you experience their pain about it. This imperative to keep the personal connection with others is what Diane DiPrima is talking about when she asks, "Who picks sorrows like lice from your heart and cracks them? Between her teeth?"

Selections

In Auden's "Funeral Blues" and Saga Nobuyuki's "Fire," lovers are so tightly tied they are virtually one. D. H. Lawrence tells a different tale: of resolute patience in forging empathetic connection. Morris Rosenfeld's "My Little Boy" and Itzik Manger's "The Bent Tree" show the emptiness that can result when love fails to meet with empathetic understanding.

W. H. Auden, *Funeral Blues*

Stop all the clocks, cut off the telephone,
Prevent the dog from barking with a juicy bone,
Silence the pianos and with muffled drum
Bring out the coffin, let the mourners come.

Let aeroplanes circle moaning overhead
Scribbling on the sky the message He Is Dead,
Put crêpe bows round the white necks of the public doves,
Let the traffic policemen wear black cotton gloves.

He was my North, my South, my East and West,
My working week and my Sunday rest,
My noon, my midnight, my talk, my song;
I thought that love would last forever: I was wrong.

The stars are not wanted now: put out every one;
Pack up the moon and dismantle the sun;
Pour away the ocean and sweep up the wood.
For nothing now can ever come to any good.

Saga Nobuyuki, *Fire*

Please don't put it out, ever—
the fire that moves out of me into you.
It is the only fire in my life.
A large bird has swooped down into the deep valley
between death and me and plucked it up.
That little fire demands nothing of you.
It protects you with perfect selflessness,
obstructing anyone's approach toward you.
And now you stand stark naked
holding up the fire on the stairway—
on the endless stairway leading to the room upstairs.

❧ D. H. LAWRENCE, *The Elephant Is Slow to Mate*

The elephant, the huge old beast,
    is slow to mate;
he finds a female, they show no haste
    they wait

for the sympathy in their vast shy hearts
    slowly, slowly to rouse
as they loiter along the river-beds
    and drink and browse

and dash in panic through the brake
    of forest with the herd,
and sleep in massive silence, and wake
    together, without a word.

So slowly the great hot elephant hearts
    grow full of desire,
and the great beasts mate in secret at last,
    hiding their fire.

Oldest they are and the wisest of beasts
    so they know at last
how to wait for the loneliest of feasts
    for the full repast.

They do not snatch, they do not tear;
    their massive blood
moves as the moon-tides, near, more near,
    till they touch in flood.

❧ MORRIS ROSENFELD, *My Little Boy*

I have a little boy
A little boy quite fine.

Whenever I see him, it seems to me
The whole world is mine.

But seldom, seldom do I see him
My pretty one, when he's awake;
I come upon him always when he's sleeping,
I see him only at night.

Work drives me out early
And lets me back late;
O, strange to me is my own flesh,
O, strange to me my child's gaze.

I come home tense,
Enveloped in darkness,
My pale wife tells me right away,
How fine the child plays,
How sweet he talks, how cleverly he asks:
"O, mama, good ma,
When comes and brings me a penny,
My good, good pa?"

I stand at his little bed,
I see and hear and—hush!
A dream moves his lips:
"O, where is, where is pa?"

I kiss his blue eyes.
They open: "O, child!"
They see me, they see me!
And close quickly.

"Here stands your papa, dear one,
A little penny for you, here!"
A dream moves his lips:
"O, where is, where is pa?"

I stay, hurt and anguished,
Embittered, and I think:
When you awaken some time, my child,
You'll find me no more.

❦ ITZIK MANGER, *The Bent Tree*

By the wayside stands a tree,
bent against the storm.
All the birds have deserted it,
leaving it alone and unprotected.

"I will become a bird and sit in the tree
to comfort it with my song during winter."

"No, my child," mother weeps,
"you will freeze to death, sitting in the tree.
But if you must, put on your scarf and galoshes;
wear your fur hat and your warm underwear."

I lift up my wings but I cannot fly.
The clothes mother puts on her weak nestling are too heavy.

Sadly I gaze into my mother's eyes,
knowing that it was her love that kept me from soaring like a bird.

bell hooks, Janice Mirikitani, and Seamus Heaney describe tender under-standing and gratitude between loving people.

❦ bell hooks, *Black Is a Woman's Color*

To her child mind old men were the only men of feeling. They did not come at one smelling of alcohol and sweet cologne. They approached one like butterflies moving light and beautiful, staying still for only a moment. She found it easy to be friends with them. They talked to her as if they understood one another, as if they were the same—nothing standing between them, not age, not sex. They were the brown skin men with serious faces who were the deacons of the church, the right hand men of God. They were the men who wept when they felt his love, who wept when the preacher spoke of the good and faithful servant. They pulled wrinkled handkerchiefs out of their pockets and poured tears into them, as if they were pouring milk into a cup. She wanted to drink those tears that like milk would nourish and help her grow.

One of these men walked with his body bent, crippled. The grown-ups frowned at her when she asked them why he didn't walk straight. Did he know how to walk straight? Had he ever learned? They never answered. Every Sunday he read the scripture for the main offering. His voice wrinkled like paper one has rolled into a ball to throw away. Sometimes it sounded as if there were already tears in it waiting to spill over, waiting to wet the thirsty throats of parched souls. She could not understand the reading. Only one part was clear. It was as though his voice suddenly found a message that eased sorrow, a message brighter than any tear. It was the part that read "It is required and understood that a man be found faithful." He was one of the faithful.

She loved the sight of him. After church she would go and stand near him, knowing that he would give her his hand, covered old bones in wrinkled brown skin that reminded her of a well worn leather glove. She would hold that hand tight, never wanting to give it back. In a wee pretend voice full of tears and longing he would ask for his hand back, saying all the while that he would love for her to keep it but could not build his house without it. She loved to hear him talk about the house that he had been building for years, a dream house, way out in the country, with trees, wild flowers and animals. She wanted to know if there were snakes. He assured her that if she came to visit the snakes would come out of their hiding places, just for her, singing and playing their enchanted flutes.

It was a hot, hot day when she went to his house. She came all by herself slowly walking down the dirt road, slowing moving up the hill.

He stood at the top waiting. The house was so funny she couldn't stop laughing. It was half finished. She could not imagine how anyone could live in a half finished house. He gave her his hand, strong and brown. She could see it sawing, nailing, putting together boards which contained the memories of all his unfulfilled dreams. She could see the loneliness in that hand. When she whispered to him that she always held that hand—the right one—because all the loneliness was stored there like dry fruit in a cool place, he understood immediately.

Sitting on the steps watching him work, she could ask all the questions about being crippled that she had ever wanted to know the answers to. Was he alone because he was crippled. Was he not married because he was crippled. Was he without children because he was crippled. Her questions, like a hot iron, smoothed the wrinkles in his brow, took the tears from his voice, wet his dreams with the promise of a woman waiting faithfully with outstretched hands.

❦ JANICE MIRIKITANI, *Soul Food*

for Cecil

We prepare
the meal together.
I complain,
hurt, reduced to fury
again by their
subtle insults
insinuations
because I am married to you.
Impossible autonomy, no mind
of my own.

You like your fish
crisp, coated with cornmeal,
fried deep,
sliced mangos to sweeten

the tang of lemons.
My fish is raw,
on shredded lettuce,
lemon slices thin as skin,
wasabe burning like green fire.
You bake the cornbread flat
and dip it in
the thick soup
I've brewed from
turkey carcass, rice gruel,
sesame oil and chervil.
We laugh over watermelon
and bubbling cobbler.

You say,
there are few men
who can stand
to have a woman equal,
upright.

This meal,
unsurpassed.

Seamus Heaney, *Act of Union*

I
To-night, a first movement, a pulse,
As if the rain in bogland gathered head
To slip and flood: a bog-burst,
A gash breaking open the ferny bed.
Your back is a firm line of eastern coast
And arms and legs are thrown
Beyond your gradual hills. I caress
The heaving province where our past has grown.
I am the tall kingdom over your shoulder

That you would neither cajole nor ignore.
Conquest is a lie. I grow older
Conceding your half-independent shore
Within whose borders now my legacy
Culminates inexorably.

Kevin Bowen reminds that even alleged enemies can, like lovers, find an unspoken, but deeply shared meeting place. W. B. Yeats and Robert Frost recognize the difficult treasure of the place of connection between two people. Carole Maso describes the poignance of empathetic understanding between a very troubled mother and her daughter.

❧ KEVIN BOWEN, *Playing Basketball with the Vietcong*

for Nguy-en Quang Sáng

You never thought it would come to this,
that afternoon in the war
when you leaned so hard into the controls
you almost became part of the landscape:
just you, the old man, old woman
and their buffalo.
You never thought then
that this grey-haired man in sandals
smoking Gauloises on your back porch,
drinking your beer, his rough cough
punctuating tales of how he fooled
the French in '54,
would arrive at your back door
to call you out to shoot some baskets, friend.
If at first he seems awkward,
before long he's got it down.
His left leg lifts from the ground,
his arms arch back then forward

from the waist to release the ball
arcing to the hoop, one, two, . . .
ten straight times. You stare at him
in his tee shirt, sandals, and shorts.
Yes, he smiles. It's a gift,
good for bringing gunships down
as he did in the Delta
and in other places where, he whispers,
there may be other scores to settle.

❦ W. B. Yeats, *When You Are Old*

How many loved your moments of glad grace,
And loved your beauty with love false or true,
But one man loved the pilgrim soul in you,
And loved the sorrows of your changing face.

❦ Robert Frost, *Home Burial*

"Let me into your grief. I'm not so much
Unlike other folk as your standing there
Apart would make me out. Give me my chance.
I do think, though, you overdo it a little.
What was it brought you up to think the thing
To take your mother-loss of a first child
So inconsolably—in the face of love.
You'd think his memory might be satisfied—"

❦ Carole Maso, *Ghost Dance*

Looking up from our tangle of cat's cradle, I noticed that Sonia's
brown eyes had turned the pale color of tea. The yellow flowers on the
wallpaper in my bedroom were beginning to disappear as if they were

being eaten off in some exquisite hunger. In the next room my father's bare feet blanched. The world was losing its color. Walking to the window, I noticed a few leaves on the backyard tree had shed their green, not for the brilliant, momentary oranges and reds of autumn but for some lesser shade, a sort of gray, the mark of a more troubled, internal season, more permanent than other seasons, colder.

This was only the beginning. In the days to come, the world would continue to empty itself slowly of color until finally, by the time my mother was handing her suitcase to my father at the top of the stairs, I would barely be able to see her at all, she would be so lost in white. This happened many times through the years of my childhood. The lake would gray and flatten into a pale square. The red-winged blackbird flying across the blue sky would lose its shock of red, its feathers would fade, and the white sky would devour it.

I began to be able to detect these changes almost immediately, no matter how subtle they were at first. I felt lucky that I could foresee my mother's departures so far in advance. With the first signs I would follow her more closely, sit nearer to her, watch her while she napped on the couch, etch her profile in my mind, hug her disappearing body as color drained from her lips and her blonde hair whitened. On these early days, her shadowy arm would curl around me like a wisp of smoke and she would whisper, "What is it, Vanessa?" But she knew well what it was.

Had I overheard telephone conversations, seen airplane or train tickets in advance, been privy to plans I had forgotten, or was it something else, something in my mother herself, some early retreat, a pulling back, a stepping away that made me aware that soon she'd be leaving again? I think I received my cue from some extreme inwardness in her, from the distant place she had already gone in preparation for her own departure, a place even beyond that place which was her normal domain. Yes, I was extremely sensitive to the timbre of my mother's existence. I loved her so much that days in advance I could see her departure in the face of a friend.

When everything had become white, I knew the time had come for my mother to go to the closet, drag her leather suitcase across the room, and lift it to the bed. She would call me into the room then, and we would sit there for a moment staring into the white. Then she would begin.

"I just don't know what to bring, Vanessa," she would say. What to pack always seemed the outward struggle of a much deeper ambivalence for both of us. We sat on the bed and looked into empty space.

"Maybe I'll pack nothing," she said finally. "Maybe I'll give the Henrietta T. Putnam Lecture in the nude! What do you think?"

"Yes, we'll only pack your hat," I said.

"Perfect," she said. "The fuchsia one with the feather."

It is one of those moments frozen in my mind forever: the hat, tilted to the side, covers one eye. Her hair, pulled up, falls over one shoulder. She stands in her lacy underwear, puckers her lips, and then laughs hysterically, shivering almost, in anticipation of the windy lecture hall.

I would keep her with me. I would keep the sparkle in her blue eyes and put it back into the lake, back into the sky she was about to leave behind. I would keep her laugh, her intonation, her hat with the feather, her hair falling down her back—her hair was yellower in those days and longer. She must have been very young.

I remained through the years an almost-silent witness to my mother's packing as I watched the mysterious rise and fall of hemlines on her lovely legs. I said very little, for language could only complicate the complicated feelings of my mother. She would sit back on the bed again and look at me and say, "I just don't know what to take," and soon she'd begin to cry in the white room. Holding her hand, I might then walk to her enormous closet with her and stand there looking at the bottoms of her dresses, and I too would begin to cry. Though I tried so hard at times, I would never be, as some children are capable of being, the grown-up my mother needed. I could not help thinking, through those years, that my friend Sonia would have been a better daughter altogether for my mother. Sonia, keeping the seasons straight and the occasion in mind, would have put together, from my mother's huge assortment of clothing, outfits— one for each day she was to be away with a change of evening clothes for the nights. But not me. We would start by carefully picking and choosing, but by the end of the day we would have moved all the clothes from the closet onto the bed. We felt unselective. We could imagine needing just about anything. And my mother had so many clothes.

My mother's attempts to stay fashionable were, I think, her one concession to life as other people know it. She worked hard not to feel out of place. We would diligently scrutinize the fashion magazines, Italian *Vogue* and *Women's Wear Daily*, make obligatory trips to Saks and Henri Bendel, watch emaciated models walk down numerous runways. "Who writes this?" she would whisper to me exasperated, as some man with a microphone told us to "imagine you are in Bali and the sun is about to set."

Fashion was frivolous in a way my mother never really could be. Despite her supreme effort, my mother was not good at dressing. Her heart was simply not in it, and yet, stubbornly, her whole life she insisted on keeping up with the fashions of the day and wearing them.

"Do you like these?" she'd ask tentatively, taking lizard shoes out of a striped shoebox. "Oh, they're really quite ridiculous, aren't they?" she laughed.

There was an urgency about her dressing. I think she believed that if she stayed current she would not get lost. If she kept one high-heeled foot in the material world, all would be fine.

I can remember thinking, after one of our many shopping sprees, as we walked down a busy street in New York, impeccably dressed, that we were misfits, and that no matter what we put on, we would never fit in. My mother must have felt that, too, but tried to douse that feeling with French cologne, to disguise it with a Christian Dior coat or a suit from the House of Chanel.

She always hated surprises, and it was some comfort to her, walking down the street, that nothing in the wide world of fashion could surprise us. When paper dresses came, we were well prepared. Fish swimming in earrings were nothing to us. And when a certain faction began dying its hair pink and green we were not fazed. My mother just smiled, pleased to be on top of the situation.

But her multitudes of clothes posed a tremendous problem when it came time to pack. She became distraught, unable to put things together. I could not help. To me, in my sorrow, each item looked like every other. I handed my mother the white dress, the white shoes, the white sweater, the white scarf, the white gloves. Did you know, she said to me, that in China white is the color of mourning? She must have seen white, too. I looked at the mountains of pale clothes on the bed. The Chinese are right, I thought, to make white the mourning color.

All those times sitting on her bed, buried under clothes, the suitcase overflowing, I found it easy to imagine that she would never come back again.

The last time I saw my mother she was waiting for me under the enormous clock in Grand Central Station where we met briefly, she on her way back from Maine and I on my way to college for the second semester. She did not see me as I approached her. She wore a large hat. Bewildered, she watched people pass her and stare. My mother could have worn anything and gotten away with it—paper dresses *and* fish earrings, snakeskin gloves, lizard shoes, parachutes, parasols. What other people saw when they passed was a large, beautiful, overdressed woman. What I saw, getting closer to her, was my mother, so ill at ease with her surroundings that she had to arm herself with layers of clothes and jewelry and makeup for protection. Her bulging suitcases flanked her.

"Hi, Mom," I said quietly, so as not to frighten her, "I'm sorry I'm late." She smiled broadly.

She was not really seeing me. "You're very nice," she said.

"Mom. Oh, Mom."

"Hmmm? What is it, honey? Vanessa?"

"Mom," I said gently. "You don't need all of this," I said, as I slipped rings from her fingers, slowly undressing her. She looked at me as though she were a child, this big woman. She was completely absorbed in me and what I was saying. "You don't need all this." Her eyes did not leave my mouth as she waited for meaning to come. I put jewelry into her large pocketbook. I removed the glasses she was wearing; there was nothing wrong with her eyes.

"How's my makeup?" she asked.

I wiped layers of color from her face. I felt the giant clock's sharp arm cutting into my back like a blade.

"I'll call you on Sunday," I said. There was so much snow—it pressed down on us. I turned to leave.

"I have loved you my whole life," she said. "Even when I was a little girl—even then."

When I turned back to look at her, she had already taken the big silver bracelet from her purse. She picked up one suitcase. It was so heavy she tipped over to one side, her leg in the air. She waved good-bye.

All those times, sitting on her bed, buried under clothes, the suitcases overflowing, I found it easy to imagine that she would not come back again, but I did not think of it that day when we parted in Grand Central Station, she on her way home to Connecticut and I back to Poughkeepsie.

Those days of packing always ended with Father coming in to close the suitcases that neither she nor I could manage, they were so full. He would then lower them to the floor. To me at this point she seemed already to be gone, though she'd be chatting away, knowing little work could be accomplished on a traveling day. If I could have changed shape, left my human life for the life of clothing, been fabric against fabric in my mother's suitcase, I would have—even to have been something frivolous, bought on a whim and never once worn.

My mother, now in a fitted dress, now in a billowy one, now in a hat, now in a veil, a scarf, a bit of plaid, my mother now in felt, now in lace, now in cashmere, smiles. My mother's shoe, one year a pump, one year flat, one year alligator, one year suede, pivots. She takes my hand in hers, one year polished, one year not, one year gloved, and we go down the stairs, she first, me following. This is how I remember her best: an extravagant, exotic figure, descending stairs or getting into the car, but always saying good-bye.

I borrowed from this scene, not on purpose, for what was the recurrent dream of my childhood. For years, nearly once a week I saw this in sleep: The room is white. My mother walks to the closet and drags the suitcase out—I recognize its smell immediately; it is like the smell of the interior of a new car. I feel as if it might suffocate me. "Mother," I say, but before completing the sentence she tells me to just relax. Breathe deeply. It's OK. She is so comforting at this moment, so maternal, that I can't believe this isn't her daily role. She looks at me, her head resting on her hand. "Shh, shh. Breathe deeply. Everything will be all right." I nod. All afternoon as she's been packing she's been uncertain, hesitant, sorrowful, but now, patting my head, comforting me, she is stronger than anyone I have ever seen. She moves with new confidence to one corner of the room. Her face has an exquisite pallor. Her chin is raised, her eyes are focused. From the corner of the room she takes a large heavy piece of white cloth and like an expert folds it into a triangle and, smiling, she gives it to me. It calms me down and I can breathe again. From the top of the stairs she passes the suitcase to my father. This is how I know the dream is nearly over. At the end of the staircase there is always fog. I hug the triangle to me. Through the fog I wait for the sound of the door closing. I can see the back of her head perfectly, even through thick fog. I listen for the engine. The lights go on. She turns to wave.

Love, across generations: Countee Cullen speaks of the enduring qualities of his grandmother. Wang Ping and Seamus Heaney reflect on the bittersweet tie that binds child with parent: how in making a life of purpose and meaning together it is not always possible to appreciate what will result. In Colin Greer's "Taking Off," father and son lose each other in the unspoken conflict between them. In "His Son, in His Arms, in Light, Aloft" Harold Brodkey tells a tale of confident, empathetic understanding of the power of going out of oneself and celebrating what is noble and emergent in someone else.

❦ COUNTEE CULLEN, *For My Grandmother*

This lovely flower fell to seed
    Work gently sun and rain;
She held it as her dying creed
    That she would grow again.

❦ WANG PING, *She Is That Reed*

Don't point at your giggling daughter
and say: My last child, her name is Reed.

Don't stop your spinning wheel, your eyes at the pond,
"Why must all girls be called flowers? I want to name her Reed."

Mother, oh my mother who called me Reed,
your story shocked me so much that I swallowed an apricot pit.

"My last daughter couldn't cry when she was born.
Your aunt made a reed flute to call you back."

"Mouth to mouth, the flute brought your first cry.
Ain't I right that I named you Reed?"

"A good name," I said, but why was I giggling again?
You pulled my ear and said: "You are still Reed even though you
    learned how to read."

Mother, oh my mother who called me Reed,
Years passed, do you still remember that reed?

You held my hand and blew the flute hard,
your tears and sweat caught me back to your dark warm cave.

How ugly I was, mother, thin and stubborn like grass in the pond,
but you knew you'd never have to worry about me again.

We roamed around valleys to pick wild fruits and pigeon eggs,
and walked fifteen miles to sell them at the fair for my tuition.

I'm probably the only person on earth saved by a reed,
I blushed every time you told the story to a stranger.

Only a crying baby could live and grow, you smiled,
I like my daughter running around the Yellow Plateau like wind.

I'm looking more and more like you, mother,
except my hair has grown beyond the river beyond the sea.

If you see a strange college girl walking down the valley,
she is that Reed, mother, who blasted out her first cry into your flute.

❧ SEAMUS HEANEY, *Follower*

My father worked with a horse-plough,
His shoulders globed like a full sail strung
Between the shafts and the furrow.
The horses strained at his clicking tongue.

An expert. He would set the wing
And fit the bright steel-pointed sock.
The sod rolled over without breaking.
At the headrig, with a single pluck

Of reins, the sweating team turned round
And back into the land. His eye
Narrowed and angled at the ground,
Mapping the furrow exactly.

I stumbled in his hob-nailed wake,
Fell sometimes on the polished sod;
Sometimes he rode me on his back
Dipping and rising to his plod.

I wanted to grow up and plough,
To close one eye, stiffen my arm.
All I ever did was follow
In his broad shadow round the farm.

I was a nuisance, tripping, falling,
Yapping always. But today
It is my father who keeps stumbling
Behind me, and will not go away.

❧ COLIN GREER, *Taking Off*

(As the comic strip tells it, Superman's parents rocketed him from home to save him from Kryptonite catastrophe.)

Your father is older than most children's fathers, his mother told him. He remembered her telling him that as if it was the first thing she said to him ever. He never could think about her without remembering that his father was older than most children's fathers. She told him that very soon after he was born, and she told him it many times afterward too. Some nights soon after he was born he remembered hearing her telling his father how much older he was than most young children's fathers. He heard her saying that while she tucked his father up in bed at night. She tucked father up like she tucked him up. Soon after he was born he noticed her tucking father up. He watched her tucking father up as he waited for her to come to him. Dad was tucked up first then she tucked him up. He didn't like waiting. He told mother he didn't like waiting. Soon after he was born he wanted her to know he didn't like waiting. As soon as he could talk he told mother he didn't like dad being tucked up first. After mother tucked him up she went back to father. He could hear them talk. He could hear mother tell dad how son wanted to be tucked up first. He wanted to tell her not to tell dad. He wished dad did not know about his wanting to be tucked up first.

Please don't tell father I wish I were first he wanted to tell mother. He wanted her to know he didn't like her telling dad about his wish to be tucked up first. He wanted mum to know, not dad. He didn't tell mother he didn't want her to tell father about his wish because he knew she would again tell dad when she returned after tucking them both up. He thought dad knew anyway. He didn't tell his mother about his wish but he was quite sure his father knew about his wanting his mother not to tell as well as about his wanting to be tucked up first. He was sure dad knew. Dad told him almost every day since soon after he was born that his father was older than most young children's fathers. He was sure his father told him this over and over because he knew about son's wishes.

Every time father said how much older he was than most young children's fathers he was sure dad knew. He wished dad did not know.

When he was told by mother that he was going to be sent away he was more sure than ever that dad knew. He could not say sorry because then dad would be sure. He had to be quiet. He had got into this trouble telling mother he wanted to be tucked up first. He had to be quiet. Dad must not know that what he already knew about son was true. He couldn't say he was sorry.

No doubt about it, dad knew. Father and mother agreed he must go away. Dad was older than most young children's fathers they told him. O how dad knew. Father could not go with him, nor could mother. Father was too old. Mother would stay with father. Mother would stay to tuck dad up. Soon you will go mother told son. She said she and dad wished it did not need to be this way. Son wished that too. Son wanted to ask dad to tuck him up. He couldn't. They said he must go. No good wanting dad to tuck him up, dad went to bed first. Father was older than most young children's fathers. No good telling dad what he wanted. Telling didn't work. Dad probably knew what he wanted anyway. No good telling dad. No good telling mother. He had to go. They told him they were sorry. They said they wished he didn't have to go.

x

Father heard himself wanting to tell son he wished they could all stay together. No use telling him when there was no choice. Father knew son had to go. There was no point in telling son that he wished they could stay together. Mother had told son that. Mother told father son had been told. No point dad saying it again. Son knew. Mother had told him. She told son he must go. She told him about how it would happen. Dad didn't say anything. Son could hear mother tell dad that she had told him about being sent away. She tucked him up as always and told him he had to go away. He couldn't say he didn't want to go. He couldn't tell mother. She would tell dad. He didn't want dad to be told he had said he didn't want to go. He knew he had to go.

Father wished his son could stay. He had wanted a son for a long time. He didn't want the boy to go. He had told mother he wanted a son. He didn't tell her how pleased he was when the boy was born. He was sure she knew how pleased he was as soon as the boy was born. He was sure as soon as she told him about how much older he was than other young children's fathers. He knew she knew.

Father wanted to tuck son up in bed. He didn't tell mother he wanted to do that. He was sure she knew he wanted to tuck son up in bed. He knew she knew what he wanted. No point in saying anything. She tucked him up in bed first at night. She told him how much older he was than other young children's fathers.

Father didn't want his son to go. He didn't tell son he wanted them all to stay together forever. Son knew what father really wanted; he knew he had to go.

❧ HAROLD BRODKEY, *His Son, in His Arms, in Light, Aloft*

We are moving, this elephant and I, we are lumbering, down some steps, across grassy, uneven ground—the spoiled child in his father's arms—behind our house was a little park—we moved across the grass of the little park. There are sun's rays on the dome of the Moorish bandstand. The evening is moist, fugitive, momentarily sneaking, half welcomed in this hour of crime. My father's neck. The stubble. The skin where the stubble stops. Exhaustion has me: I am a creature of failure, a locus of childishness, an empty skull: I am this being-young. We overrun the world, he and I, with his legs, with our eyes, with our alliance. We move on in a ghostly torrent of our being like this.

My father has the smell and feel of wanting to be my father. Guilt and innocence stream and restream in him. His face, I see now in memory, held an untiring surprise: as if some grammar of deed and purpose—of comparatively easy tenderness—startled him again and again, startled him continuously for a while. He said, "I guess we'll just have to cheer you up—we'll have to show you life isn't so bad—I guess we weren't any too careful of a little boy's feelings, were we?" I wonder if all comfort is alike.

A man's love is, after all, a fairly spectacular thing.

He said—his voice came from above me—he spoke out into the air, the twilight—"We'll make it all right—just you wait and see. . . ."

He said, "This is what you like," and he placed me on the wall that ran along the edge of the park, the edge of a bluff, a wall too high for me to see over, and which I was forbidden to climb: he placed me on the stubbed stone mountains and grouting of the walltop. He put his arm around my middle: I leaned against him: and faced outward into the salt of the danger of the height, of the view (we were at least one hundred and fifty feet; we were, therefore, hundreds of feet in the air); I was flicked at by narrow, abrasive bands of wind, evening wind, veined with sunset's sun-crispness, strongly touched with coolness.

The wind would push at my eyelids, my nose, my lips. I heard a buzzing in my ears that signaled how high, how alone we were: this view of a river valley at night and of parts of four counties was audible. I looked into the hollow in front of me, a grand hole, an immense, bellying deep sheet or vast sock. There were numinous fragments in it—birds in what sunlight was left, bits of smoke faintly lit by distant light or mist, hovering inexplicably here and there: rays of yellow light, high up, touching a few high clouds.

It had a floor on which were creeks (and the big river), a little dim, a little glary at this hour, rail lines, roads, highways, houses, silos, bridges, trees, fields, everything more than half hidden in the enlarging dark: there was the shrinking glitter of far-off noises, bearded and stippled with huge and spreading shadows of my ignorance: it was panorama as a personal privilege. The sun at the end of the large, sunset-swollen sky was a glowing and urgent orange; around it were the spreading petals of pink and stratospheric gold; on the ground were occasional magenta flarings: oh, it makes you stare and gasp; a fine, astral (not a crayon) red rode in a broad, magnificent band across the Middle Western sky: below us, for miles, shadowiness tightened as we watched (it seemed); above us, tinted clouds spread across the vast shadowing sky: there were funereal lights and sinkings everywhere. I stand on the wall and lean against Daddy, only somewhat awed and abstracted: the view does not own me as it usually does: I am partly in the hands of the jolting—amusement—the conceit—of having been resurrected—by my father.

I understood that he was proffering me oblivion plus pleasure, the end of a sorrow to be henceforth remembered as Happiness. This was to be my privilege. This amazing man is going to rescue me from any anomaly or barb or sting in my existence: he is going to confer happiness on me: as a matter of fact, he has already begun.

"Just you trust me—you keep right on being cheered up—look at that sunset—that's some sunset, wouldn't you say? Everything is going to be just fine and dandy—you trust me—you'll see—just you wait and see. . . ."

Yehuda Amichai extends empathy between lovers to a better and deeper understanding of the world. Charles Johnson extends the unspoken connection and hopefulness lovers can project into the world to the communication systems of a whole people, the Allmuseri.

❧ Yehuda Amichai, *The Aching Bones of Lovers*

The aching bones of lovers
Who rolled all day in the grass.

Their lying together, awake at night,
Brings redemption closer to the world. Not to them.

A bonfire, blind with pain, repeats in the field
The sun's act in the day.

Childhood is far away.
War is close. Amen.

❦ CHARLES JOHNSON, *Middle Passage*

It was Captain Falcon's belief that slave insurrections could be prevented if for every ten prisoners one was selected to oversee the others and keep them in line. He issued these shipboard major-domos, one of them named Ngonyama, whom I came to know well those first few weeks, old shirts and tar-splattered trousers, giving them the advantage of being clothed like the crew; they had greater freedom to roam the slippery deck, and Falcon also gave them better food and a few minor tasks such as picking old ropes apart. "The best way to control a rebellious nigger," said he, "is to give him some responsibility."

However, few slaving formulas worked with Ngonyama. Dressed he was now, in tarry breeches and a duck frock, which distinguished him from the others, despite the red bead in his right nostril, and he was quiet during our first fortnight at sea, notwithstanding wind that whipped the sails devilishly and the fact that sometimes the sea ran as high as five houses and our forward deck was invisible underwater, a thing that made the other slaves claw and wail all the more. But Ngonyama, I had the feeling, was waiting. He was so quiet sometimes he seemed to blend, then disappear into the background of shipboard life. Quiet and cunning, I'd say, because he was studying everything— everything we did, and even enlisted my aid in teaching him a smattering of English and explaining how the steerage worked, in exchange for his teaching me Allmuseri. Of all the players who promenade through this narrative, he was easily the most mysterious. At first he could not distinguish any of the white crew individually, and asked me, "How do their families tell them apart?" I suppose he selected me because I was the only Negro on board, though the distance between his people and black America was vast—his people saw whites as Raw Barbarians and me (being a colored mate) as a Cooked one. And his depth perception so differed from mine that when he looked at a portrait of Isadora I carried in my purse, he asked, "Why is her face splotched with smudges?" by which he meant the *shadows* the artist had drawn under her chin and eyes, for his tribe did not use our sense of perspective but rather the flat, depthless technique of Egyptian art. (He also asked why her nose looked like a conch, if maybe this was a trick of vision too, then saw my anger and dropped the question.)

Sometimes he helped Squibb and me in the cookroom, and the way he carved one of the skipper's pigs stopped me cold. Me, I never could carve. But Ngonyama, his shoulders relaxed, holding his breath for what seemed hours before he started, fixed his eyes as if he could see through the pig, his right hand gripping the cook's blade as if it had grown right out of his wrist. It was eerie, you ask me. It seemed, suddenly, as though the galley slipped in time and took on a transparent feel, as if everything round us were made of glass. Ngonyama began to carve. He slipped metal through meat as if it wasn't there or, leastways, wasn't solid, without striking bone, and in a pattern I couldn't follow, without hacking or rending—doing no harm—the blade guided by, I think, a knack that favored the same touch I'd developed as a thief, which let me feel safe tumblers falling a fraction of a second *before* they dropped, tracing the invisible trellis of muscles, tendons, tissues, until the pig fell apart magically in his hands. He left no knife tracks. Not a trace. The cookroom was as quiet as a tomb when he finished.

"Mirrors!" Squibb whispered to me, stunned. "It's some kinda heathen trick!"

Yet there was no trick to it. In every fiber of their lives you could sense this same quiet magic. Truth to tell, they were not even "Negroes." They were Allmuseri. Talking late at night, blue rivulets scudding back and forth on the deck, our eyes screwed up against the weather, Ngonyama unfolded before me like a merchant's cloth his tribe's official history, the story of themselves they stuck by. Once they had been a seafaring people, years and years ago, and deposited their mariners in that portion of India later to be called Harappa, where they blended with its inhabitants, the Dravidians, in the days before the Aryans and their juggernauts—"city destroyers"—leveled the civilization of Mohenjo-Daro over night. Between 1000 B.C. and 500 B.C. they sailed to Central America on North Equatorial currents that made the voyage from the west coast of Africa to the Caribbean only thirty days, bringing their skills in agriculture and metallurgy to the Olmec who, to honor these African mariners, stamped their likeness in stone and enshrined in song their prowess as warriors. Specifically, their martial-arts techniques resembled Brazilian *capoeira*. Over time these elegant moves, which Ngonyama taught me when we had time for rest, had become elements in their ceremonial dance.

I must leave their fighting arts for later, because more fascinating than their globe-spanning travels in antiquity and their style of self-defense was the peculiar, gnomic language the Allmuseri practiced. When Ngonyama's tribe spoke it was not so much like talking as the tones the savannah made at night, siffilating through the plains of coarse grass, soughing as dry wind from tree to tree. Not really a language at all, by my guess, as a melic way of breathing deep from the diaphragm that dovetailed articles into nouns, nouns into verbs. I'm not sure I know what I'm saying now, but Ngonyama told me the predication "is," which granted existence to anything, had over the ages eroded into merely an article of faith for them. Nouns or static substances hardly existed in their vocabulary at all. A "bed" was called a "resting," a "robe" a "warming." Furthermore, each verb was different depending on the nature of the object acted upon, whether it was vegetable, mineral, mammal, oblong or rotund. When Ngonyama talked to his tribesmen it was as if the objects and others he referred to flowed together like water, taking different forms, as the sea could now be fluid, now solid ice, now steam swirling around the mizzenpole. Their written language—these Africans had one—was no less unusual, and of such exquisite limpidity, tone colors, litotes, and contrapletes that I could not run my eyes across it, left to right, without feeling everything inside me relax. It consisted of pictograms. You had to look at the characters, Ngonyama taught me, as you would an old friend you've seen many times before, grasping the meaning—and relation to other characters—in a single intuitive snap. It was not, I gathered, a good language for doing analytic work, or deconstructing things into discrete parts, which probably explained why the Allmuseri had no empirical science to speak of, at least not as we understood that term. To Falcon that made them savages. Just the same, it seemed a fitting tongue for the most sought-after blacks in the world.

Compared to other African tribes, the Allmuseri were the most popular servants. They brought twice the price of a Bantu or Kru. According to legend, Allmuseri elders took twig brooms with them everywhere, sweeping the ground so as not to inadvertently step on creatures too small to see. Eating no meat, they were easy to feed. Disliking progeny, they were simple to clothe. Able to heal themselves, they required no medication. They seldom fought. They could not steal. They fell *sick*, it was said, if they wronged anyone. As I live, they so shamed me I wanted their ageless culture to be my own, if in fact Ngonyama spoke truly. But who was I fooling? While Rutherford Calhoun might envy certain features of Allmuseri folkways, he could never claim something he had no hand in creating. I respected them too much to insult them this way—particularly one woman and her eight-year-old daughter, Baleka, who'd caught a biscuit I tossed her one day when talking to Meadows. Her mother snatched it away. She studied it like a woman inspecting melons at a public market, her face growing sharp. She smelled it, she tasted it with a tiny nibble, and spat it out the side of her mouth into the sea. Presently, she stumped across the deck and dropped it back onto my lap. Sliding up behind her, half hidden behind Mama's legs, Baleka stuck out her hand. Her eyes burned a hole in my forehead. Her mother's finger wagged in my face, and in the little of their language I knew she sniffed that her baby deserved far better than one moldy biscuit. I could only agree. To square things, that night I shared my powdered beef, mustard, and tea with Baleka: a major mistake. Her expectation, and that of Mama, for sharing my *every* pan of food became an unspoken contract no less binding between us than a handshake. By and by, we were inseparable. This was how Mama wanted it, having decided her child's survival might depend on staying close to the one crew member who looked most African, asking me to decipher the strange behavior of the whites and intercede on their behalf. Thus, the child stayed at my heels as I spun rope and, when I was on larboard watch by the taffrail, leaned against my legs, looking back sadly toward Senegambia.

7
To Hear the Heartbeat of Others

COMPASSION

Plato called on us to be compassionate:

"Please, my friends, be kind, for everyone you meet is fighting a hard battle."

In order to do that, an Irish proverb tells us:

"It's easy to halve a potato where there's love."

Scarcity is the ubiquitous experience of all. It is conquered only by compassionate engagement in the world. Without compassion, scarcity gives rise to roles and conventions that are sharp and biting. Compassion is love's recognition that changes in the world take place within the lives of individuals. Compassion is how we mobilize against what Theodore Roethke called "Each malignant wish to spoil collective life." To the extent we can be sympathetic with the lives and the lot of others, so can we expect our own lives and the prospects for humanity to be bathed in the fond glow of our shared experience.

Live and let live is an essential attitude toward others, but that is not an argument for a life lived in isolation, cut off and out of sympathy with other people's lives. All too often, paranoia can seem to justify selfishness and greed. We aim to protect ourselves from the greed and selfishness of others by those same means. But, as Herman Hesse reminded us,

> Whenever we hate someone, we are hating some part of ourselves that we see in that person. We don't get worked up about anything that is not in ourselves.

It follows, then, that to be compassionate toward others, we would do well to be compassionate toward ourselves, leading, as the Bible in Psalm 133, suggests:

> Look! How good and how pleasant it is for brothers to dwell together in unity.

It is important to recognize that compassion—concern and sympathy for ourselves and others—is at the heart of our moral ideals and is about making life in society possible and meaningful. The human imperative to do this is about doing things together—doing things with others. Doing something together and reflecting on it in order to do it better and to imbue our daily effort with meaning is the long-standing legacy of storytellers, prophets, and philosophers. Lao-tzu equated compassion with soundness of heart:

> A sound heart is not shut within itself.
> But is open to other people's hearts:
> I find good people good,
> and I find bad people good
> If I am good enough;
> I trust the words of honest people,
> And I trust liars
> If I am true enough;
> I feel the heart-beats of others
> Above my own
> If I am enough of a father,
> enough of a son.

We are inevitably tied to each other. Instead of "splitting off" the bad parts of ourselves and projecting them onto others so as to blame other people for the unfortunate or evil aspects of life, we can resist the winds of hatred and keep our hearts warm. For the society of humans is most enriched when, as Adrienne Rich puts it:

> Our gifts shall bring us home; not to beginnings
> Nor always to the distinctions named
> Upon our setting forth.

Selections

Compassion, in Karen Brodine's "March 1986," is not getting in her own way through self-loathing. Hettie Jones and Sophocles' *Antigone* find compassion for parents—against the odds.

❦ KAREN BRODINE, *March 1986*

When I was a kid someone would say,
ok, what would you choose, death by fire or water?
Pragmatic, I would never play that game. Now I have to.
A new twist, the bribe is life. Life by fire, death
by percentage, life by water, drowning
all your cells just enough.

Remission is disappearance for the time being.
Cure is death by other causes.

My chances for recurrence are 35% without chemo,
half that, with. A clear choice.
Till you add barbarities or treatment. Would you
prefer to chance diabetes or heart failure,
dizziness or seeing halos round the moon?

I've never been the least religious.
Now they're tossing halos round my neck like horseshoes,

and I'm the pole, no angel, stiff and afraid,
arm protective of the missing breast.

What will happen when I swallow the poison?
Which poison should I choose?

Someone flips a coin and here I stand in my body,
one more gamble, one more statistic.

I'm like a boy on one side, a woman on the other.
Doesn't bother me so much, reminds me of running wild
and lithe through the woods like a colt.
What bothers me is I may lose my lashes
through which I look, shaded and protected,
at the world.

The dr. says he's biased toward research.
I've got another bias.
The dr. says he can't say what he would advise
if it were his wife or daughter or even himself.
Because he's not in my position.
But what are imaginations for?

Too many times I have imagined my mother, wrestling
with her tardy, errant heart, anchored to that couch
by a failing muscle. Still she came back,
dragging half her body at the leash,
into determined movement and life.

❧ HETTIE JONES, *Lottie and Oscar*

—for my parents
I like to think of them dancing
two small people in step.
He led and she followed,

but having had a leading man
I know what skill that takes.

I like to think of them stepping
in perfect time to the tune, the only time
they seemed happy together.
Mostly they never did anything right
—she the critic, he the protest—
though they kissed when he came through
  the side door to his dinner.

When, as sometimes happens, the past
leaps to the present, and the long teeth
  of their argument tear at me,
I turn at once to their waltz, their fox trot,
  their rhumba, their samba

And only because I danced with them both
  —began the beguine in the leader's arms
  and tenderly rocked the follower—

  Only because they understood the beat
  can I forgive them their battle

❦ SOPHOCLES, *Oedipus at Colonus*

OEDIPUS: Antigone, what will they do to us now?

LEADER: Out with you! Out of our country—far away!

OEDIPUS: But your promise—
won't you make good on your promise?

CHORUS: Fate will never punish a man
for returning harm first done to him.
Deceit matched by deceit, the tables turned:

treachery pays you back in pain, not kindness.
You—out of this place of rest, away, faster!
Off and gone from the land—before you fix
some greater penalty on our city.

ANTIGONE: Oh strangers,
you, with all the compassion in your hearts—
since you cannot endure my father, old as he is,
hearing the dreadful things he did against his will,
pity me at least, good strangers, my despair,
I beg you!—beg you for my father, beg you
with eyes that still can look into your eyes.
I implore you, look—
like a daughter sprung of your own blood,
I beg that my shattered father find compassion.
We throw ourselves on your mercy as on a god,
in all our misery. Hear us! Oh say Yes—
grant us the help we never dreamed to see!
I beg you now by all that you hold dear, by child,
by wife, by earthly possessions, by your gods!
Look through all humanity: you'll never find
a man on earth, if a god leads him on,
who can escape his fate.

Mayo Simon and Primo Levi recall the power of a generous heart. Shakespeare's Lady Macbeth tells starkly of the bitter loss of compassion that can flow in pursuit of grand prizes.

❧ MAYO SIMON, *The Old Lady's Guide to Survival*

NETTY: Where were you? Where did you go?

SHPRINTZY: To get you a—a— (She puts the yoghurt in Netty's hand.)

NETTY: What is it? (Laughing.) Oh, for God's sake. It's yoghurt.

SHPRINTZY: For you.

NETTY: To make me feel better. Thank you. (Eats.) Good. (Eats more then squints at Shprintzy.) Where's yours?

SHPRINTZY: I don't know.

NETTY: What do you mean, you don't know? You had a ticket for yoghurt two-for-one.

SHPRINTZY: (Trying to get Netty to stand.) Come, let's go.

NETTY: Not so fast. What happened over there?

SHPRINTZY: (Starting off.) I want to go home. Let's go.

NETTY: I'm not ready to go. I'm still eating. And I want to know why you went in with a ticket two-for-one yoghurt and you came out with one.

SHPRINTZY: I didn't want any. I'm not hungry. (A long moment of inner struggle.) It's not good anymore!

NETTY: The ticket? Who said it's not good?

SHPRINTZY: The teen-age girl.

NETTY: Another know-it-all teen-age girl.

SHPRINTZY: She showed me the little letters on the back. But I can't read the little letters.

NETTY: Well, you go in there and tell her you don't have to read the little letters on the back. You want what it says in the big letters on the front.

SHPRINTZY: You do it.

NETTY: I'm not going to do it. You're going to do it. (A little cry of fear from Shprintzy.) What are you going to do when I'm in Alaska?

SHPRINTZY: I don't know.

NETTY: Well, you better learn to stand up for yourself!

SHPRINTZY: (In tears.) I can't.

NETTY: Why can't you?

SHPRINTZY: Because my husband did that for me!

NETTY: (Standing, coming to Shprintzy.) Now you listen to me. After my husband died, I had to return a defective clock to a store, and they wouldn't give me back my money. So I said, well, my husband will come in tomorrow and he will talk to you. And you know what? They gave me back my money. I went home, and I wept bitter tears. Because I realized that my husband dead had more power than me alive. (Netty takes a breath.) That night I made myself a promise, that I would never use his name again. And I never have. Now your husband is dead, but you are alive. You are not invisible. You are an important and valuable person, and you are going back in there and you are getting another yoghurt. Now go! (Shprintzy turns around and starts walking away from Baskin-Robbins.) Stop! You can't leave!

❧ PRIMO LEVI, *Monday*

Is anything sadder than a train
That leaves when it's supposed to,
That has only one voice,
Only one route?
There's nothing sadder.

Except perhaps a cart horse,
Shut between two shafts
And unable even to look sideways.
Its whole life is walking.

And a man? Isn't a man sad?
If he lives in solitude a long time,
If he believes time has run its course,
A man is a sad thing too.

❦ WILLIAM SHAKESPEARE, *Macbeth*

Enter Macbeth's Wife, alone, with a letter.

LADY MACBETH: (Reads) "They met me in the day of success; and I have learned by the perfect'st report they have more in them than mortal knowledge. When I burnt in desire to question them further, they made themselves air, into which they vanished. Whiles I stood rapt in the wonder of it came missives from the King, who all-hailed me 'Thane of Cawdor,' by which title, before, these Weird Sisters saluted me, and referred me to the coming on of time with 'Hail, king that shalt be!' This have I thought good to deliver thee, my dearest partner of greatness, that thou mightst not lose the dues of rejoicing by being ignorant of what greatness is promised thee. Lay it to thy heart, and farewell."

Glamis thou art, and Cawdor, and shalt be
What thou art promised. Yet do I fear thy nature;
It is too full o' the milk of human kindness
To catch the nearest way. Thou wouldst be great,
Art not without ambition, but without
The illness should attend it. What thou wouldst highly,
That wouldst thou holily; wouldst not play false,
And yet wouldst wrongly win. Thou'dst have, great Glamis,
That which cries "Thus thou must do," if thou have it,
And that which rather thou dost fear to do
Than wishest should be undone. Hie thee hither,
That I may pour my spirits in thine ear
And chastise with the valor of my tongue
All that impedes thee from the golden round
Which fate and metaphysical aid doth seem
To have thee crowned withal.

Estella, in Great Expectations, *in an inside-out sense of things, sacrifices herself in order to save people who love her from the inevitable pain she believes she will bring them.* Corinthians *recalls us to compassion and a charitable attitude. Carlos*

Castaneda reminds us to do no harm, and Elie Wiesel emphasizes that there are no half measures when it comes to right living.

❦ CHARLES DICKENS, *Great Expectations*

She gradually withdrew her eyes from me, and turned them on the fire. After watching it for what appeared in the silence and by the light of the slowly wasting candles to be a long time, she was roused by the collapse of some of the red coals, and looked towards me again—at first, vacantly—then, with a gradually concentrating attention; all this time, Estella knitted on. When Miss Havisham had fixed her attention on me, she said, speaking as if there had been no lapse in our dialogue:

"What else?"

"Estella," said I, turning to her now and trying to command my trembling voice, "you know I love you. You know that I have loved you long and dearly."

She raised her eyes to my face, on being thus addressed, and her fingers plied their work, and she looked at me with an unmoved countenance. I saw that Miss Havisham glanced from me to her, and from her to me.

"I should have said this sooner, but for my long mistake. It induced me to hope that Miss Havisham meant us for one another. While I thought you could not help yourself, as it were, I refrained from saying it. But I must say it now."

Preserving her unmoved countenance, and with her fingers still going, Estella shook her head.

"I know," said I, in answer to that action; "I know."

"I have no hope that I shall ever call you mine, Estella."

"I am ignorant what may become of me very soon, how poor I may be, or where I may go. Still, I love you. I have loved you ever since I first saw you in this house."

Looking at me perfectly unmoved and with her fingers busy, she shook her head again.

"It would have been cruel in Miss Havisham, horribly cruel, to practise on the susceptibility of a poor boy, and to torture me through all these years with a vain hope and an idle pursuit if she had reflected on the gravity of what she did. But I think she did not. I think that in the endurance of her own trial, she forgot mine, Estella."

I saw Miss Havisham put her hand to her heart and hold it there, as she sat looking by turns at Estella and at me.

"It seems," said Estella, very calmly, "that there are sentiments, fancies—I don't know how to call them—which I am not able to comprehend. When you say you love me, I know what you mean, as a form of words; but nothing more. You address nothing in my breast, you touch nothing there. I don't care for what you say at all. I have tried to warn you of this; now, have I not?"

I said in a miserable manner, "Yes."

"Yes. But you would not be warned, for you thought I did not mean it. Now, did you not think so?"

"I thought and hoped you could not mean it. You, so young, untried, and beautiful, Estella! Surely it is not in Nature."

"It is in my nature," she returned. And then she added, with a stress upon the words, "It is in the nature formed within me. I make a great difference between you and all other people when I say so much. I can do no more."

"Is it not true," said I, "that Bentley Drummle is in town here, and pursuing you?"

"It is quite true," she replied, referring to him with the indifference of utter contempt.

"That you encourage him, and ride out with him, and that he dines with you this very day?"

She seemed a little surprised that I should know it, but again replied, "Quite true."

"You cannot love him, Estella?"

Her fingers stopped for the first time, as she retorted rather angrily, "What have I told you? Do you still think, in spite of it that I do not mean what I say?"

"You would never marry him, Estella?"

She looked towards Miss Havisham, and considered for a moment with her work in her hands. Then she said, "Why not tell you the truth? I am going to be married to him."

I dropped my face into my hands, but was able to control myself better than I could have expected, considering what agony it gave me to hear her say those words. When I raised my face again, there was such a ghastly look upon Miss Havisham's, that it impressed me, even in my passionate hurry and grief.

"Estella, dearest, dearest Estella, do not let Miss Havisham lead you into this fatal step. Put me aside forever—you have done so, I well know—but bestow yourself on some worthier person than Drummle. Miss Havisham gives you to him, as the greatest slight and injury that could be done to the many far better men who admire you, and to the few who truly love you. Among those few, there may be one who loves you even as dearly, though he has not loved you as long, as I. Take him, and I can bear it better for your sake!"

My earnestness awoke a wonder in her that seemed as if it would have been touched with compassion, if she could have rendered me at all intelligible to her own mind.

"I am going," she said again, in a gentler voice, "to be married to him. The preparations for my marriage are making, and I shall be married soon. Why do you injuriously introduce the name of my mother by adoption? It is my own act."

"Your own act, Estella, to fling yourself away upon a brute?"

"On whom should I fling myself away?" she retorted, with a smile. "Should I fling myself away upon the man who would the soonest feel (if people do feel such things) that I took nothing to him? There! It is done. I shall do well enough, and so will my husband. As to leading me into what you call this fatal step, Miss Havisham would have had me wait, and not marry yet; but I am tired of the life I have led, which has very few charms for me, and I am willing enough to change it. Say no more. We shall never understand each other."

"Such a mean brute, such a stupid brute!" I urged in despair.

"Don't be afraid of my being a blessing to him," said Estella; "I shall not be that. Come! Here is my hand. Do we part on this, you visionary boy—or man?"

"O Estella!" I answered, as my bitter tears fell fast on her hand, do what I would to restrain them; "even if I remained in England and could hold my head up with the rest, how could I see you Drummle's wife?"

"Nonsense," she returned, "nonsense. This will pass in no time."

"Never, Estella!"

"You will get me out of your thoughts in a week."

"Out of my thoughts! You are part of my existence, part of myself. You have been in every line I have ever read, since I first came here, the rough common boy whose poor heart you wounded even then. You have been in every prospect I have ever seen since—on the river, on the sails of the ships, on the marshes, in the clouds, in the light, in the darkness, in the wind, in the woods, in the sea, in the streets. You have been the embodiment of every graceful fancy that my mind has ever become acquainted with. The stones of which the strongest London buildings are made are not more real, or more impossible to be displaced by your hands, than your presence and influence have been to me, there and everywhere, and will be. Estella, to the last hour of my life, you cannot choose but remain part of my character, part of the little good in me, part of the evil. But, in this separation I associate you only with the good, and I will faithfully hold you to that always, for you must have done me far more good than harm, let me feel now what sharp distress I may.

"O God bless you, God forgive you!"

In what ecstasy of unhappiness I got these broken words out of myself, I don't know. The rhapsody welled up within me, like blood from an inward wound, and gushed out. I held her hand to my lips some lingering moments, and so I left her. But ever afterwards, I remembered—and soon afterwards with stronger reason that while Estella looked at me merely with incredulous wonder, the spectral figure of Miss Havisham, her hand still covering her heart, seemed all resolved into a ghastly stare of pity and remorse.

❦ I Corinthians 13

1. Though I speak with the tongues of men and of angels, and have not charity, I am become *as* sounding brass, or a tinkling cymbal.

2. And though I have *the gift of* prophecy, and understand all mysteries, and all knowledge; and though I have all faith, so that I could remove mountains, and have not charity, I am nothing.

3. And though I bestow all my goods to feed *the poor*, and though I give my body to be burned, and have not charity, it profiteth me nothing.

4. Charity suffereth long, *and* is kind; charity envieth not; charity vaunteth not itself, is not puffed up,

5. Doth not behave itself unseemly, seeketh not her own, is not easily provoked, thinketh no evil;

6. Rejoiceth not in iniquity, but rejoiceth in the truth;

7. Beareth all things, believeth all things, hopeth all things, endureth all things.

8. Charity never faileth: but whether *there be* prophecies, they shall fail; whether *there be* tongues, they shall cease; whether *there be* knowledge, it shall vanish away.

9. For we know in part, and we prophesy in part.

10. But when that which is perfect is come, then that which is in part shall be done away.

11. When I was a child, I spake as a child, I understood as a child, I thought as a child: but when I became a man, I put away childish things.

12. For now we see through a glass, darkly; but then face to face: now I know in part; but then shall I know even as also I am known.

13. And now abideth faith, hope, charity, these three; but the greatest of these *is* charity.

❧ CARLOS CASTANEDA, *Journey to Ixtlan*

"A hunter knows he will lure game into his traps over and over again, so he doesn't worry. To worry is to become accessible, unwittingly accessible. And once you worry you cling to anything out of desperation; and once you cling you are bound to get exhausted or to exhaust whoever or whatever you are clinging to."

I told him that in my day-to-day life it was inconceivable to be inaccessible. My point was that in order to function I had to be within reach of everyone that had something to do with me.

"I've told you already that to be inaccessible does not mean to hide or to be secretive," he said calmly. "It doesn't matter that you cannot deal with people either. A hunter uses his world sparingly and with tenderness, regardless of whether the world might be things, or plants, or animals, or people, or power. A hunter deals intimately with his world and yet he is inaccessible to that same world."

"That's a contradiction," I said. "He cannot be inaccessible if he is there in his world, hour after hour, day after day."

"You did not understand," don Juan said patiently. "He is inaccessible because he's not squeezing his world out of shape. He taps it lightly, stays for as long as he needs to, and then swiftly moves away leaving hardly a mark."

❧ ELIE WIESEL, *Messengers of God*

Joseph's brothers, who had sold him into slavery, many years later confronted the displeasure of Joseph, the Prince of Egypt. They turned on Jehudah—the brother who had persuaded them to sell Joseph and not to kill him. "Had you advised us to let him be, we would have been guided by you," they said.

Still the sages admonish: it is forbidden to praise Jehudah for having saved Joseph's life, or to be sympathetic to him faced with the accusation of his brothers: when human life and dignity are at stake, one has no right to settle for half-measures; Jehudah should have fought to the end to save his brother, not only from death but also from shame.

In Athol Fugard's play, compassion and understanding are in evidence when people are "moving well together." For Denise Levertov and Philip Lopate, compassion for oneself is basic to kindness in the world.

◆ ATHOL FUGARD, *Master Harold and the Boys*

SAM: There's no collisions out there, Hally. Nobody trips or stumbles or bumps into anybody else. That's what that moment is all about. To be one of those finalists on that dance floor is like . . . like being in a dream about a world in which accidents don't happen.

HALLY: (genuinely moved by Sam's image) Jesus, Sam! That's beautiful!

WILLIE: (can endure waiting no longer) I'm starting. (He dances while SAM talks.)

SAM: Of course it is. That's what I've been trying to say to you all afternoon. And it's beautiful because that is what we want life to be like. But instead, like you said, Hally, we're bumping into each other all the time. Look at the three of us this afternoon: I've bumped into Willie, the two of us have bumped into you, you've bumped into your mother, she bumping into your dad. . . . None of us knows the steps and there's no music playing. And it doesn't stop with us. The whole world is doing it all the time. Open a newspaper and what do you read? America has bumped into Russia, England is bumping into India, richman bumps into poorman. Those are big collisions, Hally. They make for a lot of bruises. People get hurt in all that bumping, and we're sick and tired of it now. It's been going on for too long. Are we never going to get it right? . . . learn to dance life like champions instead of always being just a bunch of beginners at it?

HALLY: (deep and sincere admiration of the man) You've got a vision, Sam!

SAM: Not just me. What I'm saying to you is that everybody's got it. That's why there's only standing-room left for the Centenary Hall in two weeks time. For as long as the music lasts we are going to see six couples get it right, the way we want life to be.

HALLY: But is that the best we can do, Sam . . . watch six finalists dreaming about the way it should be?

SAM: I don't know. But it starts with that. Without the dream we won't know what we're going for. And anyway, I reckon there are a few people who have got past just dreaming about it and are trying for something real. Remember that thing we read once in the paper about the Mahatma Ghandi? Going without food to stop those riots in India?

HALLY: You're right. He certainly was trying to teach people to get the steps right.

❦ DENISE LEVERTOV, *Intrusion*

After I had cut off my hands
and grown new ones

something my former hands had longed for
came and asked to be rocked.

After my plucked out eyes
had withered, and new ones grown

something my former eyes had wept for
came asking to be pitied.

❦ PHILIP LOPATE, *The Rug Merchant*

"The same reason that you don't consider buying a building has made you unwilling to get married and settle down. You live only for yourself. You are terrified of any commitment. Not only that, you have become alienated from your own people. In time of need nobody is going to be there. If you had a wife or somebody it would be different.

But this way, nobody is going to help you, nobody is going to rescue you when you are in trouble."

"But what about you, Mother? I am turning to you now."

"I, I will not always be around. Also, I have to look after myself. Because if something happens to me I don't think you are going to be able to provide for me, isn't it so?"

"Don't assume so."

"Why not? Just as you have no feelings for the community, so you have no feelings for me."

"A non sequitur if ever I heard one. I can have feelings for my mother without having them for the whole Zoroastrian community."

"But you don't. You are cut off from everyone. You are a hermit. And it is all because you are afraid of the risks of getting involved."

"I am not a hermit. I see people every day," Cyrus said mildly.

"Nevertheless, can you deny that you lead the life of a semi-recluse? It used to be that a hermit would seek out a mountain hut to get away from people, but nowadays one can retire from life in the busiest cities. Even more so. What are you laughing at?"

"I am just appreciating your turn of phrase, your perspective. Go on."

"I doubt you are going to appreciate what I say next. I will tell you what your real problem is, Kurush. You are a coward."

Cyrus shrugged. He was prepared to take any number of insults if it would put his mother into a more generous mood.

"You are afraid of life. And that makes you a coward."

"I am not the bravest person, Mother, true. I wish you would accept that about me, after all these years."

"No, I *don't* accept it," she said, "and you want to know why? Because you are not cowardly by nature. It is only that you have become so passive. Everything is fate, Kismet! You won't take your fate in your own hands."

"You keep saying that. But fate is what cannot be conquered, what is meant to be. That is the meaning of the word."

"You know what I mean, don't quibble about definitions. What I am getting at is that you don't *act* to *better* your life. You drift. Deep down you are afraid of something. That is why you never got married,

Kurush. You are afraid that if you lived with one woman, she would bore you. Certainly there are boring moments in marriage, I don't say not. But so are there in living alone. We both know that now, from experience. However, you are too wrapped up in yourself to permit anyone to get close. Probably what you are is a narcissist. Don't smirk. I read a magazine article recently about the narcissistic personality. The author was a Swiss woman; she attributed it to the mother's treatment of the child in the early years. I don't know what terrible mistakes I made, but I must have done something wrong with you. Because somehow I did not give you the courage to face life."

"It's not your fault if I am not courageous," Cyrus said. "For that I have only myself to blame."

"But if a child is frightened of life, a mother must take responsibility. "

"No, Mother, this time you're wrong."

"How, wrong?" she demanded, half irritably, half pleased to be contradicted.

"I certainly have my faults. And I repent, do penance and am sorry for all of them, believe me. But I am also kind to people, I am tender to the best of my ability, I am able to give love and to receive it. And I thank you for teaching me to be that way." He smiled at her.

Compassion in Al Young gives us a strong sense of being in the business and beauty of life. In taking a compassionate view of the harsh realities of life, Kate Green embraces the beauty and strength of people living fully no matter what the circumstances. Mary Oliver extends that embrace to the more-than-human world.

❦ AL YOUNG, *The Song Turning Back Into Itself*

Always it's either
a beginning
or some end:
the baby's being born
or its parents are
dying, fading on

like the rose
of the poem
withers, its light going out
while gardens come in
to bloom

Let us stand on streetcorners
in the desolate era
& propose a new kind
of crazyness

Let us salute one another
one by one
two by two
the soft belly
moving toward
the long sideburns
the adams apple
or no apple at all

Let there be
in this crazyness
a moon
a violin
a drum

Let the beautiful brown girl
join hands with
her black sister
her golden sister
her milkskinned sister
their eternal wombs
turning with the moon

Let there be a flute
to squeal above

the beat & the bowing
to open us up
that the greens
the blues
the yellows
the reds
the silvers &
indescribable rusts
might flow out
amazingly
& blend
with the wind

Let the wobbly spin
of the earth
be a delight
wherein
a caress forms to
the most perfect circle

Let there always be love
the beginning be love
love the only
possible
end

❦ KATE GREEN, *If the World Is Running Out*

Let me still grow this fetus in my fat belly.
Let him be among the last to die.

In the spring when he's grown fully into his new body
I'll wrap him in a plaid pastel blanket the way
black women do in my neighborhood and cover
his dark face. We'll walk up along the freeway.

Papers are blown against the cyclone fence.
Lilacs high as trees explode next to the Evangelical Temple
across from the barbecue place.

On the bridge over the freeway, stop and look, child.
I want to show you this world. See how
we ride behind glass, hands clenched to wheels,
radio tuned to jazz to soothe
the cramped and hurried spine.

Here on the corner of 94 and Lexington three years back
is where your father was falsely arrested for aggravated robbery
because he looked like another black man in sunglasses.
Memory turns every pain to love. I still see
his hands on the Monte Carlo, legs spread,
gun at his temple, the angle of his wrists
in handcuffs as they pulled him to the car with the dogs
and he looked back, crying, "Call your father."

Your world, my son, slow St. Paul by the freeway.
At the corner, St. Peter Claver Catholic School
where black parents send their kids from Milton on down.
The rest go to Maxfield. You'll be bussed to Highland
with the Jews. Indians live up back behind the capitol.

Earth, 1981. Reagan inaugurated as president,
peanut butter $2.89 a pound, the 439th day of captivity
for the hostages in Iran. Your father at the factory
cutting huge rolls of tape. He comes home smelling
of adhesive and glue in his nappy hair.
Here is the SuperAmerica where men call out, "Say baby,
you in a fine and mellow mood today." I raise my thumb.

Here's discount liquors and the giant grocery store
with boxes stacked to ceiling of all the things
we trade our time for in this life: toilet paper,
celery, milk and bread. Walk you down aisles

to say I want you to love the sad world. Love your father's
hands on the congas Saturday night full moon.
Love your mother's rice and poems cooking in the kitchen.

Love the mongrel dog in the alley and the seven birdbaths
kept clean by that shriveled woman, the one with immaculate roses.
Love the smell of barbecue Memorial Day, ten in the morning,
Cadillacs washed and shining in front of the projects.
Love the chipped jelly jar your father drinks beer from.

Love the dust on it all thrown up by the freeway.
And the green dome of the cathedral spectral in orange light
at end of day. Love your father on his knees nightly
in the pale dark. Love your own dark skin in this world
you sleep. Take all you need of breath and night to feed you.

❦ MARY OLIVER, *The Chance to Love Everything*

All summer I made friends
with the creatures nearby—
they flowed through the fields
and under the tent walls,
or padded through the door,
grinning through their many teeth,
looking for seeds,
suet, sugar; muttering and humming,
opening the breadbox, happiest when
there was milk and music. But once
in the night I heard a sound
outside the door, the canvas
bulged slightly—something
was pressing inward at eye level.
I watched, trembling, sure I had heard
the click of claws, the smack of lips
outside my gauzy house—

I imagined the red eyes,
the broad tongue, the enormous lap.
Would it be friendly too?
Fear defeated me. And yet,
not in faith and not in madness
but with the courage I thought
my dream deserved,
I stepped outside. It was gone.
Then I whirled at the sound of some
shambling tonnage.
Did I see a black haunch slipping
back through the trees? Did I see
the moonlight shining on it?
Did I actually reach out my arms
toward it, toward paradise falling, like
the fading of the dearest, wildest hope—
the dark heart of the story that is all
the reason for its telling?

Derek Walcott and Rainer Maria Rilke let themselves feel the deep hurt in the world—most clear to them in the pain and agony of the poor. Frank Bidart, Sharon Olds, and Kurt Vonnegut find ties to the lives of impoverished strangers.

❦ DEREK WALCOTT, *Another Life*

About the August of my fourteenth year
I lost my self somewhere above a valley
owned by a spinster-farmer, my dead father's friend.
At the hill's edge there was a scarp
with bushes and boulders stuck in its side.
Afternoon light ripened the valley,
rifling smoke climbed from small labourers' houses,
and I dissolved into a trance.

I was seized by a pity more profound
than my young body could bear, I climbed
with the labouring smoke,
I drowned in labouring breakers of bright cloud,
then uncontrollably I began to weep,
inwardly, without tears, with a serene extinction
of all sense; I felt compelled to kneel,
I wept for nothing and for everything,
I wept for the earth of the hill under my knees,
for the grass, the pebbles, for the cooking smoke
above the labourers' houses like a cry,
for unheard avalanches of white cloud,
but "darker grows the valley, more and more forgetting."
For their lights still shine through the hovels like litmus,
the smoking lamp still slowly says its prayer,
the poor still move behind their tinted scrim,
the taste of water is still shared everywhere,
but in that ship of night, locked in together,
through which, like chains, a little light might leak,
something still fastens us forever to the poor.

❦ RAINER MARIA RILKE, *The Song of the Leper*

See, I am one whom all have deserted.
No one knows of me in the city,
leprosy has befallen me.
And I beat upon my rattle,
knock the sorrowful sight of me
into the ears of all
who pass near by.
And those who woodenly hear it, look
not this way at all, and what's happened here
they do not want to learn.

As far as the sound of my clapper reaches
I am at home; but perhaps
you are making my clapper so loud
that none will trust himself far from me
who now shuns coming near.
So that I can go a very long way
without discovering girl or woman
or man or child.

I would not frighten animals.

❧ FRANK BIDART, *The Sacrifice*

When Judas writes the history of SOLITUDE,—
. . . let him celebrate
Miss Mary Kenwood; who, without
help, placed her head in a plastic bag,

then locked herself
in a refrigerator.

—Six months earlier, after thirty years
teaching piano, she had watched

her mother slowly die of throat cancer.
Watched her *want* to die . . .

What once had given Mary life
in the end didn't want it.

Awake, her mother screamed for help to die.
—She felt

GUILTY . . . She knew that *all* men in these situations felt
innocent—; helpless—; yet guilty.

Christ knew the Secret. Betrayal
is necessary; as is woe for the betrayer.

The solution, Mary realized at last,
must be brought out of my own body.

Wiping away our sins, Christ stained us with his blood—;
to offer yourself, yet need *betrayal*, by *Judas*, before
                    SHOULDERING

THE GUILT OF THE WORLD—;
. . . *Give me the courage not to need Judas.*

When Judas writes the history of solitude,
let him record

that to the friend who opened
the refrigerator, it seemed

death fought; before giving in.

❦ SHARON OLDS, *The Victims*

When Mother divorced you, we were glad. She took it and
took it, in silence, all those years and then
kicked you out, suddenly, and her
kids loved it. Then you were fired, and we
grinned inside, the way people grinned when
Nixon's helicopter lifted off the South
Lawn for the last time. We were tickled
to think of your office taken away,
your secretaries taken away,
your lunches with three double bourbons,
your pencils, your reams of paper. Would they take your

suits back, too, those dark
carcasses hung in your closet, and the black
noses of your shoes with their large pores?
She had taught us to take it, to hate you and take it
until we pricked with her for your
annihilation, Father. Now I
pass the bums in doorways, the white
slugs of their bodies gleaming through slits in their
suits of compressed silt, the stained
flippers of their hands, the underwater
fire of their eyes, ships gone down with the
lanterns lit, and I wonder who took it and
took it from them in silence until they had
given it all away and had nothing
left but this.

❦ KURT VONNEGUT, *Jailbird*

Mary Kathleen's shopping bags were still banked around my legs. I was as immobilized and eye-catching as Saint Joan of Arc at the stake. Mary Kathleen still grasped my wrist, and she would not lower her voice.

"Now that I've found you, Walter," she cried, "I'll never let you go again!"

Nowhere in the world was this sort of theater being done anymore. For what it may be worth to modern impresarios: I can testify from personal experience that great crowds can still be gathered by melodrama, provided that the female in the piece speaks loudly and clearly.

"You used to tell me all the time how much you loved me, Walter," she cried. "But then you went away, and I never heard from you again. Were you just lying to me?"

I may have made some responsive sound. "Bluh," perhaps, or "fluh."

"Look at me in the eye, Walter," she said.

Sociologically, of course, this melodrama was as gripping as *Uncle Tom's Cabin* before the Civil War. Mary Kathleen O'Looney wasn't the only shopping-bag lady in the United States of America. There were tens of thousands of them in major cities throughout the country. Ragged regiments of them had been produced accidentally, and to no imaginable purpose, by the great engine of the economy. Another part of the machine was spitting out unrepentant murderers ten years old, and dope fiends and child batterers and many other bad things. People claimed to be investigating. Unspecified repairs were to be made at some future time.

Good-hearted people were meanwhile as sick about all these tragic by-products of the economy as they would have been about human slavery a little more than a hundred years before. Mary Kathleen and I were a miracle that our audience must have prayed for again and again: the rescue of at least one shopping-bag lady by a man who knew her well.

Some people were crying. I myself was about to cry.

"Hug her," said a woman in the crowd.

I did so.

I found myself embracing a bundle of dry twigs that was wrapped in rags. That was when I myself began to cry. I was crying for the first time since I had found my wife dead in bed one morning—in my little brick bungalow in Chevy Chase, Maryland.

Euripides' nurse agonizes over the cruel disappointment the feelings of compassion and concern can bring. But Li-Young Lee, Otto René Castillo, and Joanna Fuhrman reflect sympathetically on the simple majesty of human endurance and caring.

❧ Euripides, *Hippolytus*

Chorus: Look! The old Nurse is coming to the door,
Bringing Phaedra into the fresh air.
How weak the queen is, how pale!
I long to know what has so wasted her.

Enter Phaedra supported by the Nurse.
Attendants bring a couch for her.

NURSE: Oh, the sickness and pain of this cruel world!
What would you like me to do, or not to do?
Here you are, in the light, under the clear sky;
We have brought your bed from the palace;
But the cloud on your brow deepens with discontent.
It was here that you begged and longed to come;
Soon you'll be fretting for your room again.
Each minute cheats you, nothing gives you pleasure;
You hate what you have, and crave what you have not.
Better to be sick, which is a single trouble,
Then wait on the sick, which troubles both heart and hand.
The whole of our life is full of pain,
And sorrow finds no relief.
And after this life, is there a happier world?
That is concealed from us, wrapped in clouds and darkness.
The truth stands plain: that we blindly love,
Such as it is, our little gleam of day.
For we know nothing of any other life;
The world below is a mystery;
And we are carried along with foolish tales.

     Servants have now placed Phaedra on her couch.

PHAEDRA: Support my body. Hold my head up.
The strength of my limbs has melted away.
Girls, hold my hands, my shapely arms.
This cap is heavy on my head—take it off;
Now let my hair fall round my shoulders.

NURSE: Patience, child! Don't tire yourself with tossing to and fro.
If you are quiet and keep a brave heart
Your illness will be easier to bear.
We are mortal, and so must suffer.

PHAEDRA: Oh! Oh! To kneel by a fountain in the fresh dew
And drink a cupful of clear water!

To lie under the poplar trees
And rest deep in the waving grass!

NURSE: What are you saying, child? Don't scatter words
So recklessly—there are people here!
Such Speech is mounted on madness.

PHAEDRA: Come, all of you, take me out to the hills!
I'm going to the woods, through the pine-forests
Where hounds pace after blood
And press close on the spotted deer.
For the gods' sake, take me! How I long to be there,
Shouting to the pack,
Lifting a lance to my hair bright in the wind,
Gripping a barbed spear!

NURSE: What is it, child, you are fretting for?
What are hounds and the hunt to you?
If you are thirsty,
Here by the palace wall a stream runs down the hill.

PHAEDRA: Artemis of the salt mere,
Goddess of the race-course and rattling hooves,
O for your level rides,
And the tamed strength of Thessaly horses under my hand!

NURSE: Again these wild words! Are you out of your mind?
A moment past you were off to the hills, Hunting as you wanted to;
Now you long for a horse on a dry sandy track.
Here's a task for a prophet indeed, to guess
Which of the gods has his bridle on you
And drives you beside yourself, my daughter!

PHAEDRA: Oh, gods have pity! Whatever did I do?
How far did I stray from sanity?
I was mad; a malign god struck me down.
What shall I do? What will become of me?
Dear Nurse, my veil again;

I am ashamed to think what I have said.
Cover me; my tears are falling,
And my face is hot with shame.
To be in my right mind is agony;
Yet to be mad was intolerable.
It is best, then, to be aware of nothing,
And die.

NURSE (VEILING HER): There, child, there!—How soon
Shall my face too be veiled with death?
I have lived long, and learnt much.
Since everyone must die, it would be better
That friends should set a limit to affection,
And never open their hearts' depths to each other.
The ties of love ought to lie loosely on us,
Easy to slip or tighten.
For one heart to endure the pain of two,
As I suffer for her, is a cruel burden.
They say that exact and scrupulous conduct
Brings with it more trouble than pleasure
And is an enemy to health.
So I'm tired of selfless devotion;
I think the best rule is, A limit to everything;
And any wise man will say the same.

❧ LI-YOUNG LEE, *My Father, In Heaven, Is Reading Out Loud*

My father, in heaven, is reading out loud
to himself Psalms or news. Now he ponders what
he's read. No. He is listening for the sound
of children in the yard. Was that laughing
or crying? So much depends upon the
answer, for either he will go on reading,

or he'll run to save a child's day from grief.
As it is in heaven, so it was on earth.

Because my father walked the earth with a grave,
determined rhythm, my shoulders ached
from his gaze. Because my father's shoulders
ached from the pulling of oars, my life now moves
with a powerful back-and-forth rhythm:
nostalgia, speculation. Because he
made me recite a book a month, I forget
everything as soon as I read it. And knowledge
never comes but while I'm mid-stride a flight
of stairs, or lost a moment on some avenue.

A remarkable disappointment to him,
I am like anyone who arrives late
in the millennium and is unable
to stay to the end of days. The world's
beginnings are obscure to me, its outcomes
inaccessible. I don't understand
the source of starlight, or starlight's destinations.
And already another year slides out
of balance. But I don't disparage scholars;
my father was one and I loved him,
who packed his books once, and all of our belongings,
then sat down to await instruction
from his god, yes, but also from a radio.
At the doorway, I watched, and I suddenly
knew he was one like me, who got my learning
under a lintel; he was one of the powerless,
to whom knowledge came while he sat among
suitcases, boxes, old newspapers, string.

He did not decide peace or war, home or exile,
escape by land or escape by sea.

He waited merely, as always someone
waits, far, near, here, hereafter, to find out:
is it praise or lament hidden in the next moment?

❧ LI-YOUNG LEE, *The City in Which I Love You*

> *I will arise now, and go*
> *about the city in the streets,*
> *and in the broad ways I will seek . . .*
> *whom my soul loveth.*

> —SONG OF SONGS 3:2

And when, in the city in which I love you,
even my most excellent song goes unanswered,
and I mount the scabbed streets,
the long shouts of avenues,
and tunnel sunken night in search of you . . .

That I negotiate fog, bituminous
rain ringing like teeth into the beggar's tin,
or two men jackaling a third in some alley
weirdly lit by a couch on fire, that I
drag my extinction in search of you . . .

Past the guarded schoolyards, the boarded-up churches, swastikaed
synagogues, defended houses of worship, past
newspapered windows of tenements, among the violated,
the prosecuted citizenry, throughout this
storied, buttressed, scavenged, policed
city I call home, in which I am a guest . . .

A bruise, blue
in the muscle, you
impinge upon me.
As bone hugs the ache home, so
I'm vexed to love you, your body

the shape of returns, your hair a torso
of light, your heat
I must have, your opening
I'd eat, each moment
of that soft-finned fruit,
inverted fountain in which I don't see me.

My tongue remembers your wounded flavor.
The vein in my neck
adores you. A sword
stands up between my hips,
my hidden fleece sends forth its scent of human oil.

The shadows under my arms,
I promise, are tender, the shadows
under my face. Do not calculate,
but come, smooth other, rough sister.
Yet, how will you know me

among the captives, my hair grown long,
my blood motley, my ways trespassed upon?
In the uproar, the confusion
of accents and inflections,
how will you hear me when I open my mouth?

Look for me, one of the drab population
under fissured edifices, fractured
artifices. Make my various
names flock overhead,
I will follow you.
Hew me to your beauty.

Stack in me the unaccountable fire,
bring on me the iron leaf, but tenderly.
Folded one hundred times and
creased, I'll not crack.
Threshed to excellence, I'll achieve you.

But in the city
in which I love you,
no one comes, no one
meets me in the brick clefts;
in the wedged dark,

no finger touches me secretly, no mouth
tastes my flawless salt,
no one wakens the honey in the cells, finds the humming
in the ribs, the rich business in the recesses;
hulls clogged, I continue laden, translated

by exhaustion and time's appetite, my sleep abandoned
in bus stations and storefront stoops,
my insomnia erected under a sky
cross-hatched by wires, branches,
and black flights of rain. Lewd body of wind

jams me in the passageways, doors slam
like guns going off, a gun goes off, a pie plate spins
past, whizzing its thin tremolo,
a plastic bag, fat with wind, barrels by and slaps
a chain-link fence, wraps it like clung skin.

In the excavated places,
I waited for you, and I did not cry out.
In the derelict rooms, my body needed you,
and there was such flight in my breast.
During the daily assaults, I called to you,

and my voice pursued you,
even backward
to that other city
in which I saw a woman
squat in the street

beside a body,
and fan with a handkerchief flies from its face.
That woman
was not me. And
the corpse

lying there, lying there
so still it seemed with great effort, as though
his whole being was concentrating on the hole
in his forehead, so still
I expected he'd sit up any minute and laugh out loud:

that man was not me;
his wound was his, his death not mine.
And the soldier
who fired the shot, then lit a cigarette:
he was not me.

And the ones I do not see
in cities all over the world,
the ones sitting, standing, lying down, those
in prisons playing checkers with their knocked-out teeth:
they are not me. Some of them are

my age, even my height and weight;
none of them is me.
The woman who is slapped, the man who is kicked,
the ones who don't survive,
whose names I do not know;

they are not me forever,
the ones who no longer live
in the cities in which
you are not,
the cities in which I looked for you.

The rain stops, the moon
in her breaths appears overhead.
The only sound now is a far flapping.
Over the National Bank, the flag of some republic or other
gallops like water or fire to tear itself away.

If I feel the night
move to disclosures or crescendos,
it's only because I'm famished
for meaning; the night
merely dissolves.

And your otherness is perfect as my death.
Your otherness exhausts me,
like looking suddenly up from here
to impossible stars fading.
Everything is punished by your absence.

Is prayer, then, the proper attitude
for the mind that longs to be freely blown,
but which gets snagged on the barb
called *world*, that
tooth-ache, the actual? What prayer

would I build? And to whom?
Where are you
in the cities in which I love you,
the cities daily risen to work and to money,
to the magnificent miles and the gold coasts?

Morning comes to this city vacant of you.
Pages and windows flare, and you are not there.
Someone sweeps his portion of sidewalk,
wakens the drunk, slumped like laundry,
and you are gone.

You are not in the wind
which someone notes in the margins of a book.
You are gone out of the small fires in abandoned lots
where human figures huddle,
each aspiring to its own ghost.

Between brick walls, in a space no wider than my face
a leafless sapling stands in mud.
In its branches, a nest of raw mouths
gaping and cheeping, scrawny fires that must eat.
My hunger for you is no less than theirs.

At the gates of the city in which I love you,
the sea hauls the sun on its back,
strikes the land, which rebukes it.
What ardor in its sliding heft,
a flameless friction on the rocks.

Like the sea, I am recommended by my orphaning.
Noisy with telegrams not received,
quarrelsome with aliases,
intricate with misguided journeys,
by my expulsions have I come to love you.

Straight from my father's wrath,
and long from my mother's womb,
late in this century and on a Wednesday morning,
bearing the mark of one who's experienced
neither heaven nor hell,

my birthplace vanished, my citizenship earned,
in league with stones of the earth, I
enter, without retreat or help from history,
the days of no day, my earth
of no earth, I re-enter

the city in which I love you.
And I never believed that the multitude
of dreams and many words were vain.

❧ OTTO RENÉ CASTILLO, *Before the Scales, Tomorrow*

And when the enthusiastic
story of our time
is told,
for those
who are yet to be born
but announce themselves
with more generous face,
we will come out ahead
—those who have suffered most from it.

And that
being ahead of your time
means suffering much from it.

But it's beautiful to love the world
with eyes
that have not yet
been born.

And splendid
to know yourself victorious
when all around you
it's all still so cold,
                    so dark.

❧ JOANNA FUHRMAN, *Domestic Comforts*

My mother is piling papers
so the housekeeper won't be

startled by the mess.
My father is talking into his miniature
tape recorder, replaying his voice
and pacing the room.
On the bookshelves,
and the table next to the bed,
the books on religion, unread,
whisper to each other.
They squabble in echoes.

If you were to come back the next day
nothing would have changed.
Except this time, my mother
might be leafing through the pale
pages of tax return forms,
and my dad might be
yelling into the phone.

By night, they're tired.
They turn the air conditioner on high
and hide themselves in bed
under a puffy down comforter,
too weary now to argue about God.

Yesterday, driving home
from their Jewish humanist group
my father said,
The problem with humanists
is that they don't
use the word God,
and the problem with
rabbis is that they do.

My mother honked the horn
at the oncoming truck and laughed.

She said *The word God is just a metaphor*
for the hand that nudges you gently into dream
or the transparent feeling you get
when you walk into a perfect lake.

My father shrugged, said nothing,
he turned the radio on high
and fiddled with the dial
looking for a perfect station,
unable, as always, to find it.

8

The Voice of the World Speaking Out

SPIRITUALITY

Henry David Thoreau clearly feared and rejected life lived on automatic: "I went to the woods because I wished to live deliberately, to front only the essential facts of life, and see if I could not learn what it had to teach, and not, when I came to die, discover that I had not lived."

Thich Nhat Hanh teaches that waking up to one's life in this way is what spirituality is about. For him, the awakened state does not require retreat from the world, but can be found by living fully in the world. He says, for example, "Even when you are walking along a path leading into a village, you can practice being fully awake ... if you are awake you will experience that path, the path leading into the village. You practice this by keeping this one thought alive, 'I'm walking along the path, the path leading into the village.'"

Hanh continues: "Whether it's sunny or rainy, whether the path is dry or wet, you keep that one thought, but not just to repeat it like a machine, over and over again. Machine-thinking is the opposite of being awake to your life. If we're really awake while walking along the path to the village, then we will consider the act of each step we take as an infinite wonder—and joy will open our hearts like a flower, enabling us to enter the world of reality."

Entering the world of reality means seeing clearly each step we take. But, of course, the path we personally tread is not the whole of life. Our life-steps are links in the complex arrangement of our experience, our work in communities and with friends, and our concern about the well-being of all who are searching for and walking to and from villages, towns, and cities all over the world. In entering the world spiritually, we aim to recognize the actuality of what surrounds us, the particularity of those who share it with us, and the larger scheme of which we are all a part. In this sense, spirituality is an expression of love at a very radical level. In it, we experience ourselves as part of a larger "we"; we experience kinship with the human and the more-than-human world.

"Behave in a manner worthy of good news," the apostle Paul admonished; stand firm "in one spirit, in one soul, striving side by side for the faith of the good news." This, for Paul, was a road to salvation. In a non-religious but spiritual sense, salvation is finding one's way to be "open" to life without dependence on the false moorings of piety or the empty promise of narrow obedience.

Instead, it is falling in love with solid ground, being closely connected to the ideal of a shared humanity, and holding hands and dancing with others in praise and preservation of life. Spirituality is a call back to the concrete and the particular of person, idea, plant, animal, and planet—and to the link between. Emily Dickinson, over and over, emphasized how in the concrete concreteness, even in the stark concreteness of everyday female chores, we can find entry into the largeness and grandeur of a much deeper—spiritual—experience:

> What liberty
> A loosened spirit brings!

The greater the presence of this spirit, the less the denial which keeps people apart. Robert Bly puts it this way:

> Breaking through the wall of denial helps us get rid of self-pity, and replaces self-pity with awe at a complicated misery of all living things.

Mechthild of Magdeburg, in the *Flowing Light of the Godhead*, said:

No one can comprehend divine gifts with human senses; therefore those persons err who do not keep their spirit open to unseen truths. What can be seen with the eyes of the flesh, heard with the ears of the flesh, and spoken with the mouth of the flesh is as different from the truth revealed to the loving soul as a candle to the bright sun.

Selections

Dame Julian of Norwich in the fourteenth century and Abraham Heschel in the twentieth century remind us of deep spiritual connections.

❦ DAME JULIAN OF NORWICH

This is the cause why we are not at rest in heart and soul: that here we seek our rest in things that are so little there is no rest in them.

❦ ABRAHAM JOSHUA HESCHEL, *The Sabbath*

The meaning of the Sabbath is to celebrate time rather than space. Six days a week we live under the tyranny of things of space; on the sabbath we try to become attuned to holiness in time. It is the day on which we are called upon to share in what is eternal in time, to turn from the results of creation to the mystery of creation; from the world of creation to the creation of the world.

Muriel Rukeyser gives a resounding "yes" to the mysteries of life. Diane Glancy recognizes the change of pace that's needed to know such things. Jay Wright and Paul Celan both reflect on the limits of what we know and the grandeur to be found in "the remotest regions of the spirit."

❦ MURIEL RUKEYSER, *Yes*

Some go local
Some go express
Some can't wait
To answer Yes

Some complain
Of strain and stress
Their answer may be
No or yes

Some like failure
Some like success
Some like Yes Yes
Yes Yes Yes

Open your eyes
Dream but don't guess.
Your biggest surprise
Comes after Yes.

❦ DIANE GLANCY, *If Indians Are Coming It Won't Start on Time*

It takes a while for the Spirits of Indians & Buffalo
To cross the highway.
It was their land.
They smell the grass
& wait for winds to bring them legs of flesh.

The Spirits of Indians & Buffalo do not easily cross
The road. The unseen
Trails they follow

Take time. They
Grapple with the new realm upon them.

Meat must be taken from bone & hides tanned.
Offerings must be made
To the Great Spirit.
It takes a while
To get used to Hope, shiny as the skin of Onion Creek.

JAY WRIGHT, *Benjamin Banneker Sends His Almanac to Thomas Jefferson*

Old now,
your eyes nearly blank
from plotting the light's
movement over the years,
you clean your *Almanac*,
and place it next
to the heart of this letter.
I have you in mind,
giving a final brush and twist
to the difficult pages,
staring down the shape of the numbers
as though you would find a flaw
in their forms.
Solid, these calculations
verify your body on God's earth.
At night,
the stars submit themselves
to the remembered way you turn them;
the moon gloats under your attention.
I, who know so little of stars,
whose only acquaintance with the moon
is to read a myth, or to listen

to the surge
of songs the women know,
sit in your marvelous reading
of all movement,
of all relations.

So you look into what we see
yet cannot see,
and shape and take a language
to give form to one or the other,
believing no form will escape,
no movement appear, nor stop,
without explanation,
believing no reason is only reason,
nor without reason.
I read all of this into your task,
all of this into the uneasy
reproof of your letter.

Surely, there must be a flaw.
These perfect calculations fall apart.
There are silences
that no perfect number can retrieve,
omissions no perfect line could catch.
How could a man but challenge God's
impartial distributions?
How could a man sit among
the free and ordered movements
of stars, and waters, beasts and birds,
each movement seen or accounted for,
and not know God jealous,
and not know that he himself must be?

So you go over the pages again,
looking for the one thing

that will not reveal itself,
judging what you have received,
what you have shaped,
believing it cannot be strange
to the man you address.
But you are strange to him
—your skin, your tongue,
the movement of your body,
even your mysterious ways with stars.
You argue here with the man and God,
and know that no man can be right,
and know that no God will argue right.
Your letter turns on what the man knows,
on what God, you think, would have us know.
All stars will forever move under your gaze,
truthfully, leading you from line to line,
from number to number, from truth to truth,
while the man will read your soul's desire,
searcher, searching yourself,
losing the relations.

PAUL CELAN, *Edgar Jené and the Dream About the Dream*

I am supposed to tell you some of the words I heard deep down in the sea where there is so much silence and so much happens. I cut my way through the objects and objections of reality and stood before the sea's mirror surface. I had to wait until it burst open and allowed me to enter the huge crystal of the inner world. With the large lower star of disconsolate explorers shining above me, I followed Edgar Jené beneath his paintings.

Though I had known the journey would be strenuous, I worried when I had to enter one of the roads alone, without a guide. One of the roads! There were innumerable, all inviting, all offering me different new eyes to look at the beautiful wilderness on the other, deeper side of existence. No wonder that, in this moment when I still had my own stubborn old eyes, I tried to make comparisons in order to be able to choose. My mouth, however, placed higher than my eyes and bolder for having often spoken in my sleep, had moved ahead and mocked me: 'Well, old identity-monger, what did you see and recognize, you brave doctor of tautology? What could you recognize, tell me, along this unfamiliar road? An also tree or almost-tree, right? And now you are mustering your Latin for a letter to old Linnaeus? You had better haul up a pair of eyes from the bottom of your soul and put them on your chest: then you'll find out what is happening here.'

Now I am a person who likes simple words. It is true, I had realized long before this journey that there was much evil and injustice in the world I had now left, but I had believed I could shake the foundations if I called things by their proper names. I knew such an enterprise meant returning to absolute *naiveté*. This *naiveté* I considered as a primal vision purified of the slag of centuries of hoary lies about the world. I remember a conversation with a friend about Kleist's *Marionette Theatre*. How could one regain that original grace, which would become the heading of the last and, I suppose, loftiest chapter in the history of mankind? It was, my friend held, by letting reason purify our unconscious inner life that we could recapture the immediacy of the beginning—which would in the end give meaning to our life and make it worth living. In this view, beginning and end were one, and a note of mourning for original sin was struck. The wall which separates today from tomorrow must be torn down so that tomorrow could again be yesterday. But what must we actually do now, in our own time, to reach timelessness, eternity, the marriage of tomorrow-and-yesterday? Reason, he said, must prevail. A bath in the *aqua regia* of intelligence must give their true (primitive) meaning back to words, hence to things, beings, occurrences. A tree must again be a tree, and its branch, on which the rebels of a hundred wars have been hanged, must again flower in spring.

Here my first objection came up. It was simply this: I knew that anything that happened was more than an addition to the given, more than an attribute more or less difficult to remove from the essence, that it changed the essence in its very being and thus cleared the way for ceaseless transformation.

My friend was stubborn. He claimed that even in the stream of human evolution he could distinguish the constants of the soul, know the limits of the unconscious. All we needed was for reason to go down into the deep and haul the water from the deep and haul the water of the dark well up to the surface. This well, like any other, had a bottom one could reach, and if only the surface were ready to receive the water from the deep, the sun of justice shining, the job would be done. But how can we ever succeed, he said, if you and people like you never come out of the deep, never stop communing with the dark springs?

I saw that this reproach was aimed at my professing that, since we know the world and its institutions are a prison for man and his spirit, we must do all we can to tear down its walls. At the same time, I saw which course this knowledge prescribed. I realized that man was not only languishing in the chains of external life, but was also gagged and unable to speak—and by speaking I mean the entire sphere of human expression—because his words (gestures, movements) groaned under an age-old load of false and distorted sincerity. What could be more dishonest than to claim that words had somehow at bottom remained the same! I could not help seeing that the ashes of burned-out meanings (and not only of those) had covered what had, since time immemorial, been striving for expression in man's innermost soul.

How could something new and pure issue from this? It may be from the remotest regions of the spirit that words and figures will come, images and gestures, veiled and unveiled as in a dream. When they meet in their heady course, and the spark of the wonderful is born from the marriage of strange and most strange, then I will know I am facing the new radiance. It will give me a dubious look because, even though I have conjured it up, it exists beyond the concepts of my wakeful thinking; its light is not daylight; it is inhabited by figures which I do not *recognize*, but *know* at first sight. Its weight has a different heaviness; its colour speaks to the new eyes which my closed lids have given one another; my hearing has wandered into my fingertips and learns to see;

my heart, now that it lives behind my forehead, tastes the laws of a new, unceasing, free motion. I follow my wandering senses into this new world of the spirit and come to know freedom. Here, where I am free, I can see what nasty lies the other side told me.

Thus I listened to my own thoughts during that last break, before facing the dangers of tramping the deep sea, of following Edgar Jené down underneath his paintings.

A Sail Leaves an Eye. One sail only? No, I see two. But the first one, which still bears the colour of the eye, cannot proceed. I know it must come back. Arduous, this return. All liquid has run out of the eye in the form of a steep waterfall. But down here (up there), the water also flows uphill, the sail climbs the steep incline of the white profile which owns nothing but this eye without a pupil and which, just because it owns nothing but this, knows and can do more than we. For this profile of a woman with hair a little bluer than her mouth (which looks up, diagonally, at a mirror we cannot see, tests its expression and judges it appropriate), this profile is a cliff, an icy monument at the access to the inner sea which is a sea of wavy tears. What can the other side of this face look like? Grey like the land we glimpse? But let us go back to our sails. The first one will come home, into the empty, yet strangely seeing socket. Perhaps the tide will carry it in the wrong direction, into the eye which stares out on the grey of the other side . . . Then the boat will bear tidings, but without much promise. And the second boat whose sail bears a fiery eye, a flaming pupil on a field, *sable*, of certainty? We enter it in our sleep: then we see what remains to be dreamed.

How many people know that the number of creatures is endless? That man created them all? May we even begin to count them? True, some know that you can give a flower to a person. But how many know that you can also give a person to a pink? And which do they consider more important? More than one will remain incredulous when you mention the son of Aurora Borealis.

Incredulous even today, when Berenice's hair has been hanging among the stars for such a long time. However, Aurora Borealis does have a son, and Edgar Jené has been the first to see him. Where man is frozen and chained in the snowy woods of his despair, he passes by. Huge. Trees do not stop him. He steps across or takes them under his wide cloak, makes them his companions on the way to the city gates where people wait for the great brother. He is the one expected. We know it by his eyes: they have seen what all have seen, and then some.

What Edgar Jené gives shape to—is its home only here? Have we not all wanted to know better the nightmare of the old reality? Have we not wanted to hear screams, our own screams louder than ever, more piercing? Look, this mirror below us makes everything show its true colour: *The Sea of Blood Covers the Land.* Devastated and grey, the hills of life. With naked feet, the spectre of war goes through the land. Now it has claws like a bird of prey, now human toes. Many are its shapes. Which one is it wearing now? A tent of blood floating in the air. Wherever it comes down, we must live between walls and shreds of blood. Where blood yawns, we get a chance to look out and see more of the same shapes of steaming blood. And we are fed: one of the claws has drilled a well of blood. There we can also mirror ourselves, lost as we are. Blood in a mirror of blood, what greater beauty, they say . . .

Many oaths have we sworn in our waking lives, in the hot shadow of impatient flags, backlighted by an alien death, at the high altar of our sanctified reason. We kept our pledges at the cost of our secret life. But when we came back to where we had made them—what did we find? The colour of the flag was the same, the shadow it threw even larger than before. Again, people raised their hands. But to whom did they pledge allegiance? To the Other, whom we had sworn to hate. And death, the alien? It was so busy it had no need of our oaths at all . . . On the altar, finally, a cock, crowing.

Now let us try to make pledges in our sleep. We are forming a tower, our face breaking through at the top, our clenched stone face. Taller than ourselves, we tower above the highest towers and can look down on ourselves, on our thousand-fold climb upwards. What a chance: to gather in hoards up there to swear our oaths, a thousand times ourselves, a great, overwhelming force. We have not quite reached the top, where our face has already become a clenched fist, a fist of eyes swearing. But we can see our way. Steep, the ascent. But if it is to tomorrow's truth that we want to pledge allegiance, we must take this route. And once up there! What a sight for an oath! What a climb into the deep! What resonance for the pledge we do not know yet!

I have tried to report some of what I saw in the deep sea of a soul.

Edgar Jené's paintings know more.

"The Horse Cursed by the Sun" and "I Watched a Snake" play out the question of whether creation follows a blessed or a cursed course. Jorie Graham and Nazim Hikmet enjoy the wonder and mystery of life that may precede or transcend our intellectual understanding.

❧ ANONYMOUS, *The Horse Cursed by the Sun*

It is said that once the Sun was on Earth, and caught the Horse to ride it. But it was unable to bear his weight, and therefore the Ox took the place of the Horse, and carried the Sun on its back. Since that time the Horse is cursed in these words, because it could not carry the Sun's weight:

"From today thou shalt have a (certain) time of dying.
This is thy curse, that thou hast a (certain) time of dying.
And day and night shalt thou eat,
But the desire of thy heart shall not be at rest,
Though thou grazest till morning and again until sunset.
Behold, this is the judgment which I pass upon thee," said the Sun.
Since that day, the Horse's (certain) time of dying commenced.

❧ ANDREW TANG, *Dust*

What is this that falls
upon our shoulders, occupies urns,
gets into our eyes to make us see

with the sight of the blessed,
or simply sleep? Scientists say that
99 percent of free-floating matter
is composed of dead skin, but is that
any less than what our flesh
leaves behind? We cannot escape it,
no matter how often we bathe, change
the sheets, or air the drapes. It all
settles on us in the end. The only way
we can see the particles is in
the light that holds them, like bees
in a jar, buzzing without direction.
Perhaps God is made of it, for we
were created in his image, and what better
way to see ourselves than in that light.
This is what we wear without thinking.
It is what collects in the quiet
meat of our hearts.

❦ JORIE GRAHAM, *I Watched a Snake*

hard at work in the dry grass
    behind the house
catching flies. It kept on
    disappearing.
And though I know this has
    something to do

with lust, today it seemed
    to have to do
with work. It took it almost half
    an hour to thread
roughly ten feet of lawn,
    so slow

between the blades you couldn't see
    it move. I'd watch
its path of body in the grass go
    suddenly invisible
only to reappear a little
    further on

black knothead up, eyes on
    a butterfly.
This must be perfect progress where
    movement appears
to be a vanishing, a mending
    of the visible

by the invisible—just as we
    stitch the earth,
it seems to me, each time
    we die, going
back under, coming back up . . .
    It is the simplest

stitch, this going where we must,
    leaving a not
unpretty pattern by default. But going
    out of hunger
for small things—flies, words—going
    because one's body

goes. And in this disconcerting creature
    a tiny hunger,
one that won't even press
    the dandelions down,
retrieves the necessary blue—
    black dragonfly

that has just landed on a pod . . .
    all this to say
I'm not afraid of them
    today, or anymore
I think. We are not, were not, ever
    wrong. Desire

is the honest work of the body,
    its engine, its wind.
It too must have its sails—wings
    in this tiny mouth, valves
in the human heart, meanings like sailboats
    setting out

over the mind. Passion is work
    that retrieves us,
lost stitches. It makes a pattern of us,
    it fastens us
to sturdier stuff
    no doubt

❧ NAZIM HIKMET, *Things I Didn't Know I Loved*

it's 1962 March 28th
I'm sitting by the window on the Prague-Berlin train
night is falling
I never knew I liked
night descending like a tired bird on a smoky wet plain
I don't like
comparing nightfall to a tired bird

I didn't know I loved the earth
can someone who hasn't worked the earth love it
I've never worked the earth
it must be my only Platonic love

and here I've loved rivers all this time
whether motionless like this they curl skirting the hills
    European hills crowned with chateaus
or whether stretched out flat as far as the eye can see
I know you can't wash in the same river even once
I know the river will bring new lights you'll never see
I know we live slightly longer than a horse but not nearly as long as a
    crow
I know this has troubled people before
                 and will trouble those after me
I know all this has been said a thousand times before
          and will be said after me

I didn't know I loved the sky
cloudy or clear
the blue vault Andrei studied on his back at Borodino
in prison I translated both volumes of *War and Peace* into Turkish
I hear voices
not from the blue vault but from the yard
the guards are beating someone again

I didn't know I loved trees
bare beeches near Moscow in Peredelkino
they come upon me in winter noble and modest
beeches are Russian the way poplars are Turkish
"the poplars of Izmir
losing their leaves . . .
they call me The Knife
       lover like a young tree . . .
I blow stately mansions sky-high"
in the Ilgaz woods in 1920 I tied an embroidered linen handkerchief
          to a pine bough for luck

I never knew I loved roads
even the asphalt kind

Vera's behind the wheel we're driving from Moscow to the Crimea
       Koktebele
   formerly "Goktepei" in Turkish
the two of us inside a closed box
the world flows past on both sides distant and mute
I was never so close to anyone in my life
bandits stopped me on the red road between Bolu and Gerede
        when I was eighteen
apart from my life I didn't have anything in the wagon they could take
and at eighteen our lives are what we value least
I've written this somewhere before
wading through a dark muddy street I'm going to the shadow play
   Ramazan night
a paper lantern leading the way
maybe nothing like this ever happened
maybe I read it somewhere an eight-year-old boy
         going to the shadow play
Ramazan night in Istanbul holding his grandfather's hand
  his grandfather has on a fez and is wearing the fur coat
    with a sable collar over his robe
and there's a lantern in the servant's hand
and I can't contain myself for joy

flowers come to mind for some reason
Poppies cactuses jonquils
in the jonquil garden in Kadikoy Istanbul I kissed Marika
fresh almonds on her breath
I was seventeen
my heart on a swing touched the sky
I didn't know I loved flowers
friends sent me three red carnations in prison

I just remembered the stars
I love them too
whether I'm floored watching them from below
or whether I'm flying at their side

I have some questions for the cosmonauts
were the stars much bigger
did they look like huge jewels on black velvet
                              or apricots on orange
did you feel proud to get closer to the stars
I saw color photos of the cosmos in Ogonek magazine now don't
be upset comrades but nonfigurative shall we say or abstract
      well some of them looked just like such paintings which is to
say they were terribly figurative and concrete
my heart was in my mouth looking at them
they are our endless desire to grasp things
seeing them I could even think of death and not feel at all sad
I never knew I loved the cosmos

snow flashes in front of my eyes
both heavy wet steady snow and the dry whirling kind
I didn't know I liked snow

I never knew I loved the sun
even when setting cherry-red as now
in Istanbul too it sometimes sets in postcard colors
but you aren't about to paint it that way

I didn't know I loved the sea
                              except the Sea of Azov
or how much

I didn't know I loved clouds
whether I'm under or up above them
whether they look like giants or shaggy white beasts

moonlight the falsest the most languid the most petite-bourgeois
strikes me
I like it

I didn't know I liked rain
whether it falls like a fine net or splatters against the glass my
heart leaves me tangled up in a net or trapped inside a drop
and takes off for uncharted countries I didn't know I loved
rain but why did I suddenly discover all these passions sitting
by the window on the Prague-Berlin train
is it because I lit my sixth cigarette
one alone could kill me
is it because I'm half dead from thinking about someone back in
  Moscow
her hair straw-blond eyelashes blue

the train plunges on through the pitch-black night
I never knew I liked the night pitch-black
sparks fly from the engine
I didn't know I loved sparks
I didn't know I loved so many things and I had to wait until sixty
 to find it out sitting by the window on the Prague-Berlin train
 watching the world disappear as if on a journey of no return

*In "I Will Not Crush the World's Corolla of Wonders," Lucian Blaga consid-
ers the fierce judgment that visits so many and leads to cosmic blame and despair.
In Rigoberta Menchú T.'s "My Martyred Homeland," pain is mediated by an
equally cosmic optimism.*

❦ Lucian Blaga, *I Will Not Crush the World's Corolla of Wonders*

I will not crush the world's corolla of wonders
and I will not kill
with reason
the mysteries I meet along my way
in flowers, eyes, lips, and graves.
The light of others

drowns the deep magic hidden
in the profound darkness.
I increase the world's engima
with my light
much as the moon with its white beams
does not diminish but increases
the shimmering mystery of night—
I enrich the darkening horizon
with chills of the great secret.
All that is hard to know
becomes a greater riddle
under my very eyes
because I love alike
flowers, lips, eyes, and graves.

❧ RIGOBERTA MENCHÚ T., *My Martyred Homeland*

I crossed the border, my love,
I do not know when I will return.
Maybe in summer
when grandmother moon and father sun
greet one another again,
on the illuminated early morning
celebrated by every star,
heralding the first rains;
the pumpkins Victor sowed that afternoon
the soldiers shot him will sprout again,
the peach orchards will bloom,
our fields will bloom.
We will plant an abundance of corn.
Corn for all the sons and daughters of our land.
The swarms of bees will return
that fled from so many massacres, so much terror.
Jar after earthenware jar will come again

from callused hand for harvesting the honey.

I crossed the border drenched in sadness.
I feel immense grief on this early morning,
rainy, dark,
so much greater than my existence.
The raccoons cry, the howler monkeys cry,
the coyotes and mockingbirds are totally silent,
the sea-snails and river-snails want to speak.
Mother Earth is dressed in mourning, swaddled in blood.
She cries day and night in such sorrow.
She will miss the lullaby of pickaxes,
the lullaby of machetes,
the lullaby of grinding-stones.
With every daybreak she will strain to hear
the laughing and singing of her exalted children.

I crossed the border burdened with dignity.
I carry a sack loaded with many things
from that rainswept land.
I carry the ancient memories of Patrocinio,
the sandals born with me,
smell of spring,
smell of moss, caress of the cornfield,
and the blessed calluses of childhood.
I carry my bright huipil
for the fiesta of my return.
I carry the bones and the last of the corn. Well, yes!
Whatever happens,
this sack will return
to the place it left behind.

I crossed the border, my love.
I will return tomorrow, when my tortured mother
weaves another huipil of many colors,

when my father burned alive rises early once more
to greet the sun from the four corners
of our small farmhouse.
Then there will be homemade rum for everyone, incense,
the laughter of children, jubilant marimbas.
There will be fires lit at every farmhouse, at every river
to wash the corn for tortillas in the early morning.
We will burn torches of pine to light the footpaths,
the rocks, the cliffs, and the fields.

(trans. Martín Espada)

Ishihara Yoshiro writes about humility in facing life's mysteries. Pete Seeger and Stephen Mitchell tell how much our spirits nourish each other. Seamus Heaney explores the meaning of human life and soul.

❦ ISHIHARA YOSHIRO, *Wheat*

Let a stalk of wheat
be your witness
to every difficult day.
Since it was a flame
before it was a plant,
since it was courage
before it was grain,
since it was determination
before it was growth,
and, above all, since it was prayer
before it was fruition,
it has nothing to point to
but the sky.
Remember the incredibly gentle wheat stalk
which holds its countless arrows fixed
to shoot from the bowstring—
you, standing in the same position
where the wind holds it.

❧ PETE SEEGER, *To My Old Brown Earth*

"To my old brown earth, and to my old blue sky I'll now give these last few molecules of I." And you who sing, and you who stand nearby, I do charge you not to cry. Guard well our human chain. Watch well you keep it strong as long as sun will shine. And this our home keep it pure and sweet and green, for now I'm yours and you are also mine.

❧ STEPHEN MITCHELL, *Psalm 133*

How wonderful it is to live
in harmony with all people:
like stepping out of the bath,
your whole body fresh and vibrant;
like the morning dew glistening
on the tiniest blade of grass.
It is god's infinite blessing,
a taste of eternal life.

❧ SEAMUS HEANEY, *On the Road*

The road ahead
kept reeling in
at a steady speed,
the verges dripped.

In my hands
like a wrested trophy,
the empty round
of the steering wheel.

The trance of driving
made all roads one:

the seraph-haunted, Tuscan
footpath, the green

oak-alleys of Dordogne
or that track through corn
where the rich young man
asked his question—

Master, what must I
do to be saved?
Or the road where the bird
with an earth-red back

and a white and black
tail, like parquet
of flint and jet,
wheeled over me

in visitation.
Sell all you have
and give to the poor.
I was up and away

like a human soul
that plumes from the mouth
in undulant, tenor,
black-letter Latin.

I was one for sorrow,
Noah's dove,
a panicked shadow
crossing the deer path.

If I came to earth
it would be by way of

a small east window
I once squeezed through,

scaling heaven
by superstition,
drunk and happy
on a chapel gable.

I would roost a night
on the slab of exile,
then hide in the cleft
of that churchyard wall

where hand after hand
keeps wearing away
at the cold, hard-breasted
votive granite.

And follow me.
I would migrate
through a high cave mouth
into an oaten, sun-warmed cliff,

on down the soft-nubbed,
clay-floored passage,
face-brush, wing-flap,
to the deepest chamber.

There a drinking deer
is cut into rock,
its haunch and neck
rise with the contours,

the incised outline
curves to a strained

expectant muzzle
and a nostril flared

at a dried-up source.
For my book of changes
I would meditate
that stone-faced vigil

until the long dumbfounded
spirit broke cover
to raise a dust
in the font of exhaustion.

Georgiana Valoyce-Sanchez wonders at our smallness, yet essentiality in all things. For the people of Ladakh, their own role and existence is intimately tied to the well-being and happiness of each other and to their surroundings.

❦ GEORGIANA VALOYCE-SANCHEZ, *The Eye of the Flute*

Enter the eye

From the north
a ribbon of geese drifts
high above the earth

    far below

beside a weathered wood shack
in the spring green foothills
of distant blue mountains
an old man sits
polishing stone

Dogs bark in the distance

Down the hill a brown horse
black mane flying
runs along the reservation road
and three children and their mother
stand beside a fence
watching

Beyond the fence a rusty tractor

sits fallow in the field
silent as the man beside it
watching the horse
run free

The eyes watching   the eye
sees   the image
held
to still-point

Silence

Silence that holds all songs
that holds the breath
to play all songs
to life

hush

listen to the music

The horse is running still
hoofbeats on pavement a drum

black mane flying
free
within the still-point
of the song
    the locus of the poem
the eye of the flute

Three children and their mother
stand beside a fence
their father close by
all watching
the horse run free

Dogs bark in the distance

An old man holds a polished stone
Up to the sun
turning it
to catch the light

High above the earth
a ribbon of geese drifts south
the call of a long journey
echoing
across the endless sky.

❧ HELENA NORBERG-HODGE, *Learning from Ladakh*

Why is the world teetering from one crisis to another? Has it always been like this? Were things worse in the past? Or better?

Experiences over more than sixteen years in Ladakh, an ancient culture on the Tibetan plateau, have dramatically changed my response to these questions. I have come to see my own industrial culture in a very different light.

Before I went to Ladakh, I used to assume that the direction of "progress" was somehow inevitable, not to be questioned. As a consequence, I passively accepted a new road through the middle of the park, a steel-and-glass bank where the two-hundred-year-old church had stood, a supermarket instead of the corner shop, and the fact that life seemed to get harder and faster with each day. I do not anymore. Ladakh has convinced me that there is more than one path into the future and given me tremendous strength and hope . . .

At the end of one summer, I went with Ngwang Paljor, a sixty-year-old *thanka* painter, to Srinagar in Kashmir. He was traditionally dressed in woolen *goncha*, hat, and yak-hair boots, and in the Kashmiris' eyes he was obviously from the "backward" region of Ladakh. Wherever we went, people made fun of him; he was constantly teased and taunted. Every taxi driver, shopkeeper, and passerby in some way managed to poke fun at him. "Look at that stupid hat!" "Look at those silly boots!" "You know, those primitive people never wash!" It seemed incomprehensible to me, but Ngawang remained completely unaffected by it all. He was enjoying the visit and never lost the twinkle in his eye. Though he was perfectly aware of what was going on, it just didn't seem to matter to him. He was smiling and polite, and when people jeeringly shouted the traditional Ladakhi greeting, *"Jule, jule!"* he simply answered *"Jule, jule!"* back. "Why don't you get angry?" I asked. *"Chi choen?"* ("What's the point?") was his reply.

Ngawang's equanimity was not unusual. The Ladakhis possess an irrepressible joie de vivre. Their sense of joy seems so firmly anchored within them that circumstances cannot shake it loose. You cannot spend any time at all in Ladakh without being won over by the contagious laughter.

At first I couldn't believe that the Ladakhis could be as happy as they appeared. It took me a long time to accept that the smiles I saw were real. Then, in my second year there, while at a wedding, I sat back and observed the guests enjoying themselves. Suddenly I heard myself saying, "Aha, they really are that happy." Only then did I recognize that I had been walking around with cultural blinders on, convinced that the

Ladakhis could not be as happy as they seemed. Hidden behind the jokes and laughter had to be the same frustration, jealousy, and inadequacy as in my own society. In fact, without knowing it, I had been assuming that there were no significant cultural differences in the human potential for happiness. It was a surprise for me to realize that I had been making such unconscious assumptions, and as a result I think I became more open to experiencing what was really there.

Of course the Ladakhis have sorrows and problems, and of course they feel sad when faced with illness or death. What I have seen is not an absolute difference; it is a question of degree. Yet the difference in degree is all-significant. As I return each year to the industrialized world, the contrast becomes more and more obvious. With so much of our lives colored by a sense of insecurity or fear, we have difficulty in letting go and feeling at one with ourselves and our surroundings. The Ladakhis, on the other hand, seem to possess an extended, inclusive sense of self. They do not, as we do, retreat behind boundaries of fear and self-protection; in fact, they seem to be totally lacking in what we would call pride. This doesn't mean a lack of self-respect. On the contrary, their self-respect is so deep-rooted as to be unquestioned.

I was with about fifteen Ladakhis and two students from Calcutta on the back of a truck taking us along the bumpy and dusty road from Zanskar. As the journey went on, the students became restless and uncomfortable and began pushing at a middle-aged Ladakhi who had made a seat for himself out of a sack of vegetables. Before long, the older man stood up so that the students—who were about twenty years younger than him—could sit down. When, after about two hours, we stopped for a rest, the students indicated to the Ladakhi that they wanted him to fetch water for them; he fetched the water. They then more or less ordered him to make a fire and herbal tea for them.

He was effectively being treated as a servant—almost certainly for the first time in his life. Yet there was nothing remotely servile in his behavior; he merely did what was asked of him as he might for a friend—without obsequiousness and with no loss of dignity. I was fuming, but he and the other Ladakhis, far from being angered or embarrassed by the way he was being treated, found it all amusing and nothing more. The old man was so relaxed about who he was that he had no need to prove himself.

I have never met people who seem so healthy emotionally, so secure, as the Ladakhis. The reasons are, of course, complex and spring from a whole way of life and world view. But I am sure that the most important factor is the sense that you are a part of something much larger than yourself, that you are inextricably connected to others and to your surroundings.

The Ladakhis belong to their place on earth. They are bonded to that place through intimate daily contact, through a knowledge about their immediate environment with its changing seasons, needs, and limitations. They are aware of the living context in which they find themselves. The movement of the stars, the sun, and moon are familiar rhythms that influence their daily activities.

Just as importantly, the Ladakhis' larger sense of self has something to do with the close ties between people. At that wedding, I watched the *paspun* group as they laughed and joked together and then sat quietly drinking tea, lost in their own thoughts for long periods without the need to exchange a word. They had shared many experiences—grieving and rejoicing. And they had worked together, supporting one another, during the ceremonies that mark the important transitions of life. I suddenly gained an insight into the depth of their relationships.

In traditional Ladakhi society, everyone, including aunts and uncles, monks and nuns, belongs to a highly interdependent community. A mother is never left on her own, separated from all her children. She always remains a part of their lives and those of their children.

Before feeling my way into Ladakhi culture, I had thought that leaving home was part of growing up, a necessary step toward becoming an adult. I now believe that large extended families and small intimate communities form a better foundation for the creation of mature, balanced individuals. A healthy society is one that encourages close social ties and mutual interdependence, granting each individual a net of unconditional emotional support. Within this nurturing framework, individuals feel secure enough to become quite free and independent. Paradoxically, I have found the Ladakhis less emotionally dependent than we are in industrial society. There is love and friendship, but it is not intense or grasping—not a possession of one person by another. I once saw a mother greeting her eighteen-year-old son when he returned home after being away for a year. She seemed surprisingly calm, as though she had not missed him. It took me a long time to understand this behavior. I thought my Ladakhi friends reacted strangely when I arrived back after being away for the winter. I had brought presents I knew they would like. I expected them to be pleased to see me and happy at the gifts. But to them it was as if I had not been gone. They thanked me for the presents, but not in the way that I was hoping. I was wanting them to look excited and confirm our special friendship. I was disappointed. Whether I had been away for six months or a day, they treated me in the same way.

I came to realize, however, that the ability to adjust to any situation, to feel happy regardless of the circumstances, was a tremendous strength. I came to appreciate the easy, relaxed attitude of my Ladakhi friends and to like being treated as though I had never been away. Ladakhis do not seem to be as attached to anything as we are. Most of them are, of course, not completely without the attachments that so affect our lives. But again, there is a difference—an all pervasive difference—in degree. One may be unhappy to see a friend leave or to lose something valuable, but not *that* unhappy.

If I ask a Ladakhi, "Do you enjoy going to Leh, or do you prefer staying in the village?" I am likely to get the answer "I am happy if I go to Leh; and if I don't go, I am also happy." It really does not matter so much one way or the other. The Ladakhis enjoy a feast more than everyday food, and they would rather be comfortable than uncomfortable, healthy rather than ill. But, finally, their contentedness and peace of mind do not seem dependent on such outside circumstances; these qualities come more from within. The Ladakhis' relationships to others and to their surroundings have helped nurture a sense of inner calm and contentedness, and their religion has reminded them that you can be healthy, warm, comfortable, and well fed, yet so long as you remain "ignorant," you will not be happy.

Contentment comes from feeling and understanding yourself to be part of the flow of life, relaxing and moving with it. If it starts to pour with rain just as you set out on a long journey, why be miserable? Maybe you would not have preferred it, but the Ladakhis' attitude is "Why be unhappy?"

PART III

If Not Now, When?

The Call to Action

If I am not for myself, who will be for me? If I am for myself alone,
    what am I?
And if not now, when?

— RABBI HILLEL

This emphasis on "now" is a common imperative of ancient wisdom
traditions. It is not enough to dream or to love. Finally, these qualities must
serve as principles for acting in specific and concrete ways in everyday life.
Action transposes dreams and feelings onto the stage of history. It is not
enough to imagine a decent future or care deeply about the pain and condition of others without doing something to make a difference. The *imagination*, mediated by *love*, is the ground of moral vision. *Love*, mediated by
imagination, is the foundation of a caring and open-hearted approach to life.

However, moral behavior, developed through vision informed by love,
must lead to action. This action can be intimate and as simple as loving a
child in trouble or supporting a friend in need. It can be as ordinary and
effective as going out of your way to help someone who loses a job. And it
can be as historic as opposing injustice and fighting for the rights of the
oppressed and exploited. Moral life is realized through what you do: "Thou
shalt not stand idly by," the prophet Isaiah warned, if we are to find peace
and fellowship in our lives together.

However, doing what you believe is right and acting according to your
most cherished visions is not always easy. There are times when self-interest overwhelms the best of intentions and fear leads one to silence or even
cowardice. Moral action is a constant challenge, and meeting that challenge
is a constant source of renewal, as Denise Levertov indicates in her poem
"Advising Myself":

When the world comes to you muffled *as through a glass
darkly*—jubilance anguish, declined into

faded postcards—remember how, seventeen, you said
you no longer felt or saw with the old
intensity, and knew that the flamelight
would not rekindle; and how Bet scoffed
and refused to believe you. And how many thousand times,
burning with joy or despair, you've known she was right.

People of sound heart, the sage Lao-tzu tells us, do not shrink from trying to live up to their ideals. "They know both ways, they can begin again."
Always beginning again, striving to get closer to our ideals and good feelings through our actions, is as complex and important a challenge for adults
as is learning to walk or speak for children. And just as learning to stand,
walk, and run are intrinsic to our becoming ourselves, so learning how to
put our ideals into practice is essential to creating and sustaining a decent
community or a good society.

Most individual acts of kindness and generosity have important but
limited consequences for others. But some have enormous significance. For
example, the wonderful story of the Good Samaritan, who stopped to tend
the sick and ailing traveler on the road after many had ignored and passed
him by—even though their tribes were adversaries. And Franz Jägerstätter
defied the Nazi regime, threatening its very foundation by defying its
authority even though, as a German Aryan, he ran no risk himself. In simple and dramatic terms, he wrote his wife when he was about to refuse
induction in 1943, "Today I am going to take the difficult step." In more
recent times in our own country, people of conscience have resigned from
rewarding and powerful positions to protest the horrors that result when
the nation shrinks from its ideals. This was the case in the Johnson administration during the Vietnam War, in the Nixon administration during
Watergate, in the Bush administration during the Gulf War, and in the
Clinton Administration over the decimation of welfare protections for the
poor. Individual actions can affect us all. But sometimes the moral course
requires collective action because we are, by definition, interdependent.
Community results from *doing*, and through action we take steps toward
making our hopes and dreams everyday realities.

Acting in community with other people can be as personally rewarding as it can be socially healing. It provides people with a sense of fullness and rootedness, and this sense of solidarity and cooperation is the practical expression of our sense of common moral purpose. This is what Desmond Tutu must have had in mind when he said,

> "We shall survive only together, black and white. We can be human only together, black and white."

It is also what Elie Wiesel means when he talks about the absolute necessity for people to fight back against intolerance and hatred in discussing how, in almost every state and in thousands of communities, Americans have in recent years created organizations to protest the burning of black churches and reject other horrific violent acts of racism, anti-Semitism, and homophobia:

> Nothing is more important. If you don't fight hate, hate wins. The only way to fight it is to speak up and denounce its ugliness. Hate is everywhere because it is a part of human nature ... the worst part. But it is also part of human nature to oppose it vigorously—with every fiber of our being. When people do that, they express what is best in us.

There is no linear progression from imagination and love to action. Some people, for example, believe that having and articulating a moral vision is the same as making that vision a living reality. Others believe that their love of "all things great and small" is enough, in and of itself, to redeem the world. Yet the troubles continue, justice is not always served, and many people suffer with no control over their lives. To get beyond dream and beyond narrow self-interest, action is necessary. Action in pursuit of a moral vision and rooted in humane understanding and concern involves our ability to demonstrate solidarity with others and faithfulness to our dreams.

In this part of the book, we have chosen selections that center around four major values that are central to unifying vision and love through action. They are *courage, responsibility, respect,* and *fairness or justice.* These values directly bring moral vision, loving-kindness, and open-heartedness into our everyday lives—into our "now"—what Thich Nhat Hanh refers to as "the present moment":

> Our true home is in the present moment. To live in the present moment is a miracle. The miracle is not to walk on water, the miracle is to walk on the green earth in the present moment, to appreciate the peace and beauty that are available now. Peace is all around us—in the world and in nature—and within us—in our bodies and in our spirits. Once we learn to touch this peace, we will be healed and transformed. It is not a matter of faith; it is a matter of practice.

9
Fear Anoints
Our Masters

COURAGE

Audre Lorde writes:

When I dare to be powerful in the service of my vision, then it becomes
less and less important why I am afraid.

Courage is most easily defined not by the absence of fear, but by our
relationship to fear, how we deal with fear—whether we turn and run,
or whether we stand and resist and by resisting transform our experience.

Frank Baum wrote *The Wizard of Oz* in part to resist the horrible degradation which threatened so many during the dark days of the Depression,
and in part to conjure more hopeful times. When the Lion asks to be given
courage by the Wizard, he is told:

"Come in," said Oz.

"I've come for my courage," announced the Lion entering the
room.

"Very well," answered the little man; "I will get it for you."

He went to a cupboard, and reaching to a high shelf took down a square green bottle, the contents of which he poured into a green-gold dish, beautifully carved. Placing this before the Cowardly Lion, who sniffed at it and did not like it, the Wizard said:

"Drink."

"What is it?" asked the Lion.

"Well," answered Oz, "if it were inside of you, it would be courage. You know, that courage is always inside one; so that this really cannot be called courage until you have swallowed it. Therefore, I advise you to drink it as soon as possible."

The Lion hesitated no longer, but drank 'til the dish was empty.

"How do you feel now?" asked Oz.

"Full of courage," replied the Lion, who went joyfully back to his friends to tell them of his good fortune.

Inside is where the potion of our possibilities gets stirred. Inside is where we can each draw from to contribute the gift of inspiration and possibility courage can bring to the world. Lillian Hellman, in her 1952 letter to the House Un-American Activities Committee, found it:

I cannot and will not act out of my conscience to fit this year's fashions.

In a similar vein, Ignazio Silone, in *The God That Failed*, writes of freedom as being built on the foundation of courage:

Liberty isn't a thing you are given as a present. You can be free under a dictatorship. It is sufficient if you struggle against it.

Sometimes courage means finding the strength to confront fear and the fortitude to risk pain, hardship, and unpopularity. Sometimes it is courageous to heed the warning of fear, to know when the risk of life and limb is foolhardy and self-indulgent. And sometimes courage means the resolve to accept the very tough task of living against inevitable and even irresistible odds.

A most insidious form of fear is that which masquerades as common sense or even wisdom, condemning as foolish, reckless, insignificant or futile the small daily acts of courage which help to preserve one's self-respect and inherent human dignity.

—Aung San Suu Kyi, Burmese recipient of the
Sakharov Prize for Freedom of Thought, 1991

It also takes courage to be honest, to face up to those odds, to take stock and to persevere. We can also speak of people being courageous when they care passionately that other people count on them and so make no idle promises—their word can be trusted. Similarly, it takes courage to dispel false beliefs, to recognize idolatry and flattering deceit, to avoid fruitless flights to recover what never was, and like Aesop's little boy to yell loudly that *"The Emperor has no clothes."*

Selections

June Jordan and Sandra Cisneros tell of raw courage—the courage to resist oppression and to meet the everyday tests of endurance that can so easily overwhelm us.

❦ JUNE JORDAN, *1977: Poem for Mrs. Fannie Lou Hamer*

You used to say, "June?
Honey when you come down here you
supposed to stay with me. Where
else?"
Meanin home
against the beer the shotguns and the
point of view of whitemen don'
never see Black anybodies without
some violent itch start up.
                The ones who
said, "No Nigga's Votin in This Town . . .
lessen it be feet first to the booth"

Then jailed you
beat you brutal
bloody/battered/beat
you blue beyond the feeling
of the terrible

And failed to stop you.
Only God could but He
wouldn't stop
you
fortress from self-
pity

Humble as a woman anywhere
I remember finding you inside the laundromat
in Ruleville
       lion spine relaxed/hell
       what's the point to courage
       when you washin clothes?

But that took courage

       just to sit there/target
       to the killers lookin
       for your singin face
       perspirey through the rinse
       and spin

and later
you stood mighty in the door on James Street
loud callin:

       "BULLETS OR NO BULLETS!
       THE FOOD IS COOKED
       AN GETTIN COLD!"

We ate
A family tremulous but fortified
by turnips/okra/handpicked
like the lilies

filled to the very living
full

one solid gospel
      (sanctified)

one gospel
      (peace)

one full Black lily
luminescent
in a homemade field

of love

❦ SANDRA CISNEROS, *Four Skinny Trees*

They are the only ones who understand me. I am the
only one who understands them. Four skinny trees with
skinny necks and pointy elbows like mine. Four who do
not belong here but are here. Four raggedy excuses planted
by the city. From our room we can hear them, but Nenny
just sleeps and doesn't appreciate these things.

Their strength is secret. They send ferocious roots
beneath the ground. They grow up and they grow down
and grab the earth between their hairy toes and bite the
sky with violent teeth and never quit their anger. This is
how they keep.

Let one forget his reason for being, they'd all droop
like tulips in a glass, each with their arms around the other.
Keep, keep, keep, trees say when I sleep. They teach.
    When I am too sad and too skinny to keep keeping,
when I am a tiny thing against so many bricks, then it is I
look at trees. When there is nothing left to look at on this
street. Four who grew despite concrete. Four who reach
and do not forget to reach. Four whose only reason is to
be and be.

Lao-tzu and Mary Wollstonecraft teach that courage is not only about physical bravery. Tricia Lande tells a story of the courage to endure great suffering. Barbara Drake, Laura Esquivel, and James Baldwin depict physical courage revealed in modest and unassuming ways.

❦ LAO-TZU, *Courage*

A man without the courage to die
Can lead others to death.
A man without the courage to bend
Will lead others to break.
A man of true courage leaves
No child unguarded,
He knows that way
Lies eternity.

❦ MARY WOLLSTONECRAFT, *Mary, A Fiction*

Unhappy, she wandered about the village, and relieved the poor; it
was the only employment that eased her aching heart; she became
more intimate with misery—the misery that rises from poverty and the
want of education. She was in the vicinity of a great city; the vicious
poor in and about it must ever grieve a benevolent contemplative mind.

One evening a man who stood weeping in a little lane, near the house she resided in, caught her eye. She accosted him; in a confused manner, he informed her that his wife was dying, and his children crying for the bread he could not earn. Mary desired to be conducted to his habitation; it was not very distant, and was the upper room in an old mansion-house, which had been once the abode of luxury. Some tattered shreds of rich hangings still remained, covered with cobwebs and filth; round the ceiling, through which the rain drop'd, was a beautiful cornice mouldering; and a spacious gallery was rendered dark by the broken windows being blocked up; through the apertures the wind forced its way in hollow sounds, and reverberated along the former scene of festivity.

It was crowded with inhabitants: som[e] were scolding, others swearing, or singing indecent songs. What a sight for Mary! Her blood ran cold; yet she had sufficient resolution to mount to the top of the house. On the floor, in one corner of a very small room, lay an emaciated figure of a woman; a window over her head scarcely admitted any light, for the broken panes were stuffed with dirty rags. Near her were five children, all young, and covered with dirt, their sallow cheeks, and languid eyes, exhibited none of the charms of childhood. Some were fighting, and others crying for food; their yells were mixed with their mother's groans, and the wind which rushed through the passage. Mary was petrified; but soon assuming more courage, approached the bed, and, regardless of the surrounding nastiness, knelt down by the poor wretch, and breathed the most poisonous air; for the unfortunate creature was dying of a putrid fever, the consequence of dirt and want.

❦ TRICIA LANDE, *White Horses*

The first time I saw Dorothea Lange's photo, *Migrant Woman*, I was ten years old and thought it was a picture of my Aunt Vergie. Aunt Vergie, who at forty-five talked to spirits and saw white horses in the night, gutted tuna for a living, pulling her sharp knife upward in the fish's soft underbelly that shined mother-of-pearl under the fish market lights.

The picture of that migrant farm woman was in *Life* or *Look*, one of those photo-heavy magazines so popular in 1941, and I ran with it through the clapboard house I shared with my grandmother and aunt.

Aunt Vergie and Grandma sat on the glassed-in front porch where they always spent their evenings. They would talk quietly, or stare off down our hill toward the west channel of the Los Angeles Harbor. Aunt Vergie always curled up on the old black car seat someone had pulled out of a '36 Ford, and my grandma sat in her wooden rocker, where she would fit a light bulb inside a cotton sock, making a hard surface to work her darning needle against, taking small, careful stitches.

My grandma must have heard me coming because she said some thing like, "fans . . . silly in November." Then she yelled, "Soody, don't you all let that screen door bang," a second before I pushed through the door, letting it slam behind me.

Then she said, "Sue Donna," as if that was all she needed to say. Sue Donna was my real name, but I was only called that when a family member was irritated with me.

"Look here what I got. Aunt Vergie, you got your picture in a magazine! "

Vergie sat fanning herself. She had a red-and-white fan with a peacock outlined in gold on its face, and I had one just like it. She and I had been given those fans by the Japanese man that owned the only Chinese restaurant in San Pedro. That was where we lived then—San Pedro, the waterfront area of Los Angeles.

I sat down next to Vergie on that hard seat, laid the magazine across her lap, and she put the fan down on the apple box that served as a coffee table. Vergie stared at that picture for a minute, then outlined it with her finger.

"Well, Soody baby, this ain't a picture of me. It looks like me, but it ain't. Hell, she looks like all of the Bybee women."

The woman in the picture held one hand up so that it lightly touched her cheek, and Vergie said, "She even got cotton-picker hands.

Look at them scars." The picture was not in color so the marks on the woman's hands showed up as dark blotches as if the film was flawed.

"How do you get cotton-picker hands, Aunt Vergie?"

"Get bad scratched from picking cotton. You out in the fields all day you cain't clean the cuts proper, so they don't heal right. That's why I'm glad I got me a different kind of job now."

The marks on my aunt's hands match those in the picture, only Vergie's were red. On days I had gone to the fish market after school just to be with her, I had watched those scarred hands work. They moved so quickly, scraping the sides of fish with a knife, sending scales flying like a shower of blue-green sequins that turned dull moments later. I could see those scars when Vergie held up the picture to my grandma.

"She looks like us, don't she, Momma?" . . .

Hiro Ikeda stood on the wharf, which smelled of creosote and diesel fuel from the tugboats docked nearby. His small white launch with its blue-and-white striped canopy was there too, lightly bouncing against a pylon. That launch was always clean, its white paint perfect. He took great care with the little boat and was as gentle with it as he was with my aunt.

It was overcast and cool that morning, and Hiro wore his navy-blue pea coat. He was a small man, no bigger than my aunt, and when he wore that pea coat with the collar turned up it hid even his nose, so that it seemed he looked at the world peering from a shell, checking to make sure things were safe before he completely emerged.

Hiro was just a kind little gray-haired man who drank lemon tea and ate steamed dumplings—vegetables wrapped in dough and drenched in sweet, thick honey sauce. To hear him tell it, nothing ever happened in his small life of work and sleep. Nothing more than a storm now and then that would blow up from Baja, and the three of us in his launch would ride the swells while Hiro gripped the small boat's wheel as if it were all there was between us and eternity.

I don't know how long Vergie and Hiro had been meeting for

these Sunday launch rides, only that it had been going on as long as I could remember, and they always took me with them. That morning they greeted each other as they always did. Vergie held out her cotton gloved hand—I never saw her remove those gloves when he was around—he took it in his small brown fingers, and bowed slightly at the waist. "I am happy to see you, Vergie." He always said it in a way that made it seem there was some doubt she would come.

Vergie, who could string enough four-letter words together to make a sailor blush, smiled and softly said, "Thank you, Hiro. It's so nice that you all asked us."

Then, as always, Hiro repeated the ritual with me, taking my hand and saying, "Little Miss Soody. You look so sweet today." He touched my hair so softly that it seemed more like the touch of a gentle breeze.

The sea was smooth that morning, and it did not take long to reach the rocks of the breakwater. We dropped anchor just inside the harbor so I could watch the fat seals that lay on the gray boulders, and the pelicans that would glide so low their bellies seemed to skim the water's surface. This was my favorite part of our voyage because Hiro would let me sit at the wheel.

Vergie and Hiro sat in the back of the boat, each wrapped in a blanket, speaking softly. Hiro said, "We could try, Vergie. If we just tried."

"Where would we live? Ain't nowhere we could live in peace. Then there's the child. I got the child to think about."

"You know how I feel about the child, Virginia. Besides, it's too late to have our own."

"It ain't too late just yet, Hiro." And my aunt laughed what sounded to me a young girl's laugh, light and soft like my friends at school. "But then we'd be in a real fine mess for sure, having a mixed-blood baby." Then she laughed again, but this time she didn't sound young at all. "Well, Momma's always yelling about the misery of family marrying family. Guess she wouldn't have nothing to yell about on our account."

Vergie said no more for a minute, then, "I got to think on it some."

"Vergie, we don't have half a lifetime left, and it seems like that's how long you've been thinking about this." It was the first time I had ever heard anger in Hiro's voice. After that he moved away from Vergie, came forward near where I sat and leaned over the railing.

I looked at him over my shoulder, and I could see that Hiro Ikeda was crying. Not loudly; there were no sobs, no deep throaty sounds. Just large drops of water that hung on his cheeks. We came home early that Sunday, Hiro and Vergie not speaking on the way in, and Vergie silent on our walk back up the hill.

That next Sunday, for the first time in my memory, Vergie and I did not go out in Hiro Ikeda's launch. That Sunday was December 7, 1941. That day Vergie Bybee cried and my grandmother rocked in her wooden chair, but did not darn socks.

The following Sunday Vergie did not put on her soft green dress, but a black one. She braided my hair, but did not weave pink ribbons into the plaits. She did not wear her white gloves, but held that red-and-white fan with the gold peacock on its face in her bare hand as we walked down the hill to the center of town and stood on the sidewalk with a crowd of other people.

A flatbed truck with wooden stakes around the sides of its bed sat idling in the street. Hiro stood in the midst of fifteen or so other Japanese men at the back of the truck, their belongings tied in white sheet bundles at their feet. There were other men too. Large white men in dark suits and wide brimmed hats. Vergie and I watched them as they yelled orders at the Japanese. We watched as they shoved this one and that. As they demanded that the small brown people climb onto the truck, Aunt Vergie leaned into me.

The crowd on the sidewalk yelled too. "Hang them! Send them to hell! Sneaky bastards!"

When Hiro climbed aboard the truck, Vergie held the closed fan over her head, not high, but just inches above her light brown hair. If Hiro saw her signal he gave no sign, but settled against the back of the truck cab and stared off toward the channel.

The truck filled with men and belongings tied into bundles and moved off down the street. Vergie said, "We ain't going see him again, Soody." And even at that young age, I knew that to be true.

❧   ❧   ❧

I ran across that picture, Migrant Woman, last summer. It was in a
book, *Collected Works of Depression Era Art*. I looked again at the picture
of that stick-thin woman with fine brown hair parted in the middle,
pulled back behind tiny ears peeling from too much sun. I saw the way
her scarred hand lightly touched her cheek, and that look in her eyes
which haunts me. Far off, as if she could not stand seeing what was in
front of her. Her small mouth, lips, made straight by anguish.

In that picture I see the image of my aunt, see her scrape at the
sides of those tuna with their sequin scales that turned dark over time.
And I think about how it must have been for Vergie on that hard-edged
day when she could no longer dream, and decided there would be no
more for her than putting that sharp knife in a fish's underbelly, pulling
it upwards so that what gave the creature life spilled out on a hard white
metal tray.

❧ BARBARA DRAKE, *When the Airplane Stopped*

When Father's airplane stopped
and we were mid-air,
the little yellow Cub continued riding
along on chilly emptiness
like a boat in a stream.
Not a heavy thing at all,
it seemed a toy plane
of paper and balsa
tossed up with no rider
but the painted outline
of a soldier, his helmet
and goggles classic, his head
bent to the controls.

Father coughed and grinned
to a grimace, and I said, "Anything wrong?"
"Damn thing went off," he answered.

The bay looked long and blue and beautiful
against the sand spit;
the air was also blue, and chilly.
"Ice," said Father,
"in the carburetor."
And still we floated
in that nothingness,
with nothing to fear,
the nothing under us.

And Father fiddled with the starter
as the ailerons rowed space
and then before we'd really lost
much altitude, maybe none, maybe
we even gained some,
the engine started and Father smiled
and said, "I could land
this plane anywhere, engine or not:
a jetty, a dune, a country
highway. I could have taken it down."

The little plane coasted
along on its rutrutrut of an engine
till we landed where Mother sat
in the car at the railing,
and, "What were you doing up there?"
she asked us. "It looked funny."
We said,
"Flying."

❦ LAURA ESQUIVEL, *Like Water for Chocolate*

When the revolutionaries arrived, they were met by Mama Elena at the entrance of the house. She had her shotgun hidden in her petticoats, and she had Rosalio and Guadalupe at her side. Her gaze met that of the captain in charge, and he knew immediately from the steeliness of her eyes that they were in the presence of a woman to be reckoned with.

"Good afternoon, senora, are you the owner of this ranch?"

"Yes, I am. What is it you want?"

"We've come to ask you to volunteer to help the cause."

"I'll volunteer to tell you to take whatever you like from the corn crib and the stable. But that is the limit; I won't allow you to touch anything inside my house. Understand? Those things are for my cause."

The captain, laughing, snapped to attention and answered her:

"Understood, my general."

This joke tickled all the soldiers, and they laughed heartily, but the captain could see you didn't fool around with Mama Elena, what she said was serious, very serious.

Trying not to be intimidated by the fierce domineering look he got from her, he ordered the soldiers to inspect the ranch. They didn't find much, a little corn for scattering and eight chickens. A frustrated sergeant came back to the captain and said, "The old lady must have everything hidden in the house. Let me go in and take a look around!"

Mama Elena put her finger on the trigger and answered:

"I'm not joking. I repeat no one is setting foot in my house!"

Laughing, swinging the chickens he was carrying in his hands, the sergeant started toward the door. Mama Elena raised the gun, braced herself against the wall so she wouldn't be knocked to the ground by the kick of the gun, and shot the chickens. Bits of chicken flew in every direction along with the smell of burnt feathers.

Shaking, Rosalio and Guadalupe got out their pistols, fully convinced that this was their last day on earth. The soldier next to the captain was going to shoot Mama Elena, but the captain motioned him to stop. They were all waiting for his order to attack.

"I have a very good aim and a very bad temper, Captain. The next shot is for you, and I assure you that I can shoot you before they can kill me, so it would be best for us to respect each other. If we die, no one will miss me very much, but won't the nation mourn your loss?"

It really was hard to meet Mama Elena's gaze, even for the captain. There was something daunting about it. It produced a nameless fear in those who suffered it; they felt tried and convicted for their offenses. They fell prisoner to a childlike fear of maternal authority.

"You're right. Don't worry, no one is going to kill you, or fail to respect you, that's for sure! Such a valiant woman will always have my admiration." He turned to his soldiers and said, "No one is to set foot in the house; see what else you can find here and let's go."

What they found was the huge dovecote formed by two slopes of the roof on the enormous house. To get to it you had to climb up a twenty-foot ladder. Three rebels climbed up and stood there stunned for some time before they were able to move. They were impressed by the dovecote's size and by the darkness and the cooing of the doves gathered there, coming and going through narrow side windows. They closed the door and the windows so none of them could get away and set about trapping the pigeons and doves.

They rounded up enough to feed the entire batallion for a week. Before the troops withdrew, the captain rode around the back patio, inhaling deep whiffs of the scent of roses that still clung indelibly to this place. He closed his eyes and was still for quite a while. Returning to Mama Elena's side, he asked her, "I understood you had three daughters. Where are they?"

"The oldest and youngest live in the United States, the other died."

The news seemed to move the captain. In a barely audible voice, he replied, "That is a pity, a very great pity."

He took leave of Mama Elena with a bow. They left peacefully, just as they had come, and Mama Elena was quite disconcerted by the way they had treated her; it didn't fit the picture of the heartless ruffians she'd been expecting. From that day on she would not express any opinion about the revolutionaries. What she never learned was that this captain was the same Juan Alejandrez who had carried off her daughter Gertrudis some months before.

They were even on that score, for the captain remained ignorant of the large number of chickens that Mama Elena had hidden behind the house, buried in ashes. They had managed to kill twenty before the troops arrived. The chickens are filled with ground wheat or oats and then placed, feathers and all, into a glazed earthenware pot. The pot is covered tightly using a narrow strip of cloth; that way the meat can be kept for more than a week.

It had been a common practice on the ranch since ancient times, when they had to preserve animals after a hunting party.

When she came out of hiding, Tita immediately missed the constant cooing of the doves, which had been part of her everyday life ever since she was born. This sudden silence made her feel her loneliness all the more. It was then that she really felt the loss of Pedro, Rosaura, and Roberto. She hurried up the rungs of the enormous ladder that went to the dovecote, but all she found there was the usual carpet of feathers and droppings.

The wind stole through the open door and lifted some feathers that fell on a carpet of silence. Then she heard a tiny sound, a little newborn pigeon had been spared from the massacre. Tita picked it up and got ready to go back down, but first she stopped for a moment to look at the cloud of dust the soldiers' horses left in their wake. She wondered why they hadn't done anything to hurt her mother. While she was in her hiding place, she had prayed that nothing bad would happen to Mama Elena, but unconsciously she had hoped that when she got out she would find her mother dead.

Ashamed of these thoughts, she placed the pigeon between her breasts to free her hands for the dangerous ladder, and climbed down from the dovecote. From then on, her main interest lay in feeding that pathetic baby pigeon. Only then did life seem to make a little sense. It didn't compare with the satisfaction derived from nursing a human being, but in some way it was similar.

❧ JAMES BALDWIN, *Tell Me How Long the Train's Been Gone*

My father looked as stunned and still and as close to madness as that, and his encircling arm began to hurt me, but I did not com-

plain. I put my hand on his face, and he turned to me; he smiled—
he was very beautiful then! And he put his great hand on top of
mine. He turned to Caleb, "That's all that happened? You didn't say
nothing?"

"What could I say? It might have been different if I had been by
myself. But I had Leo with me, and I was afraid of what they might do
to Leo."

"No, you did right man. I got no fault to find. You didn't take their
badge number?"

Caleb snickered. "What for? You know a friendly judge? We got
money for a lawyer? Somebody they going to listen to? They get us in
that precinct house and made us confess to all kinds of things and
sometimes even kill us, and don't nobody give a damn. Don't nobody
care what happens to a black man. If they didn't need us for work,
they'd have killed us all off a long time ago. They did it to the
Indians."

"That's the truth," her mother said. "I wish I could say different,
but it's the truth." She stroked our father's shoulder. "We just thank
the Lord it wasn't no worse. We just got to say: 'Well, got home safe
tonight.'"

I asked, "Daddy, how come they do us like they do?"

My father looked at us for a long time. Finally, he said, "Leo, if I
could tell you that, maybe I'd be able to make them stop. But don't let
them make you afraid. You hear?"

I said, "Yes, sir." But I knew that I was already afraid.

"Let's not talk about it no more," our mother said. "If you two is
hungry, I got some porkchops back there."

Caleb grinned at her. "Little Leo might be hungry. He stuffs himself like a pig. But I ain't hungry. Hey, old man—" he nudged my
father's shoulder; nothing would be refused us tonight—"Why don't
we have a taste of your rum? All right?"

Her mother laughed. "I'll go get it," she said. She started out of the
room.

"Reckon we can give Leo a little bit too?" our father asked. He
pulled me onto his lap.

"In a glass of water," her mother said, laughing. She took one last look at us before she went into the kitchen. "My," she said, "I sure am surrounded by some pretty men! My, my, my!"

Mbuyiseni Mtshali shows the courage to act and the courage to be generous to enemies. Shakespeare depicts the direct physical bravery of his King Henry V as does Bernard Shaw of his St. Joan.

❦ MBUYISENI MTSHALI, *The Day We Buried Our Bully*

Through years and years
of harassment
we tolerated his hideous deeds:
    girls abducted,
    women molested,
    boys assaulted,
    and men robbed.

Our fear made him our master.

One day
old warrior Death
whipped out his .38 special
from his holster
and felled our tormentor with a single shot.

    We turned his corpse
    into a piece of meat
tucked in between
the sandwich of soil
black like burnt toast
ready for ants and worms

to eat for breakfast,
and excrete as manure.

We laid wreaths
of withered flowers
to fill his grave
with an odour of decay
wafted by the wind,

As mourners smiled
through tears of relief,
"Lord! take care of his soul—
though he was but a bully."

❦ WILLIAM SHAKESPEARE, *Henry V*

WESTMORELAND: O that we now had here
But one ten thousand of those men in England
That do no work to-day !

KING: What's he that wishes so?
My cousin Westmoreland? No, my fair cousin.
If we are marked to die, we are enow
To do our country loss; and if to live,
The fewer men, the greater share of honor.
God's will! I pray thee wish not one man more.
By Jove, I am not covetous for gold,
Nor care I who doth feed upon my cost;
It yearns me not if men my garments wear;
Such outward things dwell not in my desires:
But if it be a sin to covet honor,
I am the most offending soul alive.
No, faith, my coz, wish not a man from England.
God's peace! I would not lose so great an honor

As one man more methinks would share from me
For the best hope I have. O, do not wish one more!
Rather proclaim it, Westmoreland, through my host,
That he which hath no stomach to this fight,
Let him depart; his passport shall be made,
And crowns for convoy put into his purse.
We would not die in that man's company
That fears his fellowship to die with us.
This day is called the Feast of Crispian.
He that outlives this day, and comes safe home,
Will stand a-tiptoe when this day is named
And rouse him at the name of Crispian.
He that shall see this day, and live old age,
Will yearly on the vigil feast his neighbors
And say, "To-morrow is Saint Crispian."
Then will he strip his sleeve and show his scars,
(And say, "These wounds I had on Crispin's day.")
Old men forget; yet all shall be forgot,
But he'll remember, with advantages,
What feats he did that day. Then shall our names,
Familiar in his mouth as household words—
Harry the King, Bedford and Exeter,
Warwick and Talbot, Salisbury and Gloucester—
Be in their flowing cups freshly rememb'red.
This story shall the good man teach his son;
And Crispin Crispian shall ne'er go by,
From this day to the ending of the world,
But we in it shall be remembered—
We few, we happy few, we band of brothers;
For he to-day that sheds his blood with me
Shall be my brother. Be he ne'er so vile,
This day shall gentle his condition;
And gentlemen in England now abed
Shall think themselves accursed they were not here,

And hold their manhoods cheap whiles any speaks
That fought with us upon Saint Crispin's day.

❧ GEORGE BERNARD SHAW, *Saint Joan*

LADVENU: . . . thou mayst repent thy errors in solitary
contemplation, and be shielded from all temptation to return to
them, we, for the good of thy soul, and for a penance that may wipe
out thy sins and bring thee finally unspotted to the throne of grace,
do condemn thee to eat the bread of sorrow and drink the water of
affliction to the end of thy earthly days in perpetual imprisonment.

JOAN: (rising in consternation and terrible anger) Perpetual
imprisonment! Am I not then to be set free?

LADVENU: (mildly shocked) Set free, child, after such wickedness as
yours! What are you dreaming of?

JOAN: Give me that writing. (She rushes to the table; snatches up the
paper; and tears it into fragments.) Light your fire: do you think I
dread it as much as the life of a rat in a hole? My voices were right.

LADVENU: Joan! Joan!

JOAN: Yes: they told me you were fools (the word gives great
offense), and that I was not to listen to your fine words nor trust to
your charity. You promised me my life; but you lied (indignant
exclamations). You think that life is nothing but not being stone
dead. It is not the bread and water I fear: I can live on bread: when
have I asked for more? It is no hardship to drink water if the water
be clean. Bread has no sorrow for me, and water no affliction. But to
shut me from the light of the sky and the sight of the fields and
flowers; to chain my feet so that I can never again ride with the
soldiers nor climb the hills; to make me breathe foul damp darkness,
and keep from me everything that brings me back to the love of

God when your wickedness and foolishness tempt me to hate Him: all this is worse than the furnace in the Bible that was heated seven times. I could let the banners and the trumpets and the knights and soldiers pass me and leave me behind as they leave the other women, if only I could still hear the wind in the trees, the larks in the sunshine, the young lambs crying through the healthy frost, and the blessed church bells that send my angel voices floating to me on the wind. But without these things I cannot live; and by your wanting to take them away from me, or from any human creature, I know that your counsel is of the devil, and that mine is of God.

THE ASSESSORS: (in great commotion) Blasphemy! blasphemy! She is possessed. She said our counsel was of the devil. And hers of God. Monstrous! The devil is in our midst.

D'ESTIVET: (shouting above the din) She is a relapsed heretic, obstinate, incorrigible, and altogether unworthy of the mercy we have shewn her. I call for her excommunication.

THE CHAPLAIN: (to the Executioner) Light your fire, man. To the stake with her.

The Executioner and his assistants hurry out through the court-yard.

LADVENU: You wicked girl: if your counsel were of God would He not deliver you?

JOAN: His ways are not your ways. He wills that I go through the fire to His bosom; for I am His child, and you are not fit that I should live among you. That is my last word to you.

The soldiers seize her.

Devorah Major warns us not to misread the signs of courage—the right form may not convey the real thing. Yukio Mishima writes about the courage to reject the fantasies of heroism. Thich Nhat Hanh focuses on the courage to be honest with yourself and others.

❦ DEVORAH MAJOR, *Newscast*

death is dropped
onto my plate each evening, pressed
between big game scores
and electronic weather report.

> abbreviated newsprint
> punctuated with glossy photos
> cut away to open graves.

large spiny mouthfuls
of my dead relatives
are stuffed between
my clenched teeth
and tight jaw.

tears run
from the corners
of my eyes.

they ask me
to eat my dead.
swallow them whole

> neat
> like a shot
> of two hundred year old bourbon
> distending my belly
> leaving no waste.

they ask me
to consume my dead
and maintain my peace
my place
each evening

the days counting
is brought out
skimmed across globe

        platters of dried and delicate babies
        mixed with brittle forgotten elders
        next to tureens of impaled mothers.
        those who only needed to eat
        those who rotted from man made diseases
        those who imploded because their bodies
        simply refused to fight anymore.

a roster of those killed or wounded in battle
civilization's unavoidable causalities.
a portion of suffering piled high
presented with a flourish
cacophony of applause

        now
        open wide
        chew

cut to commercial

but, i have been taught
about eating the dead.
that it is not to be done,
unless, it is the heart
for valor, the muscles
for strength, the soul
for forbearance, the mind
for history.

eating their expendable
their unneeded
their discarded,
the bones cracking beneath teeth

scratching holes into lungs,
this modern day cannibalism
is always painful.

so, i have begun
to feed on life.
watch the african honey bees
who move and nest
and move and nest
migrating across continents
gathering, building and stinging
all who dare to exploit
the sweetness of their honey.
i come, you see
from people
who have lived for eons
making peace with deadly bees
while harvesting their lush syrups.

yes, i have begun
to feed on life,
which tastes bitter
at times, and sticky
like melon juice
or sharp like tree bark.
feeding on life
studying bees
learning to sting
fashioning a stronger hive.

❦ YUKIO MISHIMA, *Confessions of a Mask*

The last year of the war came and I reached the age of twenty. Early in the year all the students at my university were sent to work at the N airplane factory, near the city of M. Eighty percent of the students became factory hands, while the frail students, who formed the remaining twenty percent, were given some sort of clerical jobs. I fell into the latter category. And yet at the time of my physical examination the year before, I had received the classification of 2(b). Having thus been declared eligible for military service, I had the constant worry that my summons would come tomorrow, if not today.

The airplane factory, located in a desolate area seething with dust, was so huge that it took thirty minutes simply to walk across it from one end to the other, and it hummed with the labor of several thousand workers. I was one of them, bearing the designation of Temporary Employee 953, with Identification No. 4409.

This great factory operated upon a mysterious system of production costs: taking no account of the economic dictum that capital investment should produce a return, it was dedicated to a monstrous nothingness. No wonder then that each morning the workers had to recite a mystic oath. I have never seen such a strange factory. In it all the techniques of modern science and management, together with the exact and rational thinking of many superior brains, were dedicated to a single end—Death. Producing the Zero-model combat plane used by the suicide squadrons, this great factory resembled a secret cult that operated thunderously—groaning, shrieking, roaring. I did not see how such a colossal organization could exist without some religious grandiloquence. And it did in fact possess religious grandeur, even to the way the priestly directors fattened their own stomachs.

From time to time the sirens of the air-raid signals would announce the hour for this perverted religion to celebrate its black mass.

Then the office would begin to stir. There was no radio in the room, so we had no way of knowing what was happening. Someone, speaking in a broad country accent, would say: "Wonder what's up?" About this time a young girl from the reception desk in the superintendent's office would come with some such report as: "Several formations of enemy planes sighted." Before long the strident voices of loud-speakers would order the girl students and the grade-school children to take shelter. Persons in charge of rescue work would walk about distributing red tags bearing the legend "Bleeding stopped: hour___ minute___." In case someone was wounded, one of these tags was to be filled in and hung about his neck, showing the time at which a tourniquet had been applied. About ten minutes after the sirens had sounded the loud-speakers would announce: "All employees take shelter."

Grasping files of important papers in their arms, the office workers would hurry to deposit them in the underground vault where essential records were stored. Then they would rush outdoors and join the swarm of laborers running across the square, all wearing air-raid helmets or padded hoods. The crowd would be streaming toward the main gate.

Outside the gate there was a desolate, bare, yellow field. Some seven or eight hundred meters beyond it, numerous shelters had been excavated in a pine grove on a gentle slope. Heading for these shelters, two separate streams of the silent, impatient, blind mob would rush through the dust—rushing toward what at any rate was not Death, no matter if it was only a small cave of easily collapsible red earth, at any rate it was not Death.

I went home on my occasional of three days, and there one night at eleven o'clock I received my draft notice. It was a telegram ordering me to report to a certain unit on February the fifteenth.

At my father's suggestion, I had taken my physical examination, not at Tokyo, but at the headquarters of the regiment located near the place where my family maintained its legal residence, in H Prefecture of the Osaka-Kyoto region. My father's theory was that my weak physique would attract more attention in a rural area than in the city, where such weakness was no rarity, and that as a result I would probably not be drafted. As a matter of fact, I had provided the examining officials with cause for an outbreak of laughter when I could not lift—not even as far as my chest—the bale of rice that the farm boys were easily lifting above their heads ten times. And still, in the end I had been classified 2(b).

So now I was summoned—to join a rough rural unit. My mother

wept sorrowfully, and even my father seemed no little dejected. As for me, hero though I fancied myself, the sight of the summons aroused no enthusiasm in me; but on the other hand, there was my hope of dying an easy death. All in all, I had the feeling that everything was as it should be.

A cold that I had caught at the factory became much worse as I was going on an inter-island steamer to join my unit. By the time I reached the home of close family friends in the village of our legal residence— we had not owned a single bit of land there since my grandfather's bankruptcy—I had such a violent fever that I was unable to stand up. Thanks, however, to the careful nursing I received in that house and especially to the efficacy of the vast quantity of febrifuge I took, I was finally able to make my way through the barracks gate, amidst a spirited send-off given me by the family friends.

My fever, which had only been checked by the medicines, now returned. During the physical examination that preceded final enlist- ment I had to stand around waiting stark naked, like a wild beast, and I sneezed constantly. The stripling of an army doctor who examined me mistook the wheezing of my bronchial tubes for a chest rattle, and then my haphazard answers concerning my medical history further con- firmed him in his error. Hence I was given a blood test, the results of which, influenced by the high fever of my cold, led to a mistaken diag- nosis of incipient tuberculosis. I was ordered home the same day as unfit for service.

Once I had put the barracks gate behind me, I broke into a run down the bleak and wintry slope that descended to the village. Just as at the airplane factory, my legs carried me running toward something that in any case was not Death—whatever it was, it was not Death. . . .

❧ THICH NHAT HANH, *Being Peace*

I wrote a poem over 30 years ago, when I was 27 or 28, about a brother who suffered so much he had to drop out of society and go to a meditation center. Since the Buddhist Temple is a place of compassion, they welcomed him. When someone is suffering so much, when he or she comes to a meditation center, the first thing is to give some kind of comfort. The people in the Temple were compassionate enough to let him come and have a place to cry. How long, how many days, how many years did he need to cry? We don't know. But finally he took up refuge in the meditation center and did not want to go back to society. He had had enough of it. He thought that he had found some peace, but one day I myself came and burned his meditation center, which was only a small hut: his last shelter! In his understanding, he had nothing else outside of that small cottage. He had nowhere to go because society was not his. He thought he had come to seek his own emancipation, but, in the light of Buddhism, there is no such thing as individual self. As we know, when you go into a Buddhist center, you bring with you all the scars, all the wounds from society, and you bring the whole society as well. In this poem, I am the young man, and I am also the person who came and burned down the cottage.

I shall say that I want it all.
If you ask me how much I want,
I shall tell you that I want it all.
You and I and everyone are flowing this
    morning
Into the marvelous stream of oneness.
Small pieces of imagination as we are,
We have come a long way to find ourselves,
And for ourselves in the dark,
The illusion of emancipation.

This morning my brother is back from his
    long adventure.
He kneels before the altar and his eyes are
    filled with tears.
His soul is looking for a shore to put an
    anchor,
My own image of long ago.
Let him kneel there and weep,

Let him cry his heart out.
Let him have his refuge for a thousand years.
Enough to dry all his tears.

Because one of these nights I shall come.
I have to come and set fire to this small
    cottage of his on a hill.
His last shelter.
My fire will destroy,
Destroy everything.
Taking away from him the only life raft he
    has, after a shipwreck.
In the utmost anguish of his soul,
The shell will break.
The light of the burning hut will witness,
    gloriously, his deliverance.
I will wait for him beside the burning cottage,
Tears will run down my cheeks.
I shall be there to contemplate his new
    existence,
And hold his hands in mine,
And ask him how much he would want.
He will smile at me and say that he wants it
    all.
Just as I did.

To me, a meditation center is where you get back to yourself, you get a clearer understanding of reality, you get more strength in understanding and love, and you prepare for your re-entry into society. If it is not like that, it is not a real meditation center. As we develop real understanding, we can re-enter society and make a real contribution.

Maurice Druon tells of the courage needed to defy other people's plans for you. In Tartuffe, *Molière recalls the threats of demagogues that must be resisted if decent and honorable living is to be achieved.*

❦ Maurice Druon, *Tistou of the Green Fingers*

In which the Author

has some very important things
to say
about the name of TISTOU

TISTOU

is a very odd name indeed and you won't find it in any Dictionary of Proper Names. There isn't even a Saint Tistou.

Nevertheless, there was a little boy whom everyone called Tistou . . . And this needs some explanation.

One day, very soon after he was born, when he was still only about the size of a bread roll in a baker's basket, his godmother, wearing a long-sleeved dress, and his godfather, wearing a black hat, took the little boy to the church and told the priest that he was to be called Jean-Baptiste. Like most babies who find themselves in this particular situation, the little boy screamed his protests and became quite red in the face with dismay. But, like all grown-ups, who never understand babies' protests and have a habit of clinging to their ready-made ideas, his godparents merely insisted that the child was to be called Jean-Baptiste.

Then the godmother in her long sleeves and the godfather in his black hat took him back to his cradle. But a very strange thing happened. The grown-ups suddenly discovered that they were quite unable to utter the names they had given him, and they found themselves calling him Tistou.

But this is not really so very strange. How many little boys and girls are baptized Anatole, Susan, Caroline or William and are never called anything else but Tolo, Susie, Caro or Billy?

This simply goes to show that ready-made ideas are badly made ideas, and that grown-ups don't really know what our names are, any more than they know, although they pretend they do, where we come from, why we are in the world, or what we are here to do in it.

This is a very important thought and requires further explanation.

If we have been put into the world merely to become a grown-up, our heads, as they grow bigger, very easily absorb ready-made ideas. And these ideas, which have been made for a long time, are to be found in books. So if we read, or listen attentively to people who have read a lot, we can very soon become a grown-up like all the others.

It is also true that there are many ready-made ideas about almost everything, and this is very convenient because it means we can change our ideas quite often.

But if we have been sent into the world on a special mission, if we have been charged with the accomplishment of some individual task, things are not quite so easy. The ready-made ideas, which other people find so useful, simply refuse to stay in our heads; they go in at one ear and come out at the other, fall on the floor and get broken.

Thus we are liable to surprise our parents very much indeed, as well as all the other grown-ups who cling with such determination to their ready-made ideas!

And this was precisely the case of the little boy who had been called Tistou without anyone having asked his permission.

❦ JEAN BAPTISTE MOLIÈRE, *Tartuffe*

ORGON: Ah, if, that day we met, you'd been on hand,
You'd feel as I do now—you'd understand.
Each day he came to church, meek as you please,
And, right across from me, fell on his knees;
He caught the eye of every person there,
Such warmth and zeal he put into his prayer;
His transports were extreme, his sighs profound;
Each moment he would stoop and kiss the ground;
And when I left, he always went before
To offer me holy water at the door.
His man, who imitates his every deed,
Informed me of his background and his need.
I gave him gifts; but in his modest way,
He'd give me back a part and humbly say:
"That is too much, that's twice too much for me;

I am not worthy of your sympathy";
And then when I refused to compromise,
He'd give half to the poor, before my eyes.
At last Heaven prompted me to take him in;
And ever since, how splendid things have been!
I see him censure everything, and take
Great interest in my wife, all for my sake;
He warns me when men ogle her on the sly,
And acts far jealouser of her than I.
Upon himself he lays his hardest sentence:
A trifle, like a sin, demands repentance;
The merest nothing fills him with dismay.
He came and blamed himself the other day
Because while praying he had caught a flea
And killed the creature much too angrily.

CLEANTE: Good Lord! Brother, you're mad, I do believe.
Are you sure you're not laughing up your sleeve?
Why, this is nonsense! Or do you insist . . . ?

ORGON: Brother, you're talking like an atheist;
Your soul's been spattered with freethinking grime.
I've warned you more than once, an ugly time
Awaits you if you will not change your mind.

CLEANTE: These are the arguments of all your kind:
Since they can't see, they think that no one ought;
Whoever does, is tainted with free thought;
Whoever balks at pious affectation
Fails to hold piety in veneration.
Come now, for all your talk, I'm not afraid;
Heaven sees my heart, and I know what I've said;
Your simulators don't disarm my wits.
Like courage, piety has its hypocrites.
Just as we see, where honor beckons most,
The truly brave are not the ones who boast;
The truly pious people, even so,

Are not the ones who make the biggest show.
What? Do you really see no difference
Between devoutness and devout pretense?
Do you want to give them both the selfsame place,
Honor the mask just as you do the face,
Equate artifice with sincerity,
And take similitude for verity?
Isn't there any difference for you
Between phantoms and men, false coins and true?
Most men are strangely made; they always stray
Out of the natural and proper way;
Rejecting reason's bounds as limitations,
They range about amid their aberrations;
Even the noblest things they often mar
By forcing them and pushing them too far.
I mention this because it's apropos.

ORGON: Oh yes, you are a learned sage, I know;
The sapience of the world within you lies;
You alone are enlightened, truly wise,
An oracle, a Cato through and through;
All other men are fools compared to you.

CLEANTE: I don't possess the wisdom of the ages,
And I am not a learned sage of sages;
My only knowledge and my only art
Is this: to tell the true and false apart.
And, as there are no heroes I revere
More than those whose devoutness is sincere,
And nothing worthier of veneration
Than genuine religious dedication,
So, nothing seems more odious to me
Than the disguise of specious piety,
Than those breast-beaters in the public square
Whose sacrilegious and deceitful air
Turns to its own advantage, with a sneer,

All that men hold most holy and most dear;
Men whom the lust for gain has so possessed
That they turn piety to interest,
And try to purchase honor and high places
By simulated zeal and false grimaces,
Those men, I say, whose vehement devotion
By way of Heaven seeks temporal promotion,
Who, while they pray, still manage to extort,
And preach of solitude—but stay at court,
Who know how to make zeal and vices mix;
Vengeful, quick-tempered, faithless, full of tricks;
And, when they want to ruin someone, make
It seem they do it all for Heaven's sake;
Most dangerous in that their bitter hate
Makes use of weapons that we venerate,
And that their zeal, which merits our applause,
Seeks to destroy us in a holy cause.
Though far too many fakers meet our eyes,
True piety's not hard to recognize.
Even today, brother, there may be found
Admirable examples all around:
Consider Ariston and Periandre,
Oronte, Alcidas, Polydore, Clitandre:
No one contests their claim to piety,
Yet they do not parade their sanctity;
Their modest zeal is never out of season,
But human and accessible to reason.
They do not lay about in all directions;
They find excessive pride in such corrections,
And leave to others all the lofty speech,
While all they do is practice what they preach.
They do not censure every bagatelle,
But judge with charity and wish men well.
They don't promote intrigue or petty strife,
But mainly seek to lead a virtuous life;

Rather than rage against a reprobate,
They think the sin alone deserves their hate,
And don't espouse, with such intensity,
The cause of Heaven beyond Heaven's own decree.
These are the men that win my admiration,
These are the models for our emulation.
You know your man is not at all like these,
And you may vaunt his fervor all you please;
I think appearances lead you astray.

10

What We're Fighting for in the End Is Each Other

RESPONSIBILITY

Responsibility is about choosing. In this sense, responsibility is a corollary of freedom. Freedom succeeds as a social principle only when citizens accept responsibility for the consequences of their actions. Otherwise self-interest rules, and freedom is reduced to license.

Mohandas Gandhi recognized the disasters that follow when we deny our responsibility and proceed in pursuit of self-interest. He summarized our responsibilities for each other in his Seven Social Sins by summarizing how social evil can run rampant:

Politics without principle
Wealth without work
Commerce without morality
Pleasure without conscience
Education without character
Science without humanity
Worship without sacrifice

For Gandhi, our responsibility to each other meant disciplining oneself to live responsibly according to this code and setting a good example for others in doing so.

In the sections that follow, we think of responsibility in three ways—responsibility for self (self-discipline), for others (generosity), and for all living beings on the planet (stewardship). Responsibility pulls us toward industrious independence, but toward each other, too—to a recognition that we are all interdependent and worthy no matter what we own and who we are. This is not always easy or comfortable, but a responsible person will go easy on oneself, adopting a generous and patient attitude.

Acting unselfishly and kindly toward others begins with taking responsibility for your impact on them. Acting unselfishly enlarges the spaces we share and makes you more comfortable to be with.

In *The Kiss of the Spider Woman*, Manuel Puig's characters discuss the nature of manhood. The two characters, one homosexual and one heterosexual, argue about what a man is. In exasperation, the gay character Molina asks, "So what finally is a man to you?" and Valentin, catching his own prejudice in operation and regretting it, replies, "A man is someone who never humiliates anybody."

That notion is at the heart of our responsibility to each other. And it begins early in life—with how we and our parents are together. Responsible parents try never to resort to blackmail: threatening to withdraw your love. That's how we erode the safety that our children find in our love for them.

Being responsibly kind requires bridging what the Israeli writer Rieha Shavit calls "the yawning gap between unlimited, sacrosanct importance which we attribute to our own lives, and the very limited sacred character we attribute to the lives of others."

A powerful reminder of the beauty and significance of the generous spirit was given us long ago by Saint Basil, Archbishop of Caesarea, in the fourth century:

> The bread that you store up belongs to the hungry; the cloak that lies in your chest belongs to the naked; the gold that you have hidden in the ground belongs to the poor.

But our responsibility is not only with "the wretched of the earth," but with the earth itself—and "all the creation thereof."

We are the stewards of that creation, and unlike Noah collecting animals only two-by-two, we need to be guided by an image of an ark like Noah's, big enough for all of us: workers, artists, singers, priests, mothers, fathers, children, dreamers—all of us, and all the parts of us.

Gary Snyder puts it this way:

> In taking responsibility for our own costs; keeping constant with the sources of the energy that flows into your own life (namely dirt, water, flesh).

David Abram, in his *Spell of the Sensuous*, pushes further. He extends the idea of "perceptual reciprocity" between people to nature:

> To listen to the forest is also, primordially, to feel oneself listened to by the forest, just as to gaze at the surrounding forest is to feel oneself exposed and visible, to feel oneself watched by the forest.

Selections

Michael Shaara's Colonel is an exemplar of responsibility. In the story of the prodigal son, we see responsibility as synonymous with generosity and gratitude. Robert Bolt's More and Norfolk struggle with their mutual and competing sense of responsibility to each other.

❧ MICHAEL SHAARA, *Killer Angels*

Glazier Estabrook was standing guard, leaning patiently on his rifle. He was a thick little man of about forty. Except for Kilrain he was the oldest man in the Regiment, the strongest man Chamberlain had ever seen. He waved happily as Chamberlain came up but went on leaning on the rifle. He pointed at one of the prisoners.

"Hey, Colonel, you know who this is? This here is Dan Burns from Orono. I know his daddy. Daddy's a preacher. You really ought to hear him. Best damn cusser I ever heard. Knows more fine swear words than any man in Maine, I bet. Hee."

Chamberlain smiled. But the Burns boy was looking at him with no expression. Chamberlain said, "You fellas gather round."

He stood in the shade, waited while they closed in silently, watchfully around him. In the background the tents were coming down, the wagons were hitching, but some of the men of the Regiment had come out to watch and listen. Some of the men here were still chewing. But they were quiet, attentive.

Chamberlain waited a moment longer. Now it was quiet in the grove and the clink of the wagons was sharp in the distance. Chamberlain said, "I've been talking with Bucklin. He's told me your problem."

Some of the men grumbled. Chamberlain heard no words clearly. He went on speaking softly so that they would have to quiet to hear him.

"I don't know what I can do about it. I'll do what I can. I'll look into it as soon as possible. But there's nothing I can do today. We're moving out in a few minutes and we'll be marching all day and we may be in a big fight before nightfall. But as soon as I can, I'll do what I can."

They were silent, watching him. Chamberlain began to relax. He had made many speeches and he had a gift for it. He did not know what it was, but when he spoke most men stopped to listen. Fanny said it was something in his voice. He hoped it was there now.

"I've been ordered to take you men with me. I've been told that if you don't come I can shoot you. Well, you know I won't do that. Not Maine men. I won't shoot any man who doesn't want this fight. Maybe someone else will, but I won't. So that's that."

He paused again. There was nothing on their faces to lead him.

"Here's the situation. I've been ordered to take you along, and that's what I'm going to do. Under guard if necessary. But you can have your rifles if you want them. The whole Reb army is up the road a ways waiting for us and this is no time for an argument like this. I tell you this: we sure can use you. We're down below half strength and we need you, no doubt of that. But whether you fight or not is up to you. Whether you come along, well, you're coming."

Tom had come up with Chamberlain's horse. Over the heads of the prisoners Chamberlain could see the Regiment falling into line out in the flaming road. He took a deep breath.

"Well, I don't want to preach to you. You know who we are and what we're doing here. But if you're going to fight alongside us there's a few things I want you to know."

He bowed his head, not looking at eyes. He folded his hands together.

"This Regiment was formed last fall, back in Maine. There were a thousand of us then. There's not three hundred of us now." He glanced up briefly. "But what is left is choice. "

He was embarrassed. He spoke very slowly, staring at the ground.

"Some of us volunteered to fight for Union. Some came in mainly because we were bored at home and this looked like it might be fun. Some came because we were ashamed not to. Many of us came . . . because it was the right thing to do. All of us have seen men die. Most of us never saw a black man back home. We think on that, too. But freedom . . . is not just a word."

He looked up into the sky, over silent faces.

"This is a different kind of army. If you look at history you'll see men fight for pay, or women, or some other kind of loot. They fight for land, or because a king makes them, or just because they like killing. But we're here for something new. I don't . . . this hasn't happened much in the history of the world. We're an army going out to set other men free."

He bent down, scratched the black dirt into his fingers. He was beginning to warm to it; the words were beginning to flow. No one in front of him was moving. He said, "This is free ground. All the way from here to the Pacific Ocean. No man has to bow. No man born to royalty. Here we judge you by what *you* do, not by what your father was. Here you can be *something*. Here's a place to build a home. It isn't the land—there's always more land. It's the idea that we all have value, you and me, we're worth something more than the dirt. I never saw dirt I'd die for, but I'm not asking you to come join us and fight for dirt. What we're all fighting for, in the end, is each other."

Once he started talking he broke right through the embarrassment and there was suddenly no longer a barrier there. The words came out of him in a clear river, and he felt himself silent and suspended in the grove listening to himself speak, carried outside himself and looking back down on the silent faces and himself speaking, and he felt the power in him, the power of his cause. For an instant he could see black castles in the air; he could create centuries of screaming, eons of torture. Then he was back in sunlit Pennsylvania. The bugles were blowing and he was done.

He had nothing else to say. No one moved. He felt the embarrassment return. He was suddenly enormously tired. The faces were staring up at him like white stones. Some heads were down. He said, "Didn't mean to preach. Sorry. But I thought . . . you should know who we are." He had forgotten how tiring it was just to speak. "Well, this is still the army, but you're as free as I can make you. Go ahead and talk for a while. If you want your rifles for this fight you'll have them back and nothing else will be said. If you won't join us you'll come along under guard. When this is over I'll do what I can to see that you get fair treatment. Now we have to move out." He stopped, looked at them. The faces showed nothing. He said slowly, "I think if we lose this fight the war will be over. So if you choose to come with us I'll be personally grateful. Well. We have to move out."

❧ STEPHEN MITCHELL, *The Prodigal Son*

Sometimes, after a day among the swine, he would be afraid to lie down in his wretched hut. Actually, the swine weren't bad company. They were intelligent animals, not any greedier than decent men he had known; he came to enjoy feeding them and hosing them down. They would close their eyes under the spray, grunt contentedly as the water washed away their grime and left them, if not whiter than snow, at least tolerably clean, then prance around in giddy pleasure, kicking up their heels.

The worst company was himself.

Sometimes he would be annoyed to a frenzy by a buzzing fly in a corner of the hut. He would stalk it from resting-place to resting-place; then, teeth clenched, he would dispatch it with a single stroke of his palm. If it had been merely stunned, he would impale it and set it on fire. He could feel his heart assuaged for an instant as the translucent wings went up in a flash and left, at the end of the pin, a tiny charred ball.

Many years later, after his own pain had been transformed in a different kind of fire, he made a vow never again to kill a fly. Whenever one of them trespassed into his house, he would trap it in a jar he kept under the sink (sometimes, with a hyperactive fly, this could take five or ten minutes). Then he would release it through a window or take it outside to freedom. It wasn't out of guilt, or out of compassion, that he made this vow, since he saw quite clearly that he was responsible for everything in his life. But simply as a reminder: to acknowledge that once upon a time he had been stopped at the crossroads of the horrible and the sacred.

❦ ROBERT BOLT, *A Man for All Seasons*

MORE: What about them?

NORFOLK: Goddammit, you're dangerous to know!

MORE: Then don't know me.

NORFOLK: Oh, that's immutable, is it? The one fixed point in a world of changing friendships is that Thomas More will not give in!

MORE: *(Urgent to explain)* To me it *has* to be, for that's myself! Affection goes as deep in me as you think, but only God is love right through, Howard; and *that's* my *self.*

NORFOLK: And who are you? Goddammit, man, it's disproportionate! *We're* supposed to be the arrogant ones, the proud, splenetic ones—and we've all given in! Why must you stand out? *(Quietly and quickly)* You'll break my heart.

MORE: *(Moved)* Well do it now, Howard: part, as friends, and meet as strangers. *(He attempts to take* NORFOLK's *hand)*

NORFOLK: *(Throwing it off)* Daft, Thomas! Why d'you want to take your friendship from me? For friendship's sake! You say we'll meet as strangers and every word you've said confirms our friendship!

MORE: *(Takes a last affectionate look at him)* Oh, that can be remedied. *(Walks away, turns; in a tone of deliberate insult)* Norfolk, you're a fool.

NORFOLK: *(Starts; then smiles and folds his arms)* *You* can't place a quarrel; you haven't the style.

MORE: Hear me out. You and your class have "given in"—as you rightly call it—because the religion of this country means nothing to you one way or the other.

NORFOLK: Well, that's a foolish saying for a start; the nobility of England has always been—

MORE: The nobility of England, my lord, would have snored through the Sermon on the Mount. But you'll labor like Thomas Aquinas over a rat-dog's pedigree. Now what's the name of those distorted creatures you're all breeding at the moment?

NORFOLK: *(Steadily, but roused towards anger by* MORE's *tone)* An artificial quarrel's not a quarrel.

MORE: Don't deceive yourself, my lord, we've had a quarrel since the day we met, our friendship was but sloth.

NORFOLK: You can be cruel when you've a mind to be; but I've always known that.

MORE: What's the name of those dogs? Marsh mastiffs? Bog beagles?

NORFOLK: Water spaniels!

MORE: And what would you do with a water spaniel that was afraid of water? You'd hang it! Well, as a spaniel is to water, so is a man to his own self. I will not give in because I oppose it—*I* do—not my

pride, not my spleen, nor any other of my appetites but *I* do—*I!*
(MORE *goes up to him and feels him up and down like an animal.*
MARGARET's *voice is heard, well off, calling her father.* MORE's
attention is irresistibly caught by this; but he turns back determinedly to
NORFOLK) Is there no single sinew in the midst of this that serves
no appetite of Norfolk's but is just Norfolk? There is! Give *that*
some exercise, my lord!

Nadine Stair poses the question of personal responsibility—namely, responsibility for how we each face our own options and make our choices.

❦ NADINE STAIR, *If I Had My Life to Live Over*

I'd dare to make more mistakes next time. I'd relax, I would limber
up. I would be sillier than I have been this trip. I would take fewer things
seriously. I would take more chances. I would climb more mountains and
swim more rivers. I would eat more ice cream and less beans. I would perhaps have more actual troubles, but I'd have fewer imaginary ones.

You see, I'm one of those people who live sensibly and sanely hour
after hour, day after day. Oh, I've had my moments, and if I had it to do
over again, I'd have more of them. In fact, I'd try to have nothing else.
Just moments, one after another, instead of living so many years ahead
of each day. I've been one of those persons who never goes anywhere
without a thermometer, a hot water bottle, a raincoat and a parachute.
If I had to do it again, I would travel lighter than I have.

If I had my life to live over, I would start barefoot earlier in the
spring and stay that way later in the fall. I would go to more dances. I
would ride more merry-go-rounds. I would pick more daisies.

In Thomas Hardy's Jude the Obscure, *we find people struggling to take
responsibility for their feelings and for their relationships. In* Bartleby the
Scrivener, *Herman Melville brings us face-to-face with both the duty and the limits of responsibility. Bertolt Brecht reminds us that responsibility might at times
mean leaving things unfinished, leaving relationships open.*

❧ THOMAS HARDY, *Jude the Obscure*

After tea that evening Phillotson sat balancing the school registers. She remained in an unusually silent, tense, and restless condition, and at last, saying she was tired, went to bed early. When Phillotson arrived upstairs, weary with the drudgery of the attendance numbers, it was a quarter to twelve o'clock. Entering their chamber, which by day commanded a view of some thirty or forty miles over the Vale of Blackmoor, and even into Outer Wessex, he went to the window, and, pressing his face against the pane, gazed with hard breathing fixity into the mysterious darkness which now covered the far-reaching scene. He was musing. "I think," he said at last, without turning his head, "that I must get the Committee to change the school-stationer. All the copy-books are sent wrong this time."

There was no reply. Thinking Sue was dozing he went on:

"And there must be a rearrangement of that ventilator in the class-room. The wind blows down upon my head unmercifully, and gives me the earache."

As the silence seemed more absolute than ordinarily he turned around. The heavy, gloomy oak wainscot which extended over the walls upstairs and down in the dilapidated "Old-Grove Place," and the massive chimney-piece reaching to the ceiling, stood in odd contrast to the new and shining brass bedstead, and the new suite of birch furniture that he had bought for her, the two styles seeming to nod to each other across three centuries upon the shaking floor.

"Soo!" he said (this being the way in which he pronounced her name).

She was not in the bed, though she had apparently been there—the clothes on her side being flung back. Thinking she might have forgotten some kitchen detail and gone downstairs for a moment to see to it, he pulled off his coat and idled quietly enough for a few minutes, when, finding she did not come he went out upon the landing, candle in hand, and said again "Soo!"

"Yes!" came back to him in her voice, from the distant kitchen quarter.

"What are you doing down there at midnight—tiring yourself out for nothing!"

"I am not sleepy; I am reading; and there is a larger fire here."

He went to bed. Some time in the night he awoke. She was not there, even now. Lighting a candle he hastily stepped out upon the landing, and again called her name.

She answered "Yes!" as before; but the tones were small and confined, and whence they came he could not at first understand. Under the staircase was a large clothes-closet, without a window; they seemed to come from it. The door was shut, but there was no lock or other fastening. Phillotson, alarmed, went towards it, wondering if she had suddenly become deranged.

"What are you doing in there?" he asked.

"Not to disturb you I came here, as it was so late."

"But there's no bed, is there? And no ventilation! Why, you'll be suffocated if you stay all night!"

"O no, I think not. Don't trouble about me."

"But—" Phillotson seized the knob and pulled at the door. She had fastened it inside with a piece of string, which broke at his pull. There being no bedstead she had flung down some rugs and made a little nest for herself in the very cramped quarters the closet afforded.

When he looked in upon her she sprang out of her lair, great eyed and trembling.

"You ought not to have pulled open the door!" she cried excitedly. "It is not becoming in you! O, will you go away; please will you!"

She looked so pitiful and pleading in her white night-gown against the shadowy lumber-hole that he was quite worried. She continued to beseech him not to disturb her.

He said: "I've been kind to you, and given you every liberty; and it is monstrous that you should feel in this way!"

"Yes," said she, weeping. "I know that! It is wrong and wicked of me, I suppose! I am very sorry. But it is not I altogether that am to blame!"

"Who is then? Am I?"

"No—I don't know! The universe, I suppose—things in general, because they are so horrid and cruel!"

"Well, it is no use talking like that. Making a man's house so unseemly at this time o' night! Eliza will hear, if we don't mind." (He meant the servant.) "Just think if either of the parsons in this town was to see us now! I hate such eccentricities, Sue. There's no order or regularity in your sentiments! . . . But I won't intrude on you further; only I would advise you not to shut the door too tight, or I shall find you stifled to-morrow."

On rising the next morning he immediately looked into the closet, but Sue had already gone downstairs. There was a little nest where she had lain, and spiders' webs hung overhead. "What must a woman's aversion be when it is stronger than her fear of spiders!" he said bitterly.

He found her sitting at the breakfast-table, and the meal began almost in silence, the burghers walking past upon the pavement—or rather roadway, pavements being scarce here—which was two or three feet above the level of the parlour floor. They nodded down to the happy couple their morning greetings, as they went on.

"Richard," she said all at once; "would you mind my living away from you?"

"Away from me? Why, that's what you were doing when I married you. What then was the meaning of marrying at all?"

"You wouldn't like me any the better for telling you."

"I don't object to know."

"Because I thought I could do nothing else. You had got my promise a long time before that, remember. Then, as time went on, I regretted I had promised you, and was trying to see an honourable way to break it off. But as I couldn't I became rather reckless and careless about the conventions. Then you know what scandals were spread, and how I was tuned out of the Training School you had taken such time and trouble to prepare me for and get me into; and this frightened me, and it seemed then that the one thing I could do would be to let the engagement stand. Of course I, of all people, ought not to have cared what was said, for it was just what I fancied I never did care for. But I was a coward—as so many women are—and my theoretic unconventionality broke down. If that had not entered into the case it would have been better to have hurt your feelings once for all then, than to marry you and hurt them all my life after. . . . And you were so generous in never giving credit for a moment to the rumour."

"I am bound in honesty to tell you that I weighed its probability, and inquired of your cousin about it."

"Ah!" she said with pained surprise.

"I didn't doubt you."

"But you inquired!"

"I took his word."

Her eyes had filled. "*He* wouldn't have inquired!" she said. "But you haven't answered me. Will you let me go away? I know how irregular it is of me to ask it—"

"It is irregular."

"But I do ask it! Domestic laws should be made according to temperaments, which should be classified. If people are at all peculiar in character they have to suffer from the very rules that produce comfort in others! . . . Will you let me?"

"But we married—"

"What is the use of thinking of laws and ordinances," she burst out, "if they make you miserable when you know you are committing no sin?"

"But you are committing a sin in not liking me."

"I *do* like you! But I didn't reflect it would be—that it would be so much more than that. . . . For a man and woman to live on intimate terms when one feels as I do is adultery, in any circumstances, however legal. There—I've said it! . . . Will you let me, Richard?"

"You distress me, Susanna, by such importunity!"

"Why can't we agree to free each other? We made the compact, and surely we can cancel it—not legally, of course; but we can morally, especially as no new interests, in the shape of children, have arisen to be looked after. Then we might be friends, and meet without pain to either. O Richard, be my friend and have pity! We shall both be dead in a few years, and then what will it matter to anybody that you relieved me from constraint for a little while? I daresay you think me eccentric, or super-sensitive, or something absurd. Well—why should I suffer for what I was born to be, if it doesn't hurt other people?"

"But it does—it hurts *me*! And you vowed to love me."

"Yes—that's it! I am in the wrong. I always am! It is as culpable to bind yourself to love always as to believe a creed always, and as silly as to vow always to like a particular food or drink!"

"And do you mean, by living away from me, living by yourself?"

"Well, if you insisted, yes. But I meant living with Jude."

"As his wife?"

"As I choose."

Phillotson writhed.

Sue continued: "She, or he, 'who lets the world, or his own portion of it, choose his plan of life for him, has no need of any other faculty than the ape-like one of imitation.' J. S. Mill's words, those are. I have been reading it up. Why can't you act upon them? I wish to, always."

"What do I care about J. S. Mill!" moaned he. "I only want to lead a quiet life! Do you mind my saying that I have guessed what never once occurred to me before our marriage—that you were in love, and are in love, with Jude Fawley!"

"You may go on guessing that I am, since you have begun. But do you suppose that if I had been I should have asked you to let me go and live with him?"

The ringing of the school bell saved Phillotson from the necessity of replying at present to what apparently did not strike him as being such a convincing *argumentum ad verecundiam* as she, in her loss of courage at the last moment, meant it to appear. She was beginning to be so puzzling and unstateable that he was ready to throw in with her other little peculiarities the extremest request which a wife could make.

They proceeded to the schools that morning as usual, Sue entering the class-room, where he could see the back of her head through the glass partition whenever he turned his eyes that way. As he went on giving and hearing lessons his forehead and eyebrows twitched from concentrated agitation of thought; till at length he tore a scrap from a sheet of scribbling paper and wrote:

"Your request prevents my attending to work at all. I don't know what I am doing! Was it seriously made?"

He folded the piece of paper very small, and gave it to a little boy to take to Sue. The child toddled off into the class-room. Phillotson saw his wife turn and take the note, and the bend of her pretty head as she read it, her lips slightly crisped, to prevent undue expression under fire of so many young eyes. He could not see her hands, but she changed her position, and soon the child returned, bringing nothing in reply. In a few minutes, however, one of Sue's class appeared, with a little note similar to his own. These words only were pencilled therein:

"I am sincerely sorry to say that it was seriously made."

Phillotson looked more disturbed than before, and the meeting-place of his brows twitched again. In ten minutes he called up the child he had just sent to her, and dispatched another missive:

"God knows I don't want to thwart you in any reasonable way. My whole thought is to make you comfortable and happy. But I cannot agree to such a preposterous notion as your going to live with your lover. You would lose everybody's respect and regard; and so should I!"

After an interval a similar part was enacted in the class-room, and an answer came:

"I know you mean my good. But I don't want to be respectable! To produce 'Human development in its richest diversity' (to quote your Humboldt) is to my mind far above respectability. No doubt my tastes are low—in your view—hopelessly low! If you won't let me go to him, will you grant me this one request—allow me to live in your house in a separate way?"

To this he returned no answer.
She wrote again:

"I know what you think. But cannot you have pity on me? I beg you to; I implore you to be merciful! I would not ask if I were not almost compelled by what I can't bear! No poor woman has ever wished more than I that Eve had not fallen, so that (as the primitive Christians believed) some harmless mode of vegetation might have peopled Paradise. But I won't trifle! Be kind to me—even though I have not been kind to you! I will go away, go abroad, anywhere, and never trouble you."

Nearly an hour passed, and then he returned an answer:

"I do not wish to pain you. How well you *know* I don't! Give me a little time. I am disposed to agree to your last request."

One line from her:

"Thank you from my heart, Richard. I do not deserve your kindness."

All day Phillotson bent a dazed regard upon her through the glazed partition; and he felt as lonely as when he had not known her.

But he was as good as his word, and consented to her living apart in the house. At first, when they met at meals, she had seemed more composed under the new arrangement; but the irksomeness of their position worked on her temperament, and the fibres of her nature seemed strained like harp-strings. She talked vaguely and indiscriminately to prevent his talking pertinently.

✧ HERMAN MELVILLE, *Bartleby the Scrivener*

He remained as ever, a fixture in my chamber. Nay—if that were possible—he became still more of a fixture than before. What was to be done? He would do nothing in the office; why should he stay there? In plain fact, he had now become a millstone to me, not only useless as a necklace, but afflictive to bear. Yet I was sorry for him. I speak less than truth when I say that, on his own account, he occasioned me uneasiness. If he would but have named a single relative or friend, I would instantly have written, and urged their taking the poor fellow away to some convenient retreat. But he seemed alone, absolutely alone in the universe. A bit of wreck in the mid-Atlantic. At length, necessities connected with my business tyrannized over all other considerations. Decently as I could, I told Bartleby that in six days' time he must unconditionally leave the office. I warned him to take measures, in the interval, for procuring some other abode. I offered to assist him in this endeavor, if he himself would but take the first step towards a removal. "And when you finally quit me, Bartleby," added I, "I shall see that you go not away entirely unprovided. Six days from this hour, remember."

At the expiration of that period, I peeped behind the screen, and lo! Bartleby was there.

I buttoned up my coat, balanced myself; advanced slowly towards him, touched his shoulder, and said, "The time has come; you must quit this place; I'm sorry for you; here is money; but you must go."

"I would prefer not," he replied, with his back still towards me.

"You *must*."

He remained silent.

Now I had an unbounded confidence in this man's common honesty. He had frequently restored to me sixpences and shillings carelessly dropped upon the floor, for I am apt to be very reckless in such shirt-button affairs. The proceeding, then, which followed will not be deemed extraordinary.

"Bartleby," said I, "I owe you twelve dollars on account; here are thirty-two; the odd twenty are yours—Will you take it?" and I handed the bills towards him.

But he made no motion.

"I will leave them here, then," putting them under a weight on the table. Then taking my hat and cane and going to the door, I tranquilly turned and added—"After you have removed your things from these offices, Bartleby, you will of course lock the door—since every one is now gone for the day but you—and if you please, slip your key underneath the mat, so that I may have it in the morning. I shall not see you again; so good-bye to you. If, hereafter, in your new place of abode, I can be of any service to you, do not fail to advise me by letter. Goodbye, Bartleby, and fare you well."

But he answered not a word; like the last column of some ruined temple, he remained standing mute and solitary in the middle of the otherwise deserted room.

As I walked home in a pensive mood, my vanity got the better of my pity. I could not but highly plume myself on my masterly management in getting rid of Bartleby. Masterly I call it, and such it must appear to any dispassionate thinker. The beauty of my procedure seemed to consist in its perfect quietness. There was no vulgar bullying, no bravado of any sort, no choleric hectoring, and striding to and fro across the apartment, jerking out vehement commands for Bartelby to bundle himself off with his beggarly traps. Nothing of the kind. Without loudly bidding Bartleby depart—as an inferior genius might have done—I *assumed* the ground that depart he must; and upon that assumption built all I had to say. The more I thought over my procedure, the more I was charmed with it. Nevertheless, next morning, upon awakening, I had my doubts—I had somehow slept off the fumes of vanity. One of the coolest and wisest hours a man has, is just after he awakes in the morning. My procedure seemed as sagacious as ever— but only in theory. How it would prove in practice—there was the rub. It was truly a beautiful thought to have assumed Bartleby's departure; but, after all, that assumption was simply my own, and none of Bartleby's. The great point was, not whether I had assumed that he would quit me but whether he would prefer so to do. He was more a man of preferences than assumptions.

After breakfast, I walked down town, arguing the probabilities *pro* and *con*. One moment I thought it would prove a miserable failure, and Bartleby would be found all alive at my office as usual; the next moment it seemed certain that I should find his chair empty. And so I kept veering about. At the corner of Broadway and Canal Street, I saw quite an excited group of people standing in earnest conversation.

"I'll take odds he doesn't," said a voice as I passed.

"Doesn't go?—done!" said I, "put up your money."

I was instinctively putting my hand in my pocket to produce my own, when I remembered that this was an election day. The words I had overheard bore no reference to Bartleby, but to the success or non-success of some candidate for the mayoralty. In my intent frame of mind, I had, as it were, imagined that all Broadway shared in my excitement, and were debating the same question with me. I passed on, very thankful that the uproar of the street screened my momentary absent-mindedness.

As I had intended, I was earlier than usual at my office door. I stood listening for a moment. All was still. He must be gone. I tried the knob. The door was locked. Yes, my procedure had worked to a charm; he indeed must be vanished. Yet a certain melancholy mixed with this: I was almost sorry for my brilliant success. I was fumbling under the door mat for the key, which Bartleby was to have left there for me, when accidentally my knee knocked against a panel, producing a summoning sound, and in response a voice came to me from within—"Not yet; I am occupied."

It was Bartleby.

I was thunderstruck. For an instant I stood like the man who, pipe in mouth, was killed one cloudless afternoon long ago in Virginia, by summer lightning; at his own warm open window he was killed, and remained leaning out there upon the dreamy afternoon, till someone touched him, when he fell.

"Not gone!" I murmured at last. But again obeying that wondrous ascendancy which the inscrutable scrivener had over me, and from which ascendancy, for all my chafing, I could not completely escape, I slowly went down stairs and out into the street, and while walking round the block, considered what I should next do in this unheard-of perplexity. Turn the man out by an actual thrusting I could not; to drive him away by calling him hard names would not do; calling in the police was an unpleasant idea; and yet, permit him to enjoy his cadaverous triumph over me—this, too, I could not think of. What was to be done? or, if nothing could be done, was there anything further that I could *assume* in the matter? Yes, as before I had prospectively assumed that Bartleby would depart, so now I might retrospectively assume that departed he was. In the legitimate carrying out of this assumption, I might enter my office in a great hurry, and pretending not to see Bartleby at all, walk straight against him as if he were air. Such a proceeding would in a singular degree have the appearance of a home-thrust. It was hardly possible that Bartleby could withstand such an application of the doctrine of assumptions. But upon second thoughts the success of the plan seemed rather dubious. I resolved to argue the matter over with him again.

"Bartleby," said I, entering the office, with a quietly severe expression, "I am seriously displeased. I am pained, Bartleby. I had thought better of you. I had imagined you of such a gentlemanly organization, that in any delicate dilemma a slight hint would suffice—in short, an assumption. But it appears I am deceived. Why," I added, unaffectedly starting "you have not even touched that money yet," pointing to it, just where I had left it the evening previous.

He answered nothing.

"Will you, or will you not, quit me?" I now demanded in a sudden passion, advancing close to him.

"I would prefer *not* to quit you," he replied, gently emphasising the *not*.

"What earthly right have you to stay here? Do you pay any rent? Do you pay my taxes? Or is this property yours?"

He answered nothing.

"Are you ready to go on and write now? Are your eyes recovered? Could you copy a small paper for me this morning? or help examine a few lines? or step round to the post-office? In a word, will you do anything at all, to give a coloring to your refusal to depart the premises?"

He silently retired into his hermitage.

I was now in such a state of nervous resentment that I thought it but prudent to check myself at present from further demonstrations. Bartleby and I were alone. I remembered the tragedy of the unfortunate Adams and the still more unfortunate Colt in the solitary office of the latter; and how poor Colt, being dreadfully incensed by Adams, and imprudently permitting himself to get wildly excited, was at unawares hurried into his fatal act—an act which certainly no man could possibly deplore more than the actor himself. Often it had occurred to me in my ponderings upon the subject that had that altercation taken place in the public street, or at a private residence, it would not have terminated as it did. It was the circumstance of being alone in a solitary office, upstairs, of a building entirely unhallowed by humanizing domestic associations—an uncarpeted office, doubtless, of a dusty, haggard sort of appearance—this it must have been, which greatly helped to enhance the irritable desperation of the hapless Colt.

But when this old Adam of resentment rose in me and tempted me concerning Bartleby, I grappled him and threw him. How? Why, simply by recalling the divine injunction: "A new commandment give I unto you, that ye love one another." Yes, this it was that saved me. Aside from higher considerations, charity often operates as a vastly wise and prudent principle—a great safeguard to its possessor. Men have committed murder for jealousy's sake, and anger's sake, and hatred's sake, and selfishness' sake, and spiritual pride's sake; but no man, that ever I heard of, ever committed a diabolical murder for sweet charity's sake. Mere self-interest, then, if no better motive can be enlisted, should, especially with high-tempered men, prompt all beings to charity and philanthropy. At any rate, upon the occasion in question, I strove to drown my exasperated feelings towards the scrivener by benevolently construing his conduct. Poor fellow, poor fellow! thought I, he don't mean anything; and besides, he has seen hard times, and ought to be indulged.

. . . What shall I do? I now said to myself buttoning up my coat to the last button. What shall I do? what ought I to do? what does conscience say I *should* do with this man, or, rather, ghost. Rid myself of him, I must; go, he shall. But how? You will not thrust him, the poor, pale, passive mortal—you will not thrust such a helpless creature out of your door? you will not dishonor yourself by such cruelty? No I will not, I cannot do that. Rather would I let him live and die here, and then mason up his remains in the wall. What, then, will you do? For all your coaxing, he will not budge. Bribes he leaves under your own paper-weight on your table; in short, it is quite plain that he prefers to cling to you.

Then something severe, something unusual must be done. What! surely you will not have him collared by a constable, and commit his innocent pallor to the common jail? And upon what ground could you procure such a thing to be done?—a vagrant, is he? What! he a vagrant, a wanderer, who refuses to budge? It is because he will *not* be a vagrant, then, that you seek to count him *as* a vagrant. That is too absurd. No visible means of support: there I have him. Wrong again: for indubitably he *does* support himself, and that is the only unanswerable proof that any man can show of his possessing the means so to do. No more then. Since he will not quit me, I must quit him. I will change my offices; I will move elsewhere, and give him fair notice, that if I find him on my new premises I will then proceed against him as a common trespasser.

❧ BERTOLT BRECHT, *About the Way to Construct Enduring Works*

I
1
How long
Do works endure? As long
As they are not completed.
Since as long as they demand effort
They do not decay.

Inviting further work
Repaying participation
Their being lasts as long as
They invite and reward.

Useful works
Require people
Artistic works
Have room for art
Wise works
Require wisdom
Those devised for completeness
Show gaps
The long-lasting
Are always about to crumble
Those planned on a really big scale
Are unfinished.

Still imperfect
Like a wall awaiting the ivy
(It was once unfinished
Long ago, before the ivy came; bare)

Still short-lived
Like a machine that is used
But is not good enough
But gives promise of a better model
Work for endurance must
Be built like
A machine full of shortcomings.

2
So too the games we invent
Are unfinished, we hope;
And the things we use in playing
What are they without the dentings from
Many fingers, those places, seemingly damaged
Which produce nobility of form;
And the words too whose
Meaning often changed
With change of users.

3
Never go forward without going
Back first to check the direction.
Those who ask questions are those
Whom you will answer, but
Those who will listen to you are
Those who then ask you

Who will speak?
He who has not spoken.
Who will enter?
He who has not yet entered.

Those whose position seems insignificant
When one looks at them
Are
The powerful ones of tomorrow
Those who have need of you
Shall have the power.

Who gives works duration?
Those who'll be alive then.
Whom to choose as builders?
Those still unborn.

Do not ask what they will be like. But
Determine it.

II
If something is to be said which will not be understood at
                          once
If advice is given which takes long to carry out
If man's infirmity is feared, or
The perseverance of enemies, all-shattering cataclysms
Then works must be given long duration.

III
The desire to make works of long duration
Is not always to be welcomed.

He who addresses himself to the unborn
Often does nothing towards their birth.
He does not fight yet wishes to win.
He sees no enemy
But oblivion.

Why should every wind endure for ever?
A good expression is worth noting

So long as the occasion can recur
For which it was good.
Certain experiences handed on in perfect form
Enrich mankind
But richness can become too much.
Not only the experiences
But their recollection too ages one.

Therefore the desire to make works of long duration is
not always to be welcomed.

Wallace Stevens reflects on our responsibility to do enough; Don Gordon explores the problem of denial: how people can refuse to consider the impact of what they do.

❧ WALLACE STEVENS, *Of Modern Poetry*

The poem of the mind in the act of finding
What will suffice. It has not always had
To find: the scene was set; it repeated what
Was in the script.
                    Then the theatre was changed
To something else. Its past was a souvenir.
It has to be living, to learn the speech of the place.
It has to face the men of the time and to meet
The women of the time. It has to think about war
And it has to find what will suffice. It has
To construct a new stage. It has to be on that stage
And, like an insatiable actor, slowly and
With meditation, speak words that in the ear,
In the delicatest ear of the mind, repeat,
Exactly, that which it wants to hear, at the sound
Of which, an invisible audience listens,
Not to the play, but to itself, expressed

In an emotion as of two people, as of two
Emotions becoming one. The actor is
A metaphysician in the dark, twanging
An instrument, twanging a wiry string that gives
Sounds passing through sudden rightnesses, wholly
Containing the mind, below which it cannot descend,
Beyond which it has no will to rise.
       It must
Be the finding of a satisfaction, and may
Be of a man skating, a woman dancing, a woman
Combing. The poem of the act of the mind.

❦ DON GORDON, *The Scientist*

He was a refugee from a continent
  strewn with limbs.
He was at home with infinity
  and with numbers,
A true believer in peace.

When the great equation flashed
  like a missile
Across his brain, he stood
  as on a nova,
Holding the future of all creatures
  in fee simple.

Did he in that instant see the terror
  in mankind,
Or know he was Genghis Khan
  incarnate
Who could not turn back,
  or would not,
From that slaughter on the plain?

He was a good man,
Not the first
Or last
To let angels die.

Responsibility and stewardship go hand in hand when we appreciate with Lance Henson and William Cowper the mutuality of need and offering that can be found in nature. Yet, as Robert Hass shows, we have reason to lament how far short we fall in honoring this standard. Annie Dillard bears witness to the more-than-human world we are a part of and that surrounds us.

❧ LANCE HENSON, *I'm Singing the Cold Rain*

for Charles White Antelope

I am singing the cold rain
I am singing the winter dawn
I am turning in the gray morning
of my life
toward home

❧ WILLIAM COWPER, *The Nightingale and the Glowworm*

A Nightingale that all day long
Had cheer'd the village with his song,
Nor yet at eve his note suspended,
Nor yet when eventide was ended,
Began to feel, as well he might,
The keen demands of appetite;
When looking eagerly around,
He spied far off, upon the ground,
A something shining in the dark,

And knew the Glowworm by his spark;
So, stooping down from hawthorn top,
He thought to put him in his crop.
The worm, aware of his intent,
Harangued him thus, right eloquent
"Did you admire my lamp," quoth he,
"As much as I your minstrelsy,
You would abhor to do me wrong,
As much as I to spoil your song:
For 'twas the self-same Power Divine
Taught you to sing, and me to shine;
That you with music, I with light,
Might beautify and cheer the night."
The songster heard this short oration,
And warbling out his approbation,
Released him, as my story tells,
And found a supper somewhere else.

❧ ROBERT HASS, *Name as a Shadow of the Predator's Wing*

They bulldozed the upper meadow at Squaw Valley
where mist rose from mountain grasses on summer
        mornings
and a few horses grazed through it in the early heat,
where moonrise threw the owl's shadow on the wood rat
and the vole crouched and not breathing in the sage smell
the earth gave back with the day's heat to the night air
And when they had gouged up the deep-rooted bunch-
        grass
and the wet alkali-scented earth had been pushed aside
or trucked someplace out of the way, they poured con-
        crete
and laid road—pleasant smell of tar in the spring sun—
and when the framers had begun to pound nails,

and the electricians and plumbers came around talk
   specs
with the general contractor, someone put up a green sign
with alpine daisies on it that said Squaw Valley Meadows.

❦ ANNIE DILLARD, *Teaching a Stone to Talk*

I

The island where I live is peopled with cranks like myself. In a cedar-shake shack on a cliff—but we all live like this—is a man in his thirties who lives alone with a stone he is trying to teach to talk.

Wisecracks on this topic abound, as you might expect, but they are made as it were perfunctorily, and mostly by the young. For in fact, almost everyone here respects what Larry is doing, as do I, which is why I am protecting his (or her) privacy, and confusing for you the details. It could be, for instance, a pinch of sand he is teaching to talk, or a prolonged northerly, or any one of a number of waves. But it is, in fact, I assure you, a stone. It is—for I have seen it—a palm-sized oval beach cobble whose dark gray is cut by a band of white which runs around and, presumably, through it; such stones we call "wishing stones," for reasons obscure but not, I think, unimaginable.

He keeps it on a shelf. Usually the stone lies protected by a square of untanned leather, like a canary asleep under its cloth. Larry removes the cover for the stone's lessons, or more accurately, I should say, for the ritual or rituals which they perform together several times a day.

No one knows what goes on at these sessions, least of all myself, for I know Larry but slightly, and that owing only to a mix-up in our mail. I assume that like any other meaningful effort, the ritual involves sacrifice, the suppression of self-consciousness, and a certain precise tilt of the will, so that the will becomes transparent and hollow, a channel for the work I wish him well. It is a noble work, and beats, from any angle, selling shoes.

Reports differ on precisely what he expects or wants the stone to say. I do not think he expects the stone to speak as we do, and describe for us its long life and many, or few, sensations. I think instead that he is trying to teach it to say a single word, such as "cup," or "uncle." For this purpose he has not, as some have seriously suggested, carved the stone a little mouth, or furnished it in any way with a pocket of air which it might then expel. Rather—and I think he is wise in this—he plans to initiate his son, who is now an infant living with Larry's estranged wife, into the work, so that it may continue and bear fruit after his death.

II

Nature's silence is its one remark, and every flake of world is a chip off that old mute and immutable block. The Chinese say that we live in the world of the ten thousand things. Each of the ten thousand things cries out to us precisely nothing.

God used to rage at the Israelites for frequenting sacred groves. I wish I could find one. Martin Buber says: "The crisis of all primitive mankind comes with the discovery of that which is fundamentally not-holy, the a-sacramental, which withstands the methods, and which has no 'hour,' a province which steadily enlarges itself." Now we are no longer primitive; now the whole world seems not-holy. We have drained the light from the boughs in the sacred grove and snuffed it in the high places and along the banks of sacred streams. We as a people have moved from pantheism to pan-atheism. Silence is not our heritage but our destiny; we live where we want to live.

The soul may ask God for anything, and never fail. You may ask God for his presence, or for wisdom, and receive each at his hands. Or you may ask God, in the words of the shopkeeper's little gag sign, that he not go away mad, but just go away. Once, in Israel, an extended family of nomads did just that. They heard God's speech and found it too loud. The wilderness generation was at Sinai; it witnessed there the thick darkness where God was: "and all the people saw the thunderings, and the lightnings, and the noise of the trumpet, and the mountain smoking." It scared them witless. Then they asked Moses to beg God, please, never speak to them directly again. "Let not God speak with us, lest we die." Moses took the message. And God, pitying their self-consciousness, agreed. He agreed not to speak to the people anymore. And he added to Moses, "Go say to them, Get into your tents again."

III

It is difficult to undo our own damage, and to recall to our presence that which we have asked to leave. It is hard to desecrate a grove and change your mind. The very holy mountains are keeping mum. We doused the burning bush and cannot rekindle it; we are lighting matches in vain under every green tree. Did the wind use to cry, and the hills shout forth praise? Now speech has perished from among the lifeless things of earth, and living things say very little to very few. Birds may crank out sweet gibberish and monkeys howl; horses neigh and pigs say, as you recall, oink oink. But so do cobbles rumble when a wave recedes, and thunders break the air in lightning storms. I call these noises silence. It could be that wherever there is motion there is noise, as when a whale breaches and smacks the water—and wherever there is stillness there is the still small voice, God's speaking from the whirlwind, nature's old song and dance, the show we drove from town. At any rate, now it is all we can do, and among our best efforts, to try to teach a given human language, English, to chimpanzees.

In the forties an American psychologist and his wife tried to teach a chimp actually to speak. At the end of three years the creature could pronounce, in a hoarse whisper, the words "mama," "papa," and "cup." After another three years of training she could whisper, with difficulty, still only "mama," "papa," and "cup." The more recent successes at teaching chimpanzees American Sign Language are well-known. Just the other day a chimp told us, if we can believe that we truly share a vocabulary, that she had been sad in the morning. I'm sorry we asked.

What have we been doing all these centuries but trying to call God back to the mountain, or, failing that, raise a peep out of anything that isn't us? What is the difference between a cathedral and a physics lab? Are not they both saying: Hello? We spy on whales and on interstellar radio objects; we starve ourselves and pray till we're blue.

IV

I have been reading comparative cosmology. At this time most cosmologists favor the picture of the evolving universe described by Lemaître and Gamow. But I prefer a suggestion made years ago by Valéry—Paul Valéry. He set forth the notion that the universe might be "head shaped."

The mountains are great stone bells; they clang together like nuns. Who shushed the stars? There are a thousand million galaxies easily seen in the Palomar reflector; collisions between and among them do, of course, occur. But these collisions are very long and silent slides. Billions of stars sift among each other untouched, too distant even to be moved, heedless as always, hushed. The sea pronounces something, over and over, in a hoarse whisper; I cannot quite make it out. But God knows I have tried.

At a certain point you say to the woods, to the sea, to the mountains, the world, Now I am ready. Now I will stop and be wholly attentive. You empty yourself and wait, listening. After a time you hear it: there is nothing there. There is nothing but those things only, those created objects, discrete, growing or holding, or swaying, being rained on or raining, held, flooding or ebbing, standing, or spread. You feel the world's word as a tension, a hum, a single chorused note everywhere the same. This is it this hum is the silence. Nature does utter a peep—just this one. The birds and insects, the meadows and swamps and rivers and stones and mountains and clouds: they all do it; they all don't do it. There is a vibrancy to the silence, a suppression, as if someone were gagging the world. But you wait, you give your life's length to listening, and nothing happens. The ice rolls up, the ice rolls back, and still that single note obtains. The tension, or lack of it, is intolerable. The silence is not actually suppression; instead, it is all there is.

V

We are here to witness. There is nothing else to do with those mute materials we do not need. Until Larry teaches his stone to talk, until God changes his mind, or until the pagan gods slip back to their hilltop groves, all we can do with the whole inhuman array is watch it. We can stage our own act on the planet—build our cities on its plains, dam its rivers, plant its topsoils—but our meaningful activity scarcely covers the terrain. We do not use the songbirds, for instance. We do not eat many of them; we cannot befriend them; we cannot persuade them to eat more mosquitoes or plant fewer weed seeds. We can only witness them— whoever they are. If we were not here, they would be songbirds falling in the forest. If we were not here, material events like the passage of seasons would lack even the meager meanings we are able to muster for them. The show would play to an empty house, as do all those falling stars which fall in the daytime. That is why I take walks: to keep an eye on things. And that is why I went to the Galápagos islands.

All this becomes especially clear on the Galápagos islands. The Galapagos islands are just plain here—and little else. They blew up out of the ocean, some plants blew in on them, some animals drifted aboard and evolved weird forms—and there they all are, whoever they are, in full swing. You can go there and watch it happen, and try to figure it out. The Galápagos are a kind of metaphysics laboratory, almost wholly uncluttered by human culture or history. Whatever happens on those bare volcanic rocks happens in full view, whether anyone is watching or not.

What happens there is this, and precious little it is: clouds come and go, and the round of similar seasons; a pig eats a tortoise or doesn't eat a tortoise; Pacific waves fall up and slide back; a lichen expands; night follows day; an albatross dies and dries on a cliff; a cool current upwells from the ocean floor; fishes multiply, flies swarm, stars rise and fall, and diving birds dive. The news, in other words, breaks on the beaches. And taking it all in are the trees. The *palo santo* trees crowd the hillsides like any outdoor audience; they face the lagoons, the lava lowlands, and the shores.

I have some experience of these *palo santo* trees. They interest me as emblems of the muteness of the human stance in relation to all that is not human. I see us all as *palo santo* trees, holy sticks, together watching all that we watch, and growing in silence.

In the Galápagos, it took me a long time to notice the *palo santo* trees. Like everyone else, I specialized in sea lions. My shipmates and I liked the sea lions, and envied their lives. Their joy seemed conscious. They were engaged in full-time play. They were all either fat or dead; there was no halfway. By day they played in the shallows, alone or together, greeting each other and us with great noises of joy, or they took a turn offshore and body-surfed in the breakers, exultant. By night on the sand they lay in each other's flippers and slept. Everyone joked, often, that when he "came back," he would just as soon do it all over again as a sea lion. I concurred. The sea lion game looked unbeatable.

But a year and a half later, I returned to those unpeopled islands. In the interval my attachment to them had shifted, and my memories of them had altered, the way memories do, like parti-colored pebbles rolled back and forth over a grating, so that after a time those hard bright ones, the ones you thought you would never lose, have vanished, passed through the grating, and only a few big, unexpected ones remain, no longer unnoticed but now selected out for some meaning, large and unknown.

Such were the *palo santo* trees. Before, I had never given them a thought. They were just miles of half-dead trees on the red lava sea cliffs of some deserted islands. They were only a name in a notebook: "*Palo santo*—those strange white trees." Look at the sea lions! Look at the flightless cormorants, the penguins, the iguanas, the sunset! But after eighteen months the wonderful cormorants, penguins, iguanas, sunsets, and even the sea lions, had dropped from my holey heart. I returned to the Galápagos to see the *palo santo* trees.

They are thin, pale, wispy trees. You walk among them on the lowland deserts, where they grow beside the prickly pear. You see them from the water on the steeps that face the sea, hundreds together, small and thin and spread, and so much more pale than their red soils that any black-and-white photograph of them looks like a negative. Their stands look like blasted orchards. At every season they all look newly dead, pale and bare as birches drowned in a beaver pond—for at every season they look leafless, paralyzed, and mute. But in fact, if you look closely, you can see during the rainy months a few meager deciduous leaves here and there on their brittle twigs. And hundreds of lichens always grow on their bark in mute, overlapping explosions which barely enlarge in the course of the decade, lichens pink and orange, lavender, yellow, and green. The *palo santo* trees bear the lichens effortlessly, unconsciously, the way they bear everything. Their multitudes, transparent as line drawings, crowd the cliffsides like whirling dancers, like empty groves, and look out over cliff-wrecked breakers toward more unpeopled islands, with their freakish lizards and birds, toward the grieving lagoons and the bays where the sea lions wander, and beyond to the clamoring seas.

Now I no longer concurred with my shipmates' joke; I no longer wanted to "come back" as a sea lion. For I thought, and I still think, that if I came back to Life in the sunlight where everything changes, I would like to come back as a *palo santo* tree, one of thousands on a cliffside on those godforsaken islands, where a million events occur among the witless, where a splash of rain may drop on a yellow iguana the size of a dachshund, and ten minutes later the iguana may blink. I would like to come back as a *palo santo* tree on the weather side of an island, so that I could be, myself, a perfect witness, and look, mute, and wave my arms.

VI

The silence is all there is. It is the alpha and the omega. It is God's brooding over the face of the waters; it is the blended note of the ten thousand things, the whine of wings. You take a step in the right direction to pray to this silence, and even to address the prayer to "World." Distinctions blur. Quit your tents. Pray without ceasing.

Michael Lerner reminds us of our responsibility to free ourselves of conventions which divert us into justifications of selfishness. Tony Hiss recalls how responsible we can, so easily, be with each other and Arthur Sze elegantly shows how watchful we need to be as we try with words to define, but can only approximate, reality.

❧ MICHAEL LERNER, *Suspect Your Neighbor as Yourself*

It is the common sense of people who have been socialized in the advanced, "dog-eat-dog" industrial world which teaches that you are naive if you trust other people to be fair in their dealings with you. Learning to "win through intimidation" may not be the only style of winning that is advocated, but there is a clear suggestion in the culture that unless you are concerned about winning, you will lose.

Given that is the conventional wisdom of our own world, perhaps it is not so hard to understand the many betrayals of daily life. At first, we might be tempted to judge those who let us down as evil people, people who are fundamentally corrupt and have no moral sense. But once we become acquainted with the betrayers, we find that they are like everyone else, with reasons, justifications and excuses.

Instead of focus on how wonderful the current reality is, increasingly the focus has been on how awful the alternatives are, or why the current reality is the only possible one, or why it is childish to hope for a less alienated existence. This has involved not just ideas but a whole new way of feeling about oneself. Increasingly we have a society producing people who don't believe that they deserve to have a better world, or people who believe that they are fundamentally incapable of getting anything that they really want. We have a society populated by people who accept the way things are because they don't believe that they could possibly make things different—not because they think things are so wonderful the way are.

It is inside our own heads, and it is recreated by us in every thought that assumes that how things are is the equivalent of "reality." It grows stronger every time we blame ourselves for having failed in some important way—and have no compassion for ourselves in light of all the ways that the structures of reality push us to be less than we want to be. And it is nourished by our endless betrayals of our loved ones, of our friends, of our own highest visions of who we should be.

❦ TONY HISS, *Experience of Place, One Recent Weekday Afternoon*

The main concourse of Grand Central—an enormous room, with fourteen entrances—is only one part of an intricate structure that was opened to the public in February of 1913 and is justly famous as a cross-roads, a noble building, an essential part of midtown Manhattan, and an ingenious piece of engineering that can handle large numbers of trains, cars, and people at once. You can buy a ticket and get train information in the concourse—and these days you can also buy a flower or a drink or a meal—but the main purpose of the room is to move people through it. It was designed to handle huge crowds and to impress people with the immensity and the dignity of enclosed public places in a modern city. From the accounts left by its builders, however, it was not designed to provide the experience actually available there today. That experience is one of the unplanned treasures of New York.

The concourse is 470 feet long and 160 feet wide, and it is 150 feet—fifteen stories, perhaps—from the floor to the peak of the vaulted ceiling. The room has arched windows 33 feet wide and 60 feet high, which are deep enough to have corridors running through them—a series of walkways built between the outer glass and the inner glass in each window—and it has constellations painted on the ceiling, with sixty of the stars really glowing, because they are small light bulbs. A balcony 30 feet wide and 20 feet above the floor runs along every wall except the south one. From the west balcony a marble staircase pours down and then divides in two to flow around steps that lead from the concourse to a lower concourse for suburban trains. The main concourse is bigger than the nave of Notre Dame, and it is sometimes called awe-inspiring or referred to as an American cathedral, but the experience it offers has to do with day-to-day urban living: It's a sort of introductory course (or, for old-timers, a refresher course) in how to join the choreography of New York City.

The experience of the concourse seems to have changed very little in the last seventy-seven years. At least, what I find there now is substantially true to the continuing experience I found there forty-three

years ago, when I was six and a newcomer to the city. Two major atten-
tion-grabbing additions to this huge room since the late 1940s—a big
illuminated clock and stock ticker on the south wall and an oversize
illuminated Kodak photograph on the east wall—have recently been
removed, and the gigantic windows have been washed. These days,
though, there are much sadder sights in the concourse than there used
to be: In the mid-1980s, Grand Central became a principal hangout for
large numbers of homeless people, as well as for some of those who
prey on the homeless.

One recent weekday afternoon around three-thirty, I entered the
concourse from the east, through one of the two long, nearly straight
passageways that lead in from Lexington Avenue. I came out of the East
Side IRT subway into the more southerly of the two straightaways and
immediately found myself part of a stream of people, four and five
abreast, all of them looking straight ahead and moving at a fast New
York clip toward the concourse along the right-hand side of a tunnel
only twice the width of the stream itself. Toward me along the left-
hand side of the corridor—which is well lighted, has a low white ceiling
and a beige marble floor, and is lined with convenience stores—came a
second stream of people, just as wide, and moving at the same speed
and with the same look. Though I could hear my own footsteps, nearby
footfalls and normal tones of voice registered as loud but blurred, indeterminate noises, and although no one was touching me, or even brushing past, I kept feeling that I was about to be bumped into. People
sounded closer than they looked, and they seemed closer still, because
my eyes and ears couldn't determine whether the people I was looking
at were the people making the sounds I could hear.

I felt hurried along. My breathing was shallow and slightly con-
stricted; my neck and shoulders were tight. I could smell cookies and
pizza baking in the shops around me, but it seemed difficult to look to
either side. I could see maybe twelve feet ahead of me—a view consisting entirely of backs of heads and oncoming faces. There was nothing
in any of the faces to suggest that they had just come from a different
kind of place. The only alternative to hurrying forward seemed to be to
swerve right at random and come to rest in front of a shop.

Then these two streams of people crossed a second pair of streams, running at a right angle to them. The stream I was in entered a space with a slightly higher, cross-vaulted ceiling, and I had a moment to feel alarmed in retrospect, wondering why no one had bumped into anyone else during the crossing. The whole journey so far had taken something like fifteen seconds.

Crossing this new space in the next five or six seconds, I was aware of a slight diminution in the noise around me, felt a slight lightening in my shoulders, noticed that the stores on either side were a vitamin shop and a snack bar, and saw in front of me a different light: grayer, clearer, brighter, less intense. I felt that something in me and near me was about to change.

In another step, I was in the concourse. I knew this first not by sight but by body sensation, sounds, the absence of a smell, and breathing. I felt as if some small weight suspended several feet above my head that I had not till then even been aware of, had just shot fifteen stories into the air. I straightened up, my breathing slowed down, and I noticed that the scentless air around me was warm. I was walking at the same fast clip, and on the same kind of marble floor, but now, and for the rest of the minute it took me to walk the length of the concourse, I could no longer distinguish the sounds of my own footsteps. All the sounds that reached me seemed to have been fused into a single sound. Vast and quiet, it seemed to be evenly distributed throughout the great room. This sound, pleasant in all its parts, regular in all its rhythms, and humorous and good-natured, seemed also to have buttoned me into some small, silent bubble of space. I felt that I wasn't quite walking but was paddling—or somehow propelling—this bubble across the floor. I became aware that my pace had slowed.

This sound was produced by five hundred or more people talking and walking on marble through the bottom part of eleven million cubic feet of air. Within two or three feet of where I stood, I could hear separate voices: "Take care, now" and "Yep, see you tomorrow" and "All 'board!" And quite often, and from quite far away, I could hear laughing. The rest of what I heard was just the single commingled sound. I could see, quite clearly, two things: an unmoving framework made up of marble floor, tall piers, arched windows, high barrel vault, daylight, and faint electric stars; and the swirling, living motion of five hundred people walking, two and three abreast, from and toward the fourteen entrances and exits of the concourse. Moving silently, as it seemed, within that sound, I noticed once again that no one was bumping into anyone else—that every time I thought I myself might be about to bump into people near me, both I and they were already accelerating slightly, or decelerating, or making a little side step, so that nobody ever collided. On top of this, the weightless sensation in my head gave me the feeling that I could look down on all this movement, in addition to looking out at it. I had a sense that the cooperation I was a part of kept repeating itself throughout the vast room around me and the vaster city beyond it.

I thought, as I have many times in the concourse, that if I were a stranger to this overwhelming city, it would be helpful to me to know that something in me and in everyone around me already knew how to fit in with all the people circulating through the city and going about their business. After emerging onto Vanderbilt Avenue, I found that when I crossed over and walked along the south side of Forty-third Street, I could for a while keep with me this awareness of the cooperation that makes a city possible. It lasted about a block and a half—until, as I was standing at a stoplight at Fifth Avenue, a screaming ambulance and the rest of the traffic brought me back to a more ordinary sense of separateness and disjointedness. At the same time, waiting for the light to change, I could see that even though I no longer felt it, some form of cooperation was continuing to govern the movements of people near me on the sidewalk. People moving in four different directions passed one another without colliding, and in each minute, hundreds of accidents never occurred. Still, the overall level of cooperation seemed diminished, because there was no sense of connectedness between the people on foot and the people in vehicles.

❧ ARTHUR SZE, *The Network*

In 1861, George Hew sailed in a rowboat
from the Pearl River, China, across

the Pacific Ocean to San Francisco.
He sailed alone. The photograph of him
in a museum disappeared. But, in the mind,
he is intense, vivid, alive. What is
this fact but another fact in a world
of facts, another truth in a vast network
of truths? It is a red maple leaf
flaming out at the end of its life,
revealing an incredibly rich and complex
network of branching veins. We live
in such a network: the world is opaque,
translucent, or, suddenly, lucid,
vibrant. The air is alive and hums
then. Speech is too slow to the mind.
And the mind's speech is so quick it breaks
the sound barrier and shatters glass.

11

The Sacred Grove

RESPECT AND CONNECTION

Self-respect, respect for other people and cultures, and respect for nature itself are forms of connectedness. They are a way of affirming one's welcome place in history, culture, the family, among friends, and on the earth. Respect is an affirmation of life that affects the way people act. It leads to honoring the elderly for their experience and wisdom and nurturing the growth of children for the possibility they represent. It provides the grounds upon which people fight to keep culture and language alive, to work for balanced ecosystems and take risks for trees, rivers, a frog on the verge of extinction or a place about to be destroyed for the benefit of a few. It is not the same as love however, as it is possible to respect people you don't love, and even, in the case of dysfunctional relationships, to love people you don't respect.

Respect cannot be legislated. It is produced by the quality and nature of the life you live, the behavior of people you encounter, and by the quality of nature itself. Rosellen Brown expresses the fundamental source of respect in *Cora Fry's Pillow Book:*

I think you have one life, I told him, sorry to say it.
You cup your hands and drink it deep,
or you pour it out on strange ground
like so much spilled water.

Respect is an acknowledgment of the potential specialness of everyone and everything, and of the grace and blessing of life itself. Among people, it must be mutual to be nurtured. Respect can be destroyed when one person treats another as a disposable object, as someone not worthy of consideration. It can be eroded when greed leads to the disruption of the fabric of community or the coherence of the natural world. Disrespect for a person's feelings or property, for a public place, for a group of people or even for a species is all too characteristic of contemporary life. When disrespect is pervasive, it disrupts the fabric of coherent social life.

Traditionally, there have been many images of places where respect and reverence rule. The sacred grove of trees or magic circle of stones, the Ark or holy mountain or lake—all are places where we can expunge the worst in ourselves, the greedy impulses, the moments when self-indulgence and careless disregard for consequences make us forget our own vulnerability.

As Annie Dillard says in her essay "Teaching a Stone to Talk," the whole of which is reprinted elsewhere in this book:

> We have trained the light from the boughs in the sacred grove and snuffed it in the high places and along the banks of sacred streams.

Too often we have destroyed the sacred groves, not only in the environment, but in each other's hearts. We have learned how to see other people as less than fully human, have turned animals into objects, and the earth into an economic resource instead of a common habitat. The selections in this part of the book reflect how respect, beginning with the self and moving out to the world, can restore a sense of connectedness. Without this sense of belonging, of comfort among others that honors them simply for being, character is impoverished, deficient in meaning, and open to meanness. It is difficult if not impossible to be good without being connected.

Selections

This first long poem is on connectedness, which is the ground of respect.

❧ DIANE DI PRIMA, *The Loba as Eve*

> *I am Thou & Thou art I*
> *and where Thou art I am*
> *and in all things am I dispersed*
>
> *and from wherever Thou willst*
> *Thou gatherest Me*
>
> *but in gathering Me*
> *Thou Gatherest Thyself*

—GOSPEL OF EVE

I am Thou & Thou art I

where tossing in grey sheets you weep
I am
where pouring like mist you

                              scatter among the stars

I shine
where in black oceans of sea & sky
        you die
        you die
I chant
a voice like angels from the heart
of virgin gold,
                plaint of the unicorn caught
in the boundless circle

            where you confront
broken glass, lost trees & men
                      tossed up
on my beaches, hear me pray:
                    your words

slip off my tongue, I am pearl

of yr final tears, none other
than yr flesh, though it go soft

I am worm
           in the tight bud, burst
of starcloud that covers your dream & morning
I am sacred mare grazing
    in meadow of yr spirit & you run
in my wind. Hear the chimes
that break from my eyes like infants
struggling eternally against

                              these swaddling clothes

and where Thou art, I am

astride the wind, or held
by two hoodlums under a starting truck.
crocheting in the attic.
striding forever out of the heart of quartz
immense, unhesitant, monotonous
as galaxies; or rain; or
lost cities of the dinosaurs now sunk
in the unopening rock.

who keeps the bats from flying in your window?
who rolls the words you drop back into seed?
                           who picks
sorrows like lice from your heart & cracks them
                  between her teeth?
who else blows down your chimney with the moon
scattering ashes from your dismal hearth to show
the sleeping Bird in the coals, or is it
garnet you lost?

        What laughter spins you
around in the windy street?

& in all things am I dispersed

gold fleece on the hunted deer.
the Name of everything.
sweet poison eternally churned
from the milky ocean.
futurity's mirror.   ivory gate
of death.
the fruit I hold out spins
the dharma wheel.
I weep
I weep
dry water I am, cold fire, "our"
Materia, mother & matrix
                        eternally in labor.
The crescent I stand on rocks
like a shaky boat, it is
the winking eye of God.

& from wherever Thou willst
Thou gatherest Me

steel, from the belly of Aries.
Or that cold fire which plays
above the sea.
White sow munching acorns in graveyards where roots
of oaks wrap powdery bones of the devas.
There, suckle at my tits. Crucify
me like a beetle on yr desk. Nod out
amidst the rustling play of lizards, recognize
epics the lichen whisper, read twigs
& leaves as they fall.

Nurture my life with quartz & alabaster
& drink my blood from a vein in my lower leg.

I neigh, I nuzzle you, I explode
          your certain myth.
I crawl slimy from a cave beneath yr heart
I hiss, I spit oracles at yr front door
in a language you have forgotten. I unroll
the scroll of yr despair, I blind your children with it.

It is for this you love me.
It is for this
you seek me everywhere.

Because I gave you apples out of season
Because I gnaw at the boundaries of the light

but in gathering Me
Thou Gatherest Thyself

daystar that hovers
over the heavy waters of that Sea
bright stone that fell
out of the fiery eye of the Pyramid

it grows
out of the snake as out of the crescent:
apple you eternally devour
forever in your hand. I lock
the elements around you where you walk:

        earth from my terror
        water from my grief
        air my eternal flight
        & fire / my lust

I am child who sings
uninjured in the furnace of your flesh.

Blue earth am I & never on this earth
have I been naked
Blue light am I that runs
like marrow in the thin line yr breath

I congeal
waterlilies on the murky pond
I hurl
the shafts of dawn like agony
                              down the night

Paul Celan's agonizing poem about the Nazi Holocaust perpetrated against the Jews, "Death Fugue" is an unbearable cry against the horrors that can result when the fabric of respect and connectedness between peoples is broken and all humane dimensions are destroyed in an orgy of hatred.

Paul Celan, *Death Fugue*

Black milk of daybreak we drink it at evening
we drink it at midday and morning we drink it at night
we drink and we drink
we shovel a grave in the air there you won't lie too cramped
A man lives in the house he plays with his vipers he writes
he writes when it grows dark to Deutschland your golden hair
                    Marguerite
he writes it and steps out of doors and the stars are all sparkling
                              he whistles his hounds to come close
he whistles his Jews into rows has them shovel a grave in the ground
he orders us strike up and play for the dance

Black milk of daybreak we drink you at night
we drink you at morning and midday we drink you at evening
we drink and we drink

A man lives in the house he plays with his vipers he writes
he writes when it grows dark to Deutschland your golden hair
      Marguerite
your ashen hair Shulamith we shovel a grave in the air
                        there you won't lie too cramped
He shouts jab this earth deeper you lot there you others sing up and
    play
he grabs for the rod in his belt he swings it his eyes are blue
jab your spades deeper you lot there you others play on for the
    dancing

Black milk of daybreak we drink you at night
we drink you at midday and morning we drink you at evening
we drink and we drink
a man lives in the house your goldenes Haar Marguerite
your aschenes Haar Shulamith he plays with his vipers
He shouts play death more sweetly Death is a master from
    Deutschland
he shouts scrape your strings darker you'll rise then in smoke to the
    sky
you'll have a grave then in the clouds there you won't lie too
    cramped

Black milk of daybreak we drink you at night
we drink you at midday Death is a master aus Deutschland
we drink you at evening and morning we drink and we drink
this Death is ein Meister aus Deutschland his eye it is blue
he shoots you with shot made of lead shoots you level and true
a man lives in the house your goldenes Haar Margarete
he looses his hounds on us grants us a grave in the air
he plays with his vipers and daydreams
                      der Tod ist ein Meister aus Deutschland
dein goldenes Haar Margarete
dein aschenes Haar Shulamith

Respect can be manifested in small as well as large ways; can be implicit as well as explicit. N. Scott Momaday's story and Sharon Olds' and Jaime Jacinto's poems illustrate the ways in which people acknowledge each other's specialness and create binding and nurturing relationships.

❦ N. SCOTT MOMADAY, *Billy the Kid Offers a Kindness to an Old Man at Glorieta (In the Presence of the Sun)*

He was a broken-down old man, a twist of rawhide. When you looked at him you had the sense that you were looking at a ruin, something of prehistoric character, like a shard of pottery or the remnant of an ancient wall. His face, especially, was an archaeology in itself. The shadows of epochs come and go in such a face.

He was a cowboy, he allowed. He had broken horses all his life, and not a few of them had broken him. And he had known men and women, good and bad—singular men and singular women. He was more than willing to talk about these and other things. We listened, Billy and I. The old man's real existence was at last invested in his stories; there he lived, and not elsewhere. He was nothing so much as the story of himself, the telling of a tale to which flesh was gathered incidentally. It was no wonder Billy liked him.

We passed the time of day with him, and he created us over and over again in his stories, fashioned us into myriad wonderful things that we should not otherwise have been. Now we were trick-shot artists in a Wild West Show, and the old man, his guns blazing, shot the buttons off our vests. Again we dined on the most exotic and delicious fruits in the golden palaces of the Orient. We were there at the Battle of the Wilderness, at the very point of the Bloody Angle, following the old man into legend. Christmas was coming on, and we were the Magi, the old man said. Laughing, we half believed him. And then it was time to go.

Billy fetched a plug of tobacco from his coat pocket, cut it in two with a jackknife, and gave the old man half. We said goodbye and left the old man there at Glorieta, before his fire. The leading edge of a dream was moving like a distant, migrant bird across his eyes.

Later, on the way to Santa Fe, I said to Billy:

"Say, amigo, I have never seen you chew tobacco."

"No, and it isn't likely that you ever will," he said. "I have no use for the weed."

Then, seeing that I was perplexed, he went on:

"I bought the tobacco at La Junta because I knew that we were coming this way and I hoped to see the old man, who is my true friend. He has a taste for it. And I offered him the half instead of the whole because he should prefer that I did not give him something outright; it pleased him that I should share something of my own with him. As it happens, I have thrown away my share, in which the ownership consists—it lies back there in a snowdrift. But that is an unimportant matter, a trivial conceit—and this the old man understands and appreciates more even than the tobacco itself."

He started to say something more, but apparently he thought better of it and fell silent. He seemed lost in thought, but it was impossible to say. This brief sojourn into language had been for him extraordinary, and he seemed spent, and indeed almost remorseful and contrite, as if he had squandered something of which he had too little in store. His eyes were precisely equal color to the sky at that moment, and the sky was curdled with snow.

"Indeed we are the Magi," I said, but I said it softly, that his thoughts, whatever they were, should not be disturbed.

❧ SHARON OLDS, *Grandmother Love Poem*

Late in her life, when we fell in love,
I'd take her out from the nursing home
for a chaser and two bourbons. She'd crack
a joke sharp as a tin lid
hot from the teeth of the can-opener,
and cackle her crack-corn laugh. Next to her
wit, she prided herself on her hair,
snowy and abundant. She would lift it up
at the nape of the neck, there in the bar,

and under the white, under the salt-and-
pepper, she'd show me her true color,
the color it was when she was a bride:
like her sex in the smoky light she would show me
the pure black.

❦ JAIME JACINTO, *Visitation*

It is spring today
and I think of him
kneeling beside me
this companion
who was my father's father,
who appeared one day
and stayed with us,
never to leave the house—
all day dressed in pajamas
shuffling in his slippers
down the back stairs
to the garden where we'd watch him
bunching the dead leaves
tamping the pulpy soil
flicking the hollow shells of dead beetles.
He would tend his garden
day by day, little by little
brushing away the loose earth,
the soggy crumbs of moss
until his fingers found
what they had wanted.
From a fist full of black earth—
the pale green sprouts
more delicate than morning light.
Now years later when I'm nearly asleep
listening to the slow movements
of animals, the rustle of leaves

where their paws might fall,
he returns, ancient, waving
his leathery hands,
knuckles nicked by thorns.
I hear him whispering
our names, and the night breeze passes
over us with the first sliver of moonlight.

Self-respect, delight in one's own being and connectedness, is an abiding source of strength. The following three poems are statements of such proper self-love. They also indicate how difficult it is to walk the line between self-aggrandizement and appropriate affection for the person one is and can be.

❧ DEVORAH MAJOR, *Shine*

have you ever seen somebody
walking down any street
strutting
clothes laying just so
picked out just the right colors
to set off their tone
taking the street
like they own it
like they think they something
like they think they special
like they going somewhere

just announcing it to the world
loud and sassy as you please

ever seen those people
that move like they just
two inches taller
or that much smarter

or something more
proud people
make you say
"you ain't no better than me"
make you pull up
and stick out your chest
strut your colors too
because you want them to know
that that's plenty fine
that they think they somebody
but they need to know
that you, why you plenty fine too
so you just polish up your aura
straighten out your back
and tell everybody

to put on they sunglasses
and watch you shine
yeah
ever seen somebody
like that
who think they something
important
just like you
yeah
someone
going somewhere
doing something
righteous
yeah
just like you
yeah
ever seen that

you
watching

them
watching
you
shine
Shine
and shine on through

❦ WENDELL BERRY, *The Recognition*

You put on my clothes
and it was as though
we met some other place
and I looked and knew
you. This is what we keep
going through, the lyrical
changes, the strangeness
in which I know again
what I have known before.

❦ STEVIE SMITH, *The Frog Prince*

I am a frog,
I live under a spell,
I live at the bottom
Of a green well.

And here I must wait
Until a maiden places me
On her royal pillow,
And kisses me,
In her father's palace.

The story is familiar,
Everybody knows it well,

But do other enchanted people feel as nervous
As I do? The stories do not tell,

Ask if they will be happier
When the changes come,
As already they are fairly happy
In a frog's doom?

I have been a frog now
For a hundred years
And in all this time
I have not shed many tears,

I am happy, I like the life,
Can swim for many a mile
(When I have hopped to the river)
And am for ever agile.

And the quietness,
Yes, I like to be quiet
I am habituated
To a quiet life,

But always when I think these thoughts,
As I sit in my well
Another thought comes to me and says:
It is part of the spell

To be happy
To work up contentment
To make much of being a frog
To fear disenchantment

Says, It will be *heavenly*
To be set free,
Cries, *Heavenly* the girl who disenchants

And the royal times, *heavenly*,
And I think it will be.

Come, then, royal girl and royal times,
Come quickly,
I can be happy until you come
But I cannot be heavenly,
Only disenchanted people
Can be heavenly.

One component of self-respect is respect for the cultures that contribute to the formation of one's character. Sometimes the contributions are negative, but most often they can be abiding sources of strength and affirmations of identity as Victor Hernandez Cruz, Ray A. Young Bear, and Jimmie Durham's poems indicate.

❧ VICTOR HERNANDEZ CRUZ, *Problems with Hurricanes*

A campesino looked at the air
And told me:
With hurricanes it's not the wind
or the noise or the water.
I'll tell you he said:
it's the mangoes, avocados
Green plantains and bananas
flying into town like projectiles.

How would your family
feel if they had to tell
The generations that you
got killed by a flying
Banana.

Death by drowning has honor
If the wind picked you up

and slammed you
Against a mountain boulder
This would not carry shame
But
to suffer a mango smashing
Your skull
or a plantain hitting your
Temple at 70 miles per hour
is the ultimate disgrace.

The campesino takes off his hat—
As a sign of respect
towards the fury of the wind
And says:
Don't worry about the noise
Don't worry about the water
Don't worry about the wind—

If you are going out
beware of mangoes
And all such beautiful
sweet things.

❦ RAY A. YOUNG BEAR, *From The Spotted Night*

In the blizzard
while chopping wood
the mystical whistler
beckons my attention.
Once there were longhouses
here. A village.
In the abrupt spring floods
swimmers retrieved our belief.
So their spirit remains.

From the spotted night
distant jets transform
into fireflies who float
towards me like incandescent
snowflakes.
The leather shirt
which is suspended
on a wire hanger
above the bed's headboard
is humanless; yet when one
stands outside the house,
the strenuous sounds
of dressers and boxes
being moved can be heard.
We believe someone wears
the shirt and rearranges
the heavy furniture
although nothing
is actually changed.
Like the Plains Indian shirts
which repelled lead bullets,
ricocheting from them
in fiery sparks,
this shirt is the means;
this shirt *is* the bullet.

❧ JIMMIE DURHAM, *Tarascan Guitars*

In Texas, at that old Comanche place called White Flint,
I found the skull of an armadillo.
Maybe some new hunter killed an armadillo with a .22 rifle.
I asked rocks and other things around.
It was probably that way, they said.

I painted the armadillo's skull bright turquoise and orange,
Blue and red, black, green, like tiles and aztec flowers.
Where his old eyes had been, I put an agate
and a seashell;
For seeing in all directions.

Now he can go to the festival of the dead
In Tarasco where they make those guitars,
And where a wildman made the first ocarina,
To make the women fall in love with him.

In Tarasco, Mexico, where fields are covered with flowers,
They sometimes make guitars from the armor of armadillos.
So if he goes there to the festival of the dead
He can dance like a flower to the music of his brothers.

Everyone will be glad to see him, and will say,
That Cherokee guy sent me here.

If we do not let our memories fail us
The dead can sing and be with us.
They want us to remember them.
And they can make festivals in our struggles.

Someday we will find those Cherokees
Who tried to escape Texas into Mexico
But were killed by Sam Houston's hunters

I have already found an armadillo's skull
And like Sequoia who was lost in Mexico
I write to remember.

Respect for human life implies refusing to turn a person into a commodity or an object of convenience. It involves respect for the way in which our days are shaped and our work is done. This excerpt from E. F. Schumacher's Small Is Beautiful *points toward a respectful redefinition of work, one that is radically different than what is common in our society.*

❦ E. F. Schumacher, *Economics as if People Mattered*

There is universal agreement that a fundamental source of wealth is human labour. Now, the modern economist has been brought up to consider "labour" or work as little more than a necessary evil. From the point of view of the employer, it is in any case simply an item of cost, to be reduced to a minimum if it cannot be eliminated altogether, say, by automation. From the point of view of the workman, it is a "disutility"; to work is to make a sacrifice of one's leisure and comfort, and wages are a kind of compensation for the sacrifice. Hence the ideal from the point of view of the employer is to have output without employees, and the ideal from the point of view of the employee is to have income without employment.

The consequences of these attitudes both in theory and in practice are, of course, extremely far-reaching. If the ideal with regard to work is to get rid of it, every method that "reduces the workload" is a good thing. The most potent method, short of automation, is the so-called "division of labour" and the classical example is the pin factory eulogised in Adam Smith's *Wealth of Nations*. Here it is not a matter of ordinary specialisation, which mankind has practised from time immemorial, but of dividing up every complete process of production into minute parts, so that the final product can be produced at great speed without anyone having had to contribute more than a totally insignificant and, in most cases, unskilled movement of his limbs.

The Buddhist point of view takes the function of work to be at least threefold: to give a man a chance to utilise and develop his faculties; to enable him to overcome his egocenteredness by joining with other people in a common task; and to bring forth the goods and services needed for a becoming existence. Again, the consequences that flow from this view are endless. To organise work in such a manner that it becomes meaningless, boring, stultifying, or nerve-racking for the worker would be little short of criminal; it would indicate a greater concern with goods than with people, an evil lack of compassion and a soul-destroying degree of attachment to the most primitive side of this worldly existence. Equally, to strive for leisure as an alternative to work would be considered a complete misunderstanding of one of the basic truths of human existence, namely that work and leisure are complementary parts of the same living process and cannot be separated without destroying the joy of work and the bliss of leisure.

From the Buddhist point of view, there are therefore two types of mechanisation which must be clearly distinguished: one that enhances a man's skill and power and one that turns the work of man over to a mechanical slave, leaving man in a position of having to serve the slave. How to tell the one from the other? "The craftsman himself," says Ananda Coomaraswamy, a man equally competent to talk about the modern west as the ancient east, "can always, if allowed to, draw the delicate distinction between the machine and the tool. The carpet loom is a tool, a contrivance for holding warp threads at a stretch for the pile to be woven round them by the craftsmen's fingers; but the power loom is a machine, and its significance as a destroyer of culture lies in the fact that it does the essentially human part of the work." It is clear, therefore, that Buddhist economics must be very different from the economics of modern materialism, since the Buddhist sees the essence of civilisation not in a multiplication of wants but in the purification of human character. Character, at the same time, is formed primarily by a man's work. And work, properly conducted in conditions of human dignity and freedom, blesses those who do it and equally their products. The Indian philosopher and economist J. C. Kumarappa sums the matter up as follows:

> If the nature of the work is properly appreciated and applied, it will stand in the same relation to the higher faculties as food is to the physical body. It nourishes and enlivens the higher man and urges him to produce the best he is capable of. It directs his free will along the proper course and disciplines the animal in him into progressive channels. It furnishes an excellent back-

ground for man to display his scale of values and develop his personality.

If a man has no chance of obtaining work he is in a desperate position, not simply because he lacks an income but because he lacks this nourishing and enlivening factor of disciplined work which nothing can replace. A modern economist may engage in highly sophisticated calculations on whether full employment "pays" or whether it might be more "economic" to run an economy at less than full employment so as to ensure a greater mobility of labour, a better stability of wages, and so forth. His fundamental criterion of success is simply the total quantity of goods produced during a given period of time. "If the marginal urgency of goods is low," says Professor Galbraith in *The Affluent Society*, "then so is the urgency of employing the last man or the last million men in the labour force." And again: "If . . . we can afford some unemployment in the interest of stability—a proposition, incidentally, of impeccably conservative antecedents—then we can afford to give those who are unemployed the goods that enable them to sustain their accustomed standard of living."

From a Buddhist point of view, this is standing the truth on its head by considering goods as more important than people and consumption as more important than creative activity. It means shifting the emphasis from the worker to the product of work, that is, from the human to the subhuman, a surrender to the forces of evil.

Disrespect and lack of connectedness can lead to the disintegration of character and the destruction of the environment. Mary Tall Mountain's poem shows how violation of respect is both sad and infuriating.

❦ MARY TALL MOUNTAIN, *The Last Wolf*

the last wolf hurried toward me
through the ruined city
and I heard his baying echoes

down the steep smashed warrens
of Montgomery Street and past
the few ruby-crowned highrises
left standing
their lighted elevators useless

passing the flicking red and green
of traffic signals
baying his way eastward
in the mystery of his wild loping gait
closer the sounds in the deadly night
through clutter and rubble of quiet blocks

I heard his voice ascending the hill
and at last his low whine as he came
floor by empty floor to the room
where I sat
in my narrow bed looking west, waiting
I heard him snuffle at the door and
I watched
he trotted across the floor

he laid his long gray muzzle
on the spare white spread
and his eyes burned yellow
his small dotted eyebrows quivered

Yes, I said.
I know what they have done.

Mutual respect leads to the ability to communicate across barriers and boundaries. People have dreamed of communicating with animals and even teaching stones to talk. Pablo Neruda's poem and Gary Snyder's essay both manifest respect for how much we have to learn from this complex and beautiful world and how the quality of our lives and character is illuminated by the respect we show for people and nature.

❦ Pablo Neruda, *Bestiary*

If I were able to speak with the birds,
with oysters and with little lizards,
with the foxes of Selva Oscura,
with penguin representatives,
if sheep could understand me,
and tired woollen dogs,
and great cart-horses,
if I could have words with cats,
if chickens would listen to me!

It has never occurred to me to speak
with the genteel animals.
I have no interest in
the opinions of wasps
nor of racehorses.
Let them get on with their flying,
let them win racing colours!
I want to speak to flies,
to the bitch newly delivered,
and have conversation with serpents.

When my feet were able to walk
through threefold nights, now vanished,
I followed the dogs of the dark,
these squalid vagabonds
who pad about in silence
hurrying towards nowhere,
and I followed them for hours;
they were distrustful of me,
the poor insensitive beasts.
They lost the opportunity
of telling me their troubles,
of tailing wretchedly through
the ghost-crowded streets.

I was always curious
about the erotic rabbit.
Who stirs it up, who whispers
in its genital ears?
It never stops procreating,
goes unnoticed in San Francisco,
has no time for trivia.
The rabbit is always at it
with its inexhaustible mechanism,
I would like to speak with the rabbit.
I love its randy habits.

Spiders have been explained away
in imbecilic texts
by exasperating simplifiers
who take the fly's point of view,
who describe them as voracious,
carnal, unfaithful, lascivious.
For me, that reputation
reflects on those who bestow it.
The spider is an engineer,
a divine watchmaker.
For one fly more or less
the foolish can detest them;
I wish to speak with spiders.
I want them to weave me a star.

Fleas interest me so much
that I let them bite me for hours.
They are perfect, ancient as Sanscrit,
relentless as machines.
They bite not in order to eat,
they only bite to go jumping,
the gymnasts of the globe,
the most delicate and accomplished
acrobats in the circus.

Let them gallop across my skin,
let them unbare their feelings,
let them enjoy my blood,
but let someone introduce me;
I want to know them closely,
I want to know what to count on.

I have not been able to form
close friendships with the ruminants.
Of course, I am a ruminant;
I don't see why they misread me.
I shall have to take up this theme
grazing with cows and oxen,
plotting with the bulls.
Somehow I shall know
so many intestinal things
which are concealed inside
deeply, like secret passions.

What do pigs think of the dawn?
They do not sing but bear it up
with their huge pink bodies,
with their small hard hooves.

Pigs bear up the dawn.

Birds gobble up the night.

And in the morning the world
is deserted—spiders and men,
dogs and the wind, all sleep;
pigs grunt and a day breaks.

I want to talk to the pigs.

Frogs, soft, raucous, sonorous—
I always wanted to be a frog,
I always loved the pools and the leaves
slender as filaments,
the green world of watercress
with the frogs lords of the sky.

The serenade of frogs
starts in my dream and illumines it,
starts up like a climbing plant
to the balconies of my childhood,
to my cousin's growing nipples,
to the astronomic jasmine
of black Southern nights,
and now that time has passed,
let them not ask me for the sky;
it seems I still have not learned
the harsh speech of frogs.

If all this is so, how am I a poet?
What do I know of the intimate
geography of the night?

In this world, rushing, subsiding,
I need more communication,
other languages, other signs;
I want to know this world.

Everyone has remained satisfied
with the sinister pronouncements
of capitalists in a hurry
and systematic women.
I want to speak with many things
and I will not leave this planet
without knowing what I came to find,

without solving this affair,
and people are not enough.
I have to go much farther
and I have to go much closer.

So, gentlemen, I am going
to converse with a horse;
let the poetess excuse me,
the professor give me leave.
I shall be busy all week,
I have to listen incessantly.
What was that cat there called?

❦ GARY SNYDER, *Reinhabitation*

I came to the Pacific slope by a line of people that somehow
worked their way west from the Atlantic over 150 years. One grandfather ended up in the Territory of Washington and homesteaded in
Kitsap County. My mother's side were railroad people down in Texas,
and before that they'd worked the silver mines in Leadville, Colorado.
My grandfather being a homesteader and my father a native of the state
of Washington put our family relatively early in the Northwest. But
there were people already there, long before my family, I learned as a
boy. An elderly Salish Indian gentleman came by our farm once every
few months in a Model T truck, selling smoked salmon. "Who is he?"
"He's an Indian," my parents said.

Looking at all the different trees and plants that made up my sec-
ond-growth Douglas fir forest plus cow pasture childhood universe, I
realized that my parents were short on a certain kind of knowledge.
They could say, "That's a Doug fir, that's a cedar, that's bracken fern,"
but I perceived a subtlety and complexity in those woods that went far
beyond a few names.

As a child I spoke with the old Salishan man a few times over the
years he made these stops—then, suddenly, he never came back. I

sensed what he represented, what he knew, and what it meant to me: he knew better than anyone else I had ever met *where I was*. I had no notion of a white American or European heritage providing an identity; I defined myself by relation to the place. Later I also understood that "English language" is an identity—and later, via the hearsay of books, received the full cultural and historical view—but never forgot, or left, that first ground, the "where" of our "who are we?"

There are many people on the planet now who are not "inhabitants." Far from their home villages; removed from ancestral territories; moved into town from the farm; went to pan gold in California—work on the pipeline—work for Bechtel in Iran. Actual inhabitants—peasants, paisanos, paysan, peoples of the land, have been dismissed, laughed at, and overtaxed for centuries by the urban-based ruling elites. The intellectuals haven't the least notion of what kind of sophisticated, attentive, creative intelligence it takes to "grow food." Virtually all the plants in the gardens and the trees in the orchards, the sheep, cows, and goats in the pastures were domesticated in the Neolithic, before "civilization." The differing regions of the world have long had—each—their own precise subsistence pattern developed over millennia by people who had settled in there and learned what particular kinds of plants the ground would "say" at that spot.

Humankind also clearly wanders. Four million years ago those smaller protohumans were moving in and out of the edges of forest and grassland in Africa—fairly warm, open enough to run in. At some point moving on, catching fire, sewing clothes, swinging around the arctic, setting out on amazing sea voyages. During the middle and late Pleistocene, large-fauna hunting era, a fairly nomadic grassland-and-tundra hunting life was established, with lots of mobility across northern Eurasia in particular. With the decline of the Ice Age—and here's where we are—most of the big-game hunters went out of business. There was possibly a population drop in Eurasia and the Americas, as the old techniques no longer worked.

Countless local ecosystem habitation styles emerged. People developed specific ways to *be* in each of those niches: plant knowledge, boats, dogs, traps, nets, fishing—the smaller animals and smaller tools.

From steep jungle slopes of Southwest China to coral atolls to barren arctic deserts—*a spirit of what it was to be* there evolved that spoke of a direct sense of relation to the "land"—which really means, the totality of the local bioregion system, from cirrus clouds to leaf mold.

Inhabitory peoples sometimes say, "This piece of land is sacred"— or "all the land is sacred." This is an attitude that draws on awareness of the mystery of life and death, of taking life to live, of giving life back— not only to your own children but to the life of the whole land.

Abbé Breuil, the French prehistorian who worked extensively in the caves of southern France, has pointed out that the animal murals in those twenty-thousand-year-old caves describe fertility as well as hunting—the birth of little bison and cow calves. They show a tender and accurate observation of the qualities and personalities of different creatures, implying a sense of the mutuality of life and death in the food chain and what I take to be a sense of the sacramental quality of that relationship.

Inhabitation does not mean "not traveling." The term does not of itself define the size of a territory. The size is determined by the bioregion type. The bison hunters of the great plains are as surely in a "territory" as the Indians of northern California, though the latter may have seldom ventured farther than thirty miles from where they were born. Whether a vast grassland or a brushy mountain, the Peoples knew their geography. Any member of a hunting society could recall and visualize any spot in the surrounding landscape and tell you what was there, how to get there. "That's where you'd get some cattails." The bushmen of the Kalahari Desert could locate a buried ostrich egg full of emergency water in the midst of a sandy waste—walk right up and dig it out: "I put this here three years ago, just in case."

As always, Ray Dasmann's terms are useful to make these distinctions: "ecosystem-based cultures" and "biosphere cultures." By that Dasmann means societies whose life and economies are centered in terms of natural regions and watersheds, as against those who discovered—seven or eight thousand years ago in a few corners of the globe— that it was "profitable" to spill over into another drainage, another watershed, another people's territory, and steal away its resources, natural or human. Thus, the Roman Empire would strip whole provinces for the benefit of the capital, and villa owning Roman aristocrats would have huge slave-operated farms in the south using giant wheeled plows. Southern Italy never recovered. We know the term *imperialism*— Dasmann's concept of "biosphere cultures" helps us realize that biological exploitation is a critical part of imperialism, too: the species made extinct, the clear-cut forests.

All that wealth and power pouring into a few centers had bizarre results. Philosophies and religions based on fascination with society, hierarchy, manipulation, and the "absolute." A great edifice called "the state" and the symbols of central power—in China what they used to call "the true dragon"; in the West, as Mumford says, symbolized perhaps by that Bronze Age fort called the Pentagon. No wonder Lévi-Strauss says that civilization has been in a long decline since the Neolithic.

So here in the twentieth century we find Occidentals and Orientals studying each other's wisdom, and a few people on both sides studying what came before both—before they forked off. A book like *Black Elk Speaks*, which would probably have had zero readership in 1900, is perceived now as speaking of certain things that nothing in the Judeo-Christian tradition, and very little in the Hindu-Buddhist tradition, deals with. All the world religions remain primarily human-centered. That next step is excluded or forgotten—"Well, what do you say to Magpie? What do you say to Rattlesnake when you meet him?" What do we learn from Wren, and Hummingbird, and Pine Pollen, and how? Learn what? Specifics: how to spend a life facing the current; or what it is perpetually to die young; or how to be huge and calm and eat *anything* (Bear). But also, that we are many selves looking at each other, through the same eye.

The reason many of us want to make this step is simple, and is explained in terms of the forty-thousand-year looping back that we seem to be involved in. Sometime in the last twenty years the best brains of the Occident discovered to their amazement that we live in an Environment. This discovery has been forced on us by the realization that we are approaching the limits of something. Stewart Brand said that the photograph of the earth (taken from outer space by a satellite) that shows the whole blue orb with spirals and whorls of cloud was a great landmark for human consciousness. We see that it has a shape, and it has limits. We are back again, now, in the position of our Mesolithic forebears— working off the coasts of southern Britain, or the shores of Lake Chad, or the swamps of Southeast China, learning how to live by the sun and the green at that spot. We once more know that we live in a system that is enclosed in a certain way, that has its own kinds of limits, and that we are interdependent with it.

The ethics or morality of this is far more subtle than merely being nice to squirrels. The biological-ecological sciences have been laying out (implicitly) a spiritual dimension. We must find our way to seeing the mineral cycles, the water cycles, air cycles, nutrient cycles as sacramental—and we must incorporate that insight into our own personal spiritual quest and integrate it with all the wisdom teachings we have received from the nearer past. The expression of it is simple: feeling gratitude to it all; taking responsibility for your own acts; keeping contact with the sources of the energy that flow into your own life (namely dirt, water, flesh).

Another question is raised: is not the purpose of all this living and studying the achievement of self-knowledge, self-realization? How does knowledge of place help us know the Self? The answer, simply put, is that we are all composite beings, not only physically but intellectually, whose sole individual identifying feature is a particular form or structure changing constantly in time. There is no "self" to be found in that, and yet oddly enough, there is. Part of you is out there waiting to come into you, and another part of you is behind you, and the "just this" of the ever-present moment holds all the transitory little selves in its mirror. The Avatamsaka ("Flower Wreath") jeweled-net-interpenetration-ecological-systems-emptiness-consciousness tells us no self-realization without the Whole Self, and the whole self is the whole thing.

Thus, knowing who we are and knowing where we are are intimately linked. There are no limits to the possibilities of the study of *who* and *where*, if you want to go "beyond limits"—and so, even in a world of biological limits, there is plenty of open mind-space to go out into.

Summing Up

In Wendell Berry's essay "The Unsettling of America," he points out that the way the economic system works now, you're penalized if you try to stay in one spot and do anything well. It's not just that the integrity of Native American land is threatened, or national forests and parks; it's *all* land that's under the gun, and any person or group of people who tries to stay there and do some one thing well, long enough to be able to say, "I really love and know this place," stands to be penalized. The economics of it works so that anyone who jumps at the chance for quick profit is rewarded—doing proper agriculture means *not* to jump at the most profitable chance—proper forest management or game management means doing things with the far future in mind— and the future is unable to pay us for it right now. Doing things right means living as though your grandchildren would also be alive, in this land, carrying on the work we're doing right now, with deepening delight.

I saw old farmers in Kentucky last spring who belong in another century. They are inhabitants; they see the world they know crumbling and evaporating before them in the face of a different logic that declares, "Everything you know, and do, and the way you do it, mean nothing to us." How much more the pain and loss of elegant cultural skills on the part of the nonwhite Fourth World primitive remnant cultures—who may know the special properties of a certain plant or how to communicate with dolphins, skills the industrial world might never regain. Not that special, intriguing knowledges are the real point: it's the sense of the magic system, the capacity to hear the song of Gaia *at that spot*, that's lost.

Reinhabitory refers to the tiny number of persons who come out of the industrial societies (having collected or squandered the fruits of eight thousand years of civilization) and then start to turn back to the land, back to place. This comes for some with the rational and scientific realization of interconnectedness and planetary limits. But the actual demands of a life committed to a place, and living somewhat by the sunshine green-plant energy that is concentrating in that spot, are so physically and intellectually intense that it is a moral and spiritual choice as well.

Mankind has a rendezvous with destiny in outer space, some have predicted. Well: we are already traveling in space—this is the galaxy, right here. The wisdom and skill of those who studied the universe firsthand, by direct knowledge and experience, for millennia, both inside and outside themselves, are what we might call the Old Ways. Those who envision a possible future planet on which we continue that study, and where we live by the green and the sun, have no choice but to bring whatever science, imagination, strength, and political finesse they have to the support of the inhabitory people—natives and peasants of the world. In making common cause with them, we become "rein-habitory." And we begin to learn a little of the Old Ways, which are outside of history, and forever new.

12

The Common Problem

FAIRNESS AND A COMMITMENT TO JUSTICE

Being fair implies accepting other people's rights as well as claiming one's own. It implies a commitment to action and is not merely a matter of belief. As Robert Browning phrased it in "Bishop Blougram's Apology":

The common problem, yours, mine, everyone's
Is—not to fancy what were fair in life
Provided it could be—but finding first
What may be, then find how to make it fair
Up to our means.

To be fair is to incorporate values such as generosity, compassion, and respect into everyday behavior. It is to balance giving other people their voice and their share of resources while maintaining your own part. It is a matter of reciprocity—of living in ways that encourage the development of a convivial common life in which people support rather than take advantage of each other.

The rationale for acting fairly has been debated. For some people it is a matter of acting without self-interest, of being committed to fundamental ideals of democracy that imply that all people have, as the African-American gospel song puts it, "a right to the tree of life." For others, fairness does have a component of self-interest as it provides the social context in which individuals can flourish.

In either case, being fair implies an obligation to act without favoritism or prejudice and holding other people in the same high regard you hold yourself, your family, and your circle of friends. It means being engaged in other people's lives in a caring manner.

Fairness plays itself out in many simple and immediate ways, such as treating all of one's own children in the same way or sharing wealth and resources within the family. It functions in business by paying people the same wage for equal work or making sure that everyone has an equal opportunity for employment. It works through refusing to accept the prejudices of society and treating all people, regardless of gender, sexual orientation, or background, in a equitable manner. Being fair also implies resistance and opposition to intolerance and prejudice in all of their manifestations.

There are many temptations to limit the scope of fairness in one's life: to act out of self-interest, hoard precious resources, or treat one's loved ones in privileged ways when it comes to work and opportunity. Being fair and remaining fair is a constant struggle that has many contradictions, especially when resources are limited or social and economic pressures make one's own life difficult.

Commitment to justice takes fairness even a step further and implies that one is willing to stand up and speak out for the fundamental rights of all people throughout the world, whether or not it has any specific effect on your personal life. It goes beyond fairness in voting or in having access to facilities, and reaches toward universal values and rights that encompass economic as well as social and political aspects of life. It implies engaging oneself with larger issues in the world, such as lack of free expression or human rights, poverty, unreasonable imprisonment, ethnic- or gender-based hatred, and economic exploitation.

Commitment to fairness and justice requires keeping your eyes open to other people's realities as well as to your own experiences. It requires speaking out when it might be more comfortable to stay silent and being discontent so long as people are hungry or being treated unfairly, no matter how well your life might be going. It requires keeping memories alive and not looking away when horrible things happen. The Russian poet Anna

Akhmatova, who suffered the horrors of Stalinism, beautifully expressed this complex and courageous act of witness:

> No foreign sky protected me,
> no stranger's wing shielded my face.
> I stand as witness to the common lot,
> survivor of that time, that place.

Witness, however, is just the beginning. Action is often necessary and people willing to risk their resources, reputations, and lives for issues of fairness and justice are moral exemplars, models of the kind of people we can aspire to become. Sometimes such moral quality is manifested in simple acts, as Martín Espada illustrates in this short poem:

> Julio cheats
> signing his name,
> copying slowly
> from his Social Security card,
> man's hand
> scratching letters child-crooked.

> But Julio's black hand
> was schooled for lettuce-picking,
> not lawsuits.

Selections

The selections that follow illustrate the dangers of being passive in the face of oppression and unfairness, as well as the complex nature and consequences of taking justice to one's heart. They speak not merely to the risks of speaking out, but to the fundamental joy and sense of belonging that result from acting according to conscience instead of succumbing to the whims of self-indulgence.

The first poem speaks to the danger of yielding to the temptations of power untempered and unchecked by a sense of fairness.

Miroslav Holub, *Parasite*

It rises somewhere in the inner dark
like the fruit of a surplus morning star.
It eats with a worm's tiny mouth,
sweetly round, lined with hooklets
of embryonic exactitude.

It grows, releasing one segment after another,
impregnated by the drowsy ballads of mucosae,
embedded in agreement's protective slime,
it grows, swells, expands,

outgrows the body of its host
as a child outgrows its mother,
ingesting and digesting affectionately
the last epics dealing with
the life of the Lord of the Flies,

and now it grows bigger and still bigger,
larger than life-sized,
the original body's inside now,
the host is the parasite's parasite,
breathing out night and mucus
like a leaf breathing oxygen,
condensing dew-drops, agreeably crunching
with a scarcely audible smacking
the stiff reality of tombstones without
    inscriptions.

It spills out from house to town,
and from town into landscape, releasing articles
agreeing in principle with Vesuvius's eruption,
with the Krebs cycle and the cutting off
of right hands and left ears,

agreeing in principle with mercilessness,
agreeing in principle with evolution,
the laws of which it ignores
because of the principles of parasitology,

it attains a philosophical dimension
in which it's the only form of matter,
in which it's the only proportion of
    disproportion.

and when it shrinks again
to the size of a sigmoid loop,
in the derelict landscape of tombstones and
    mercilessness
there will be a draft, as in a tunnel,
for years the eruption will die away
and little spores of imbecile agreement
will bore into granite and wait there
like wet dynamite.

The poem by Anna Akhmatova is about resolve, the deep passion to struggle for others as well as for oneself.

❧ ANNA AKHMATOVA, *I Have Learned How Faces Fall to Bone*

I have learned how faces fall to bone,
how under the eyelids terror lurks,
how suffering inscribes on cheeks
the hard lines of its cuneiform texts,
how glossy black or ash-fair locks
turn overnight to tarnished silver,
how smiles fade on submissive lips,
and fear quavers in a dry titter.

And I pray not for myself alone . . .
for all who stood outside the jail,
in bitter cold or summer's blaze,
with me under that blind red wall.

It is possible to act with scrupulous fairness in everyday life and still not devote time and effort to issues of justice. This commitment to justice, to standing up and opposing abuse and oppression wherever they manifest themselves, is expressed in this moving prayer by Vahan Tekeyan.

❧ VAHAN TEKEYAN, *Prayer on the Threshold of Tomorrow*

Look. New sprouts push through the fields.
But which are thorns and which wheat
I do not know. Perhaps to the appetite
that is sated, all is chaff,
while to the hungry all is wheat.

Undistinguishable sounds, blows, footfalls
thud in the distance, an agonizing attack,
where the oppressed plant red
flames with their blood.
And the rains sweat and expand
into floods that shake the walls
of the oldest dams.

Lord, now is the time to send
your wisdom and kindness
to the tortured who, although
they have forgotten, need you as they hurl
themselves closer to the precipice.

Oh, God, who trimmed the wick of the mind
and poured the oil of life, do not let

your lamps be overturned.
Let them illuminate paths to your truth.

Plant love in the eyes of today's
and tomorrow's mighty. Do not let
their hearts close.

And do not let the hearts of the child
and the aged be strangers
to tenderness and hope.

Let the struggle of our time be short.
Let it be settled with justice.

Let the fortress of egos,
that huge barricade,
crumble. And let every treasure
go to every man. Let every garden
gate be open. But let no flower be crushed.
No single branch fall.

Here is a series of poems speaking from different cultural backgrounds, perspectives, and times, about keeping one's ears, eyes, and heart open to issues of fairness and justice. They are also about resistance to oppression and taking a stand based on values. Some are painful statements about other people's pain; others are ironic and even humorous. They represent some of the many modalities of resistance that sustain people who choose to make a commitment to fairness and justice fundamental aspects of their own character.

❧ FEDERICO GARCÍA LORCA, *Casida of Sobbing*

I have shut my balcony door
because I don't want to hear the sobbing,
but from behind the grayish walls
nothing else comes out but sobbing.

Very few angels are singing,
very few dogs are barking,
a thousand violins fit into the palm of my hand.

But the sobbing is a gigantic dog,
the sobbing is a gigantic angel,
the sobbing is a gigantic violin,
tears close the wind's jaws,
all there is to hear is sobbing.

❦ WILLIAM WANTLING, *Rune for the Disenchanted*

What if:

—In a moment of pure terror I refused the call of Beauty
by stuffing bank notes in my ear?

—In a moment of pure intuition I bit and scratched my
cat and sought to learn her secret?

—In a moment of pure compassion I refused to hate my
enemy?

—In a moment of pure vision I awoke from out of my
lonely dream?

—In a moment of pure understanding I howled with
laughter which never ceased, flinging roses all about
me?

—In a moment of pure decision I called our game a
draw?

—In a moment of pure sophistication I refused to play
my role and pierced my ears with seashells?

—In a moment of pure inspiration I began to love my
dream of life, and thus resumed my game and role?

❦ IRINA RATUSHINSKAYA, *But Only Not to Think*

. . . But only not to think about the journey
On roads hot, dusty, to be walked all day.
Preserve me, my uncompromising reason,
Don't let the reins go now, only half-way.

A long time yet we must fight off together
The suffocating nights, the prison airs,
The prison dreams—hallucinations, almost,
The senseless gibes of executioners,

The treachery of the wearied, and their kisses'
Poison . . . Die, but afterwards fight on—
Not knowing how long the term, and not possessing
The right yet to declare our strength is done.

Don't let us weaken; punish with refusal
Each childish "Can't take any more, I'm through . . . "
Preserve me in this midnight age, my reason.
Keep me from harm—and I'll watch over you.

❦ GWENDOLYN BROOKS, *First Fight. Then Fiddle*

First fight. Then fiddle. Ply the slipping string
With feathery sorcery; muzzle the note
With hurting love; the music that they wrote
Bewitch, bewilder. Qualify to sing
Threadwise. Devise no salt, no hempen thing
For the dear instrument to bear. Devote
The bow to silks and honey. Be remote
A while from malice and from murdering.
But first to arms, to armor. Carry hate

In front of you and harmony behind.
Be deaf to music and to beauty blind.
Win war. Rise bloody, maybe not too late
For having first to civilize a space
Wherein to play your violin with grace.

❦ LUCILLE CLIFTON, *Turning*

turning into my own
turning on in
to my own self
at last
turning out of the
white cage. turning out of the
lady cage
turning at last
on a stem like black fruit
in my own season
at last

❦ QUINCY TROUPE, *After Hearing a Radio Announcement*

yesterday, in new york city
the gravediggers went on strike
& today, the undertakers went on strike
because, they said, of the overwhelming
number of corpses
stretched out on tables
in the overworked, embalming rooms
(unnecessarily, they said, because of wars
& plenty stupid killings in the streets
& et cetera & et cetera, et cetera)

sweating up the world, corpses
propped up straight in living room chairs

ensconced at dinner tables, jamming up cars
on freeways, clogging up rivers, stopping up elevators
grinning toothless in stairwells
taking up kids' space in front of tvs
standing in line for bank tellers
stinking up bedrooms
in the gutters, dead as rudders
corpses, everywhere you turn

& the undertakers said they were being overworked
with all this goddamned killing going on
said they couldn't even enjoy all the money they was making
like a bandit, said that this shit has got to stop

& today eye just heard, on the radio, that
the coffin makers are waiting, in the wings, for their chance
to do the very same thing, & tomorrow & if things keep going
this way, eye expect to hear of the corpses
themselves, boycotting death
until things get better
or at least, getting themselves
together, in some sort of union
espousing self-determination, for better
funerals & burial conditions, or something
extraordinarily heavy & serious, like that

❧ AMITAVA KUMAR, *Primary Lessons in Political Economy*

For every ten bushels of paddy she harvests
    the landless laborer takes home one.

This woman, whose name is Hiria, would have to starve
    for three days to buy a liter of milk.

If she were to check her hunger and not eat
    for a month, she could buy a book of poems.

And if Hiria, who works endlessly, could starve
    endlessly, in ten years she could buy that piece

Of land on which during short winter evenings
    the landlord's son plays badminton.

It is not unusual for struggles for justice to be misrepresented as personal actions taken out of anger and frustration at a particular moment. Rosa Parks's refusal to move to the back of a segregated bus, which was the precipitating event that led to the Montgomery bus boycott in 1955 during the Civil Rights Movement, is an example. Many textbooks claim that Mrs. Parks's action was taken because she was tired and angry, but the following essays shows how in fact it was part of a larger, planned, and very risky struggle for justice.

❧ HERBERT KOHL, *The Story of Rosa Parks and the Montgomery Bus Boycott*

The story of Rosa Parks and the Montgomery bus boycott is a cultural myth in the United States. Here is a generic version of the myth, one I made up after reading dozens of school textbooks and children's books dealing with the Civil Rights Movement of the 1950's and 1960's.

"Rosa Was Tired: The Story of the Montgomery Bus Boycott"

Rosa Parks was a poor seamstress. She lived in Montgomery, Alabama, during the 1950's. Those days there still was segregation in parts of the United States. That meant that African-Americans and European Americans were not allowed to use the same public facilities such as restaurants or swimming pools. It also meant that whenever it was crowded on the city buses African-Americans had to give up seats in front to European Americans and move to the back of the bus.

One day on her way home from work Rosa was tired and sat down in the front of the bus. As the bus got crowded she was asked to give up her seat to a European American man and she refused. The bus driver told her she had to go to the back of the bus and she still refused to move. It was a hot day and she was tired and angry, and became very stubborn.

The driver called a policeman who arrested Rosa.

When other African-Americans in Montgomery heard this they became angry too, so they decided to refuse to ride the buses until everyone was allowed to ride together. They boycotted the buses.

The boycott, which was led by Martin Luther King, Jr., succeeded. Now African-Americans and European Americans can ride the buses together in Montgomery.

Rosa Parks was a very brave person.

This story seems innocent enough. Rosa Parks is treated with respect and dignity and the African-American community is given credit for running the boycott and winning the struggle. However, on closer examination the story reveals some distressing characteristics that serve to turn an organized and carefully planned movement for social change into a spontaneous outburst based upon frustration and anger. The following annotations on "Rosa Was Tired" suggest that we need a new story, one more in line with the truth and directed at showing the organizational intelligence and determination of the African-American community in Montgomery, as well as the role of the bus boycott in the larger struggle to desegregate Birmingham and the South.

The Annotated "Rosa Was Tired"

1. Rosa Parks was a seamstress who was poor. She lived in Montgomery, Alabama, during the 1950s.

Rosa Parks was the Executive Secretary of the Montgomery NAACP at the time of the boycott, which she considered her main job. She had also worked for E. D. Nixon, vice president of the Brotherhood of Sleeping Car Porters, in the union's office. Her work as a seamstress in a large department store was secondary to her community work. In addition she had, as she says in an interview printed in *My Soul is Rested* (Howard Raines, Bantam, 1978, p. 35), "almost a life history of being rebellious against being mistreated because of my color." She was well-known to all of the African-American leaders in Montgomery for her opposition to segregation, her leadership abilities, and her moral strength. She attended an interracial meeting at the Highlander Folk School in Tennessee a few months before the boycott and indicated there that she intended to become an active participant in attempts to overcome segregation. Finally Rosa Parks had the active support of her mother and her husband in her civil rights activities. To call Rosa Parks a poor tired seamstress and not talk about her role as a community leader as well is to turn an organized struggle for freedom into a personal act of frustration. It is a thorough misrepresentation of the Civil Rights Movement in Montgomery. Here is another way of beginning a children's version of the Montgomery bus boycott:

It was 1955. Everyone in the African-American community in Montgomery, Alabama, knew Rosa Parks. She was a leader and people admired her courage. All throughout her life she had opposed prejudice, even if it got her into trouble with European American people.

2. Those days there still was segregation in parts of the United States. That meant that African-Americans and European Americans were not allowed to use the same public facilities.

The existence of legalized segregation in the South during the 1950's is integral to the story of the Montgomery bus boycott, yet it is an embarrassment to many school people and difficult to explain to children without accounting for the moral corruption of the majority of the European-American community in the South. The sentence I composed is one way of avoiding direct confrontation with the moral issues of segregation. First it says "Those days there was still segregation" as if segregation is no longer an issue. This is particularly pernicious at a time when overt racism is once again becoming a common phenomenon and children have to be helped to understand and eliminate it.

Describing integration passively ("there was still segregation" instead of "European Americans created segregated facilities and enforced their use") also ignores the issue of legalized segregation even though Mrs. Parks was arrested for a violation of the Alabama state law. It doesn't talk overtly about racism. And it refers to "parts" of the United States, softening the tone and muddying the reference to the South.

This softening of the tone is also evident in the next sentence, which says that "African-Americans and European Americans were not allowed to use the same public facilities." It puts "African-Americans" and "European Americans" on the same footing, as if there was some symmetry there and both were punished by the segregation laws. A more appropriate way of describing the situation would be "African-American people were prevented by law from using the same public facilities as European Americans. In addition, the African-American facilities were vastly inferior to the ones made available to European Americans."

Even this rewriting is generous given the pervasive, brutal, and total nature of segregation in the pre–civil rights South. Perhaps the best analogy that could be used here is apartheid.

Recasting of the third and fourth sentences of "Rosa Was Tired" is called for:

Those days Alabama was legally segregated. That means that African-American people were prevented by the state law from using the same swimming pools, schools, and other public facilities as European Americans. There also were separate entrances, toilets, and drinking fountains for African-Americans and European Americans in places such as bus and train stations. The facilities African-Americans were allowed to use were not only separate from the ones European Americans used, but they were also inferior. The reason for this was racism, the belief that European Americans were superior to African-Americans and that, therefore, European Americans deserved better facilities.

3. Whenever it was crowded on the city buses, African-American people had to give up seats in front to European Americans and move to the back of the bus.

Actually, African-Americans were never allowed to sit in the front of the bus in the South in those days. The front seats were reserved for European Americans. Between five and ten rows back, the "colored" section began. When the front of the bus filled up, African-Americans seated in the "colored" section had to give up their seats and move toward the back of the bus.

The next sentence should be expanded as follows:

Those days public buses were divided into two sections: The one at the front for European Americans, which was supposed to be "for whites only." From five to ten rows back the section for African-Americans began. That part of the bus was called the "colored" section.

Whenever it was crowded on the city buses, African-American people were forced to give up seats in the "colored" section to European Americans and move to the back of the bus. For example, an elderly African-American woman would have to give up her seat to a European American teenage male. If she refused, she could be arrested for breaking the segregation laws.

4. One day on her way home from work, Rosa was tired and sat down in the front of the bus.

Rosa Parks did not sit in the front of the bus. She sat in the front row of the "colored" section. When the bus got crowded, she refused to give up her seat in the "colored" section to a European American.

At this point, the story lapses into the familiar and refers to Rosa Parks as "Rosa." However, given that it was a sanctioned social practice in the South during the time of the story for European Americans to call African-American adults by their first names as a way of reinforcing the African-Americans' inferior status, it is not wise to use that practice in the story. The following is more respectful and historically accurate:

One day on her way home from work, Rosa Parks was tired and sat down in the front row of the "colored" section of the bus she usually rode home on.

5. As the bus got crowded, she was asked to give up her seat to a European American man and she refused. The bus driver told her she had to go to the back of the bus and she still refused to move. It was a hot day and she was tired and angry and became very stubborn.

The driver called a policeman who arrested Rosa.

This is the way that Rosa Parks described her experiences with buses:

> I had problems with bus drivers over the years because I didn't see fit to pay my money into the front and then go around to the back. Sometimes bus drivers wouldn't permit me to get on the bus, and I had been evicted from the bus. But as I say, there had been incidents over the years. One of the things that made this . . . (incident) . . . get so much publicity was the fact that the police were called in and I was placed under arrest.

Mere anger and stubbornness could not account for the clear resolve with which Rosa Parks acted. She knew what she was doing, understood the consequences, and was prepared to confront segregation head on at whatever sacrifice she had to make. A more accurate account of the event, taking into consideration Rosa Parks' past history, might be:

As the bus got crowded, the driver demanded that she give up her seat to a European American man and move to the back of the bus. This was not the first time that this had happened to Rosa Parks. In the past, she refused to move and the driver simply put her off the bus.

Mrs. Parks hated segregation, and along with many other African-American people refused to obey many of its unfair rules. She refused to do what the bus driver demanded.

The bus driver commanded her once more to go to the back of the bus, and she stayed in her seat, looking straight ahead and not moving an inch. It was a hot day and the driver was angry and became very stubborn. He called a policeman who arrested Mrs. Parks.

6. When other African-Americans in Montgomery heard this they became angry too, so they decided to refuse to ride the the buses until everyone was allowed to ride together. They boycotted the buses.

The connection between Rosa Parks's arrest and the boycott is a mystery in most accounts of what happened in Montgomery. Community support for the boycott is portrayed as being instantaneous and miraculously effective the very day after Mrs. Parks was arrested. It is an insult to the intelligence and courage of the African-American community in Montgomery to turn their planned resistance to segregation into a spontaneous emotional response. The actual situation was more interesting and complex.

According to E. D. Nixon, in the three months preceding Mrs. Parks's arrest at least three other African-American people had been arrested in Montgomery for refusing to give up their bus seats. In each case, people in leadership positions in the African-American community in Montgomery investigated the background of the person arrested. They were looking for someone who had the respect of the community and the strength to deal with all of the publicity that would result from being at the center of a bus boycott. This leads to the most important point left out in popularized accounts of the Montgomery bus boycott: *The boycott had been planned and organized before Rosa Parks was arrested.*

The story goes back at least as far as 1949. In Montgomery, there was an African-American women's organization headed by Jo Ann Gibson Robinson, a professor at Alabama State College, and called the Woman's Political Council (WPC). In 1949, Professor Gibson was put off a bus in Montgomery for refusing to move from her seat in the fifth row of an almost empty bus. She says in her book *The Montgomery Bus Boycott and the Women Who Started It: The Memoir of Jo Ann Gibson Robinson* (University of Tennessee Press, 1987) that "it was during the period of 1949–1955 that the Women's Political Council of Montgomery . . . prepared to stage a bus boycott when the time was ripe and the people were ready."

This story of collective decision making, willed risk, and coordinated action is more dramatic than the story of an angry individual who sparked a demonstration; one that has more to teach children who themselves may have to organize and act collectively against oppressive forces in the future. Here's one way to tell this complex story to young children:

Mrs. Parks was not the first African-American person to be arrested in Montgomery for refusing to move to the back of the bus. In the months before her refusal, at least three other people were arrested for the same reason. In fact, African-American leaders in Montgomery were planning to overcome segregation. One way they wanted to do this was to have every African-American person boycott the buses. Since most of the bus riders in the city were African-American, the buses would go broke if they refused to let African-Americans and European Americans ride the buses as equals.

From 1949 right up to the day Mrs. Parks refused to move, the Woman's Political Council of Montgomery prepared to stage a bus boycott because of how African-Americans were treated on the bus. They were just waiting for the time to be ripe and the African-American people in Montgomery were ready to support the boycott. The right time was 1955.

However, none of the people who were arrested before Mrs. Parks were leaders. She was, and the day she was arrested the leadership called a meeting at the Dexter Avenue Baptist Church. They decided to begin their refusal to ride the buses the next morning. They knew Mrs. Parks had the courage to deal with the pressure of defying segregation and would not yield even if her life was threatened.

The next day the Montgomery bus boycott began.

7. The boycott, which was led by Martin Luther King, Jr., succeeded. Now African-Americans and European Americans can ride the buses together in Montgomery.

Rosa Parks was a very brave person.

The boycott was planned by the WPC, E.D. Nixon, and others in Montgomery. Martin Luther King, Jr., was a new member of the community. He had just taken over the Dexter Avenue Baptist Church, and when Nixon told him that Rosa Parks's arrest was just what everybody was waiting for to kick off a bus boycott and assault the institution of segregation, King was reluctant to join in at first. However, the community people chose him to lead and he accepted their call. The boycott lasted 381 days, something not usually mentioned in children's books. It did succeed and was one of the events that sparked the entire Civil Rights Movement. People who had been planning an overt attack on segregation for years took that victory as a sign that the time was ripe. Here's one possible way to convey this to children:

There was a young new minister in Montgomery those days. His name was Martin Luther King, Jr. People in the community felt that he was a special person and asked him to lead the boycott. At first he wasn't sure. He worried about the violence that might result from the boycott. However, he quickly made up his mind that it was time to destroy segregation and accepted the people's call for him to be their leader.

The Montgomery bus boycott lasted 381 days. For over a year, the African-American people of Montgomery, Alabama, stayed off the buses. Some walked to work, others rode bicycles or shared car rides. It was very hard for them, but they knew that what they were doing was very important for all African-American people in the South.

The boycott succeeded, and by the end of 1956 African-Americans and European Americans could ride the buses in Montgomery as equals. However, the struggle for the complete elimination of segregation had just begun.

We all owe a great deal to the courage and intelligence of Rosa Parks and the entire African-American community of Montgomery, Alabama. They took risks to make democracy work for all of us.

Concluding Thoughts

What remains then, is to retitle the story. The revised version is still about Rosa Parks, but it is also about the African-American people of Montgomery, Alabama. This does not diminish Rosa Parks in any way. It places her, however, in the midst of a consciously planned movement for social change, and reminds me of the freedom song "We shall not be moved," for it was precisely Rosa Parks's and the community's refusal to be moved that made the boycott possible. For that reason, the new title, *She Would Not Be Moved: The Story of Rosa Parks and the Montgomery Bus Boycott* makes sense.

When the story of the Montgomery bus boycott is told merely as a tale of a heroic person, it leaves children hanging. Not everyone is a hero or heroine. Of course, the idea that only special people can create change is useful if you want to prevent mass movements and keep change from happening. Not every child can be a Rosa Parks, but everyone can imagine herself or himself as a participant in the boycott. As a tale of a social movement and a community effort to overthrow injustice, the Rosa Parks story opens the possibility of every child identifying herself or himself as an activist, as someone who can help make justice happen. And it is that kind of empowerment that people in the United States desperately need.

Sara Evans's Personal Politics *provides a sense of what it is like to be actively engaged in a movement for justice. It is about the courageous young women who chose to go South to participate in the Civil Rights Movement.*

✦ SARA EVANS, *Personal Politics*

Frightened parents used every weapon they could muster: "We'll cut off your money," or "You don't love us!" Even activist parents, who themselves had taken serious risks for causes they believed in, were troubled. Mimi Feingold learned years later that when she joined the freedom rides her mother became ill with worry. Heather Tobis's uncle wrote that her work in Mississippi compared with the struggle against fascism in the 1930s and 1940s. "We are proud to claim you as our own," he said. But her parents asked angrily over the phone, "Did you know how much it takes to make a child?" Whether they kept their fears to themselves or openly opposed their children's participation, the messages from such parents, both overt and subliminal, were mixed: "We believe in what you're doing—but don't do it." Their parental love and concern could only heighten their daughter's ambivalences. In the face of pressures like these, women who volunteered to go south had to have the strength to handle the emotional fallout of strained relationships. The decision itself often represented a forceful act of self-assertion. Compared with male volunteers, the women tended to be more qualified and to have more political experience.

For the young women who went south, the difficulties they faced in deciding to become involved were overridden by the moral excitement and vision that the civil rights movement generated. The rhetoric used reinforced the spirit of idealism that characterized northern middle-class student involvement, as it had the southern students' religious commitment. Phrases like "freedom," "equality," and "community" fired the imaginations of young people who believed they would participate in changing the course of history. "I have a dream," "we shall overcome." Again and again in their applications to come south they conveyed a sense of urgency, "I can't stand on the sidelines," "I can't sit by any longer." A generation steeped in ideas drawn from existential theology and philosophy translated the concept, "beloved community," into a belief in the power of transforming human relationships. . . .

The songs of the movement constituted one of the strongest forces sustaining the spirit of insurgency in the south. Vivian Leburg reflected years afterward, "I got a lot of my politics from the songs." Sally Belfrage described "We Shall Overcome" as "the only song that has no clapping, because the hands are holding all the other hands. A suspension from color, hate, recrimination, guilt, suffering—a kind of lesson in miniature of what it's all about. The song begins slowly, and somehow, without anticipation of these things: just the song, the last one, before we separate. You see the others, and the instant when it comes to each one to think what the words mean, when each nearly breaks, wondering, shall we overcome? The hands hold each other tighter, Mrs. Hamer is smiling, ringing out the words, and crying at once. 'Black and white together.' She leads the next verse, and a sort of joy begins to grow in every face; 'we are not afraid'—and for just that second no one is afraid, because they are free."

The first of these selections is the U.S. government document that ordered all people of Japanese ancestry into internment camps during World War II. Following it is a poem in response to the document written by a Japanese-American poet who, while keeping that memory alive, talks about fairness, justice, and the larger commitments that work to avoid the oppression of any peoples.

❦ PRESIDIO OF SAN FRANCISCO, CALIFORNIA, MAY 3, 1942, *Instructions to All Persons of Japanese Ancestry Living in the Following Area*

All of that portion of the City of Los Angeles, State of California, within that boundary beginning at the point at which North Figueroa Street meets a line following the middle of the Los Angeles River; thence southerly and following the said line to East First Street; thence westerly on East First Street to Alameda Street; thence southerly on Alameda Street to East Third Street; thence northwesterly on East Third Street to Main Street; thence northerly on Main Street to First Street; thence northwesterly on first Street to Figueroa Street; thence northwesterly on Figueroa Street to the point of beginning.

Pursuant to the provisions of Civilian Exclusion Order No. 33, this Headquarters, dated May 3, 1942, all persons of Japanese ancestry, both alien and non-alien, will be evacuated from the above area by 12 o'clock noon, P.W.T., Saturday, May 9, 1942.

No Japanese person living in the above area will be permitted to change residence after 12 o'clock noon, P.W.T., Sunday, May 3, 1942, without obtaining special permission from the representative of the Commanding General, Southern California Sector, at the Civil Control Station located at:

Japanese Union Church,
120 North San Pedro Street,
Los Angeles, California

Such permits will only be granted for the purpose of uniting members of a family, or in cases of emergency.

The Civil Control Station is equipped to assist the Japanese population affected by this evacuation in the following ways:

1. Give advice and instructions on the evacuation.

2. Provide services with respect to the management, leasing, sale, storage or other disposition of most kinds of property, such as real estate, busi-

ness and professional equipment, household goods, boats, automobiles and livestock.

3. Provide temporary residence elsewhere for all Japanese in family groups.

4. Transport persons and a limited amount of clothing and equipment to their new residence.

The Following Instructions Must Be Observed:

1. A responsible member of each family, preferably the head of the family, or the person in whose name most of the property is held, and each individual living alone, will report to the Civil Control Station to receive further instructions. This must be done between 8:00 A.M. and 5:00 P.M. on Monday, May 4, 1942, or between 8:00 A.M. and 5:00 P.M. on Tuesday, May 5, 1942.

2. Evacuees must carry with them on departure for the Assembly Center, the following property:

    A. Bedding and linens (no mattress) for each member of the family;

    B. Toilet articles for each member of the family;

    C. Extra clothing for each member of the family;

    D. Sufficient knives, forks, spoons, plates, bowls and cups for each member of the family;

    E. Essential personal effects for each member of the family.

    All items carried will be securely packaged, tied and plainly marked with the name of the owner and numbered in accordance with instructions obtained at the Civil Control Station. The size and number of packages is limited to that which can be carried by the individual or family group.

3. No pets of any kind will be permitted.

4. No personal items and no household goods will be shipped to the Assembly Center.

5. The United States Government through its agencies will provide for the storage, at the sole risk of the owner, of the more substantial household items, such as iceboxes, washing machines, pianos and other heavy furniture. Cooking utensils and other small items will be accepted for storage if crated, packed and plainly marked with the name and address of the owner. Only one name and address will be used by a given family.

6. Each family, and individual living alone, will be furnished transportation to the Assembly Center or will be authorized to travel by private automobile in a supervised group. All instructions pertaining to the movement will be obtained at the Civil Control Station.

> Go to the Civil Control Station between the hours of 8:00 A.M. and 5:00 P.M., Monday, May 4, 1942, or between the hours of 8:00 A.M. and 5:00 P.M., Tuesday, May 5, 1942, to receive further instructions.
> Civilian Exclusion Order No. 33

J. L. DeWITT
Lieutenant General, U.S. Army
Commanding

❦ LAWSON FUSAO INADA, *Instructions to All Persons*

Let us take
what we can
for the occasion:

> Ancestry. *(Ancestry)*
> All of that portion. *(Portion)*
> With the boundary. *(Boundary)*
> Beginning. *(Beginning)*
> At the point. *(Point)*
> Meets a line. *(Line)*
> Following the middle. *(Middle)*
> Thence southerly. *(Southerly)*
> Following the said line. *(Following) (Said)*

Thence westerly. *(Westerly)*
Thence northerly. *(Northerly)*
To the point. *(Point)*
Of beginning. *(Beginning) (Ancestry)*

Let us bring
what we need
for the meeting:

Provisions. *(Provisions)*
Permission. *(Permission)*
Commanding. *(Commanding)*
Uniting. *(Uniting)*
Family. *(Family)*

Let us have
what we have
for the gathering

Civil. *(Civil)*
Ways. *(Ways)*
Services. *(Services)*
Respect. *(Respect)*
Management. *(Management)*
Kinds. *(Kinds)*
Goods. *(Goods)*
For all. *(All)*

Let us take
what we can
for the occasion:

Responsible.

Individual.

Sufficient.

Personal.

Securely.

Civil.

Substantial.

Accepted.

Given.

Authorized.

Let there be
Order.

Let us be
Wise.

This essay by Kwame Dawes illustrates the complexities of communication across race and the resentment and hatred that can result from lack of awareness of other people's perspectives. It also suggests some ways out of our racial conundrums.

❦ KWAME DAWES, *Diary*

. . . A southern writer had just done a successful reading from a new book on my university campus. My Division hosted a reception at which he began to speak of some of the sources of his fiction. I was the only black in the room, but there was nothing unusual about this in a school with only three black faculty members. He said that in his historical novels he wrote about family, about friends, about people he knew. Someone asked him whether people got upset when he wrote such awful things about them. He laughed and said that for the most part they were pleased because he really toned down the truth a lot—he had to make it more palatable. It was a great joke—his characters are hardly the stuff of decorous living. He offered an example of the kind of scandal-infested reality that was part of his history. It was his grandfather, he said, smiling, who on becoming sheriff, picked six black males at random from the gaol and lynched them. People laughed. I smiled. I was embarrassed for him, for his family, for his people, for his race. It didn't appear to bother too many people, this story. Yet, later that afternoon, he confided in two of my colleagues that he thought he had offended me; that by telling this story he had "lost a potential friend." They assured him that I was not so dismissive and that I understood the business of story-telling quite well. Still, they let me know that he was worried, so I wrote to him.

I explained that I was not offended but startled. I explained that I could not stop thinking about the families of those six men, I could not stop thinking of their grandchildren, people who are still alive today and, maybe, working in the same town as his family. I said I was fascinated by the story and impressed that he could tell it so candidly. I admitted that it horrified me and that I wanted to talk to him because I wanted to know more of these horror stories that clearly litter the Southern landscape. His reply was prompt. He said he had sensed fear in me, in the way I crossed my legs to protect my genitals, the way I turned my body away from him. It was, he said, the first time—despite having lived in the South all his life, despite having worked with blacks all his life, despite having written about racial issues all his writing life— that he really understood the fear that blacks felt in the face of racism.

I was confused. On the one hand, I was touched that he recognized that he was in some way implicated in the horror he described, both because he carried its memory in his soul, in his genes, and because he carried the story and was willing to repeat it—to keep it alive, regardless of his motives. But I was furious at the assumption that my reaction was one of fear. It did not occur to him that I may have been embarrassed for him; that I may have felt shame for him to be sitting there, in front of a black man, telling a story like that. It did not occur to him because he was not ashamed—and that bothered me. It bothered me that he thought I was afraid, but I had to understand what it was he assumed I was afraid of. Did he think I was afraid of him? Did he think I was reacting with a primordial fear, a genetic fear? I resented the fact that he assumed I was afraid and went on to speak about it, and I reacted by telling him that I did not grow up in the South with that legacy of fear, but in Ghana and Jamaica with a legacy of pride. I could only understand such fear as an admission of weakness, of helplessness, of shame—the shame of the oppressed and the abused.

Above all, I felt angry that he thought he had seen me standing there naked before him and that he could only grasp my reaction to his story in that light. It made sense, though, because the historical reality of the story, and its retelling as myth, were about the invocation of fear. He had learned that story not in a context of shame or regret, but as part of a mythic understanding of the dynamics of race. He understood it as a story about creating fear, and a cult of fear, that would stay in families for generations. So when he saw what he thought was fear in me, he was enacting a tragic habit that went back a long way, and I resented the fact that he was doing this. It left me naked, vulnerable, my genitals exposed, while he stood there fully clothed and watched my shame with some regret, but more amazement. And yet, he had told me all this as an expression of sadness, a way of saying that he had learnt something about the kind of fear that blacks felt. I wanted more. To be comfortable with him, I had to have more. Indeed, the difference between the two of us at that point was that he was well protected, completely free of any vulnerability—layered, clothed—while I stood naked. I did not like the arrangement.

It was at that point that a number of other things about race began to make sense to me. I understood, for instance, that Farrakhan was the way he was because of his need to stave off the shame of fear. Farrakhan decided long ago to wear clothes, layers and layers of them, and the rhetoric of aggression, of being on the offensive, is the form this clothing has taken. Admitting that one is a victim of racism is, for many blacks, an expression of profound shame. Many white people do not understand this. To say I have been a victim of racism leaves me vulnerable; it means that they have got me by the balls and are squeezing me and that the pain is so much I have to scream out. Admitting that I am a victim of racism amounts to standing naked before the world and saying I am helpless. The solution, at that point, is to put on clothes, or to change the arrangement and deploy an aggressive rhetoric that will strip the white person of what he or she is wearing. Farrakhan is a product of white racism, not a product of anything he has made of himself. White racism has left him with few alternatives but to assert his pride and put on clothes. Anything else will be laced with shame—the kind of shame that ate away at Martin Luther King in his private moments, the shame that haunts many black people struggling for equality through non-violence and reconciliation. There's no question about it, the "good blacks," the loving blacks, all of us, have to contend with that shame in our quietest moments.

Farrakhan's power is founded on a reaction to shame, a reaction to profound powerlessness. Farrakhan seems most threatening to whites because they suddenly feel uncomfortable with a black male fully garbed in the anger for which they know he has good reason. I am not denying the monstrousness of some of his statements, but nor will I deny what his existence says about white racism. The truth is that the instinct not to sit at a table with a white man and talk about reconciliation and peaceful coexistence is founded on a suspicion that the conversation will turn on what he has done to me and my people, on what his people think about me and my people, on why I am angry, on why I am ashamed—and that I will find myself naked. He, on the other hand, need not be naked in the same way, even if he admits he has been a racist, that he has always been afraid to give up power and allow himself to be vulnerable. And the chances are that he won't in any case. So I don't speak. He doesn't speak, and there is an impasse. Voilà, America.

I recently saw a video called *The Colour of Fear* directed by a Chinese American, Lee Munwah. Seven or eight American-born men of different races sat in a circle and talked about race. I watched as one of the two white men became the centre of the discussion. He did not buy the idea that whites had done anything to make minorities feel ashamed or used or oppressed. He was convinced that it was all in their heads. The others gave examples, told stories, got angry, cried, shouted, stood naked before him, and he remained quite calm, confident in his view that this was all their construction. It was the kind of talk I have heard again and again coming from whites. I began to regard the film as a failure. One of the two black men then spoke what I was feeling. "I feel like shit," he said. "I feel like going outside and running my head into a wall. I have made myself vulnerable in front of this guy, I have explained why I feel such shame in the face of racism, and he has turned it back on me, made it my problem—denied any culpability. I feel like shit." There was an eclectic, ugly, uncomfortable silence; Munwah kept the camera rolling.

That moment represented the basic dilemma of American racism. When white America insists on denying its racism—when "normal," right-thinking, decent whites insist on not confronting the source of their prejudices—blacks recognize quite quickly that talking about race will only embarrass them and leave them vulnerable. The blacks just won't speak, won't come to the table. They know what is going to happen already and they have no reason to expect the white man to allow himself to feel "like shit," to feel in any way like the victim who needs the forgiveness and tolerance of the black to continue living.

But things changed in the film. The white male slowly came around, he slowly faced his own fears, and then suddenly, in a flood of regret, he began to speak of his childhood, of a father who taught him racism, of a life spent denying the presence of racism for fear of the shame and responsibility he would feel if he admitted that he was part of a system that made so many people like shit. He wept. I waited to see the reaction of the other men. Incredibly (but given the history of how minorities have reacted to well-meaning, liberal whites in this country, understandably), they were willing to forgive him, to embrace him, to count this a moment of hope, of possibility. I had to ask myself if I would have done this? or would I have looked at him and said: "Yes, you need to cry some more, you need to cry for your father, for your grandfather, for your goddamned great grandfather, 'cause none of them ever cried to my father, to my grandfather, to my great grandfather!"

Two older white men watched the video after me. Like me, they were reviewing it to see if a recommendation that local legislatures be asked to watch it to raise their racial consciousness was a viable and useful one. One of the men, whom I expected to hate the video and dismiss it as just another "white bashing" exercise, reacted in a manner that baffled and humbled me. He began to talk about his childhood, to second-guess his assumptions about what minorities felt. "Thought-provoking, very thought-provoking," he said at the end. It is probably a reflection of the depth of my pessimism about Southern racism that I saw this as a miracle—as a genuine triumph of hope, as evidence that perhaps things could get better.

Finally, Si Kahn, a modern songwriter and community leader, and Frederick Douglass, abolitionist and former slave, pose the most practical and profound of moral questions: Which side are you on? For Si Kahn, the ultimate truth is in the actions we take; Douglass goes farther in reminding us that action alone is not enough—equally key are the questions: On whose behalf and for what purpose?

❦ SI KAHN, *What You Do with What You've Got*

You must know someone like him, he was tall & strong & lean,
Body like a greyhound, mind so sharp and keen
But his heart just a laurel grew twisted on itself,
'Til almost everything he did brought pain to someone.

It's not just what you're born with, it's what you choose
    to bear.
It's not how large your share is, but how much you can
    share.
It's not the fights you dream of, but those you really
    fought.
It's not just what you're given, but what you do with
    what you've got.

For what's the use of two strong legs if you only run away
What good is the finest voice if you've nothing good to say.
What good are strength & muscles if you only push & shove,
What's the use of two good ears if you can't hear those you
    love.

Between those who those use their neighbors & those who use a
    cane
Between those in constant power & those in constant pain
Between those who run to evil &

Those who cannot run
Tell me which ones are the cripples & which ones touch the
    sun.

It's not just what you're born with, it's what you choose
    to bear.
It's not how large your share is, but how much you can
    share.
It's not the fights you dream of, but those you really
    fought.
It's not just what you're given, but what you do with
    what you've got.

❦ FREDERICK DOUGLASS, *Life and Times of Frederick Douglass*

I have thus far told my story without copious quotations from my letters, speeches, or other writings, and shall not depart from this rule in what remains to be told, except to insert here my speech, delivered at Arlington, near the monument to the "Unknown Loyal Dead," on Decoration Day, 1871. It was delivered under impressive circumstances, in presence of President Grant, his Cabinet, and a great multitude of distinguished people, and expresses, as I think, the true view which should be taken of the great conflict between slavery and freedom to which it refers.

"Friends and Fellow Citizens: Tarry here for a moment. My words shall be few and simple. The solemn rites of this hour and place call for no lengthened speech. There is, in the very air of this resting ground of the unknown dead a silent, subtle and all-pervading eloquence, far more touching, impressive, and thrilling than living lips have ever uttered. Into the measureless depths of every loyal soul it is now whispering lessons of all that is precious, priceless, holiest, and most enduring in human existence.

"Dark and sad will be the hour to this nation when it forgets to pay

grateful homage to its greatest benefactors. The offering we bring today is due alike to the patriot soldiers dead and their noble comrades
who still live; for, whether living or dead, whether in time or eternity,
the loyal soldiers who imperiled all for country and freedom are one
and inseparable.

"Those unknown heroes whose whitened bones have been piously
gathered here, and whose green graves we now strew with sweet and
beautiful flowers, choice emblems alike of pure hearts and brave spirits,
reached, in their glorious career that last highest point of nobleness
beyond which human power cannot go. They died for their country.

"No loftier tribute can be paid to the most illustrious of all the
benefactors of mankind than we pay to these unrecognized soldiers
when we write above their graves this shining epitaph.

"When the dark and vengeful spirit of slavery, always ambitious,
preferring to rule in hell than to serve in heaven, fired the Southern
heart and stirred all the malign elements of discord, when our great
Republic, the hope of freedom and self-government throughout the
world, had reached the point of supreme peril, when the Union of these
States was torn and rent asunder at the center, and the armies of a
gigantic rebellion came forth with broad blades and bloody hands to
destroy the very foundation of American society, the unknown braves
who flung themselves into the yawning chasm, where cannon roared
and bullets whistled, fought and fell. They died for their country.

"We are sometimes asked, in the name of patriotism, to forget
the merits of this fearful struggle, and to remember with equal admiration those who struck at the nation's life and those who struck to
save it, those who fought for slavery and those who fought for liberty
and justice.

"I am no minister of malice. I would not strike the fallen. I would
not repel the repentant; but may my 'right hand forget her cunning and
my tongue cleave to the roof of my mouth,' if I forget the difference
between the parties to that terrible, protracted, and bloody conflict.

"If we ought to forget a war which has filled our land with widows
and orphans; which has made stumps of men of the very flower of our
youth; which has sent them on the journey of life armless, legless,
maimed and mutilated; which has piled up a debt heavier than a moun-

tain of gold, swept uncounted thousands of men into bloody graves and planted agony at a million hearthstones—I say, if this war is to be forgotten, I ask, in the name of all things sacred, what shall men remember?

"The essence and significance of our devotions here to-day are not to be found in the fact that the men whose remains fill these graves were brave in battle. If we met simply to show our sense of bravery, we should find enough on both sides to kindle admiration. In the raging storm of fire and blood, in the fierce torrent of shot and shell, of sword and bayonet, whether on foot or on horse, unflinching courage marked the rebel not less than the loyal soldier.

"But we are not here to applaud manly courage, save as it has been displayed in a noble cause. We must never forget that victory to the rebellion meant death to the republic. We must never forget that the loyal soldiers who rest beneath this sod flung themselves between the nation and the nation's destroyers. If to-day we have a country not boiling in an agony of blood, like France, if now we have a united country, no longer cursed by the hell-black system of human bondage, if the American name is no longer a by-word and a hissing to a mocking earth, if the star-spangled banner floats only over free American citizens in every quarter of the land, and our country has before it a long and glorious career of justice, liberty, and civilization, we are indebted to the unselfish devotion of the noble army who rest in honored graves all around us."

INDEX

Fleur Adcock, "Epitaph" and "Outwood" from *The Incident Book,* © Oxford University Press, 1986.

Anna Akhamatova, "Requiem" and "I Have Learned How Faces Fall to Bone" from her poem "Requiem," translated by Stanley Kunitz and Max Hayward. Reprinted by permission of Stanley Kunitz.

Yehuda Amichai, "In-Between" from *Even a Fist Was Once an Open Palm with Fingers,* selected and translated by Barbara and Benjamin Harshav. Copyright © 1991 Yehuda Amichai. English-language translation copyright © 1991 HarperCollins Publishers, Inc. "The Aching Bones of Lovers" from TIME, copyright © 1979 by Yehuda Amichai. Reprinted by permission of HarperCollins Publishers, Inc.

Maya Angelou, "Praise Poem" from *The Pulse of the Morning,* copyright © Random House, Inc. 1993, reprinted by permission of Random House, Inc.

W. H. Auden, "Funeral Blues" from "Twelve Songs," no. XXXIV from *Stop All Clocks: Poems 1931–1936,* copyright © Random House, Inc.

James Baldwin, from *Tell Me How Long the Train's Been Gone,* copyright © 1968 by James Baldwin. Copyright renewed. Reprinted by permission of the James Baldwin Estate.

David Bergman, "Urban Renewal, Baltimore," copyright © David Bergman. First published in *Cracking the Code.* Published by permission of the author.

Wendell Berry, "The Recognition" from *The Country of Marriage,* copyright © 1971 by Wendell Berry. Reprinted by permission of Harcourt Brace & Company.

Frank Bidart, "The Sacrifice" from *The Sacrifice,* copyright © 1983 by Frank Bidart. Reprinted by permission of the publisher.

Lucian Blaga, "Psalm" from *At the Court of Yearning: Selected Poems by Lucian Blaga,* translated by Andrei Codrescu, Ohio State University Press, 1988. Reprinted with the permission of Andrei Codrescu.

Ernst Bloch, from *The Principle of Hope,* reprinted by permission of MIT Press, 1986.

Robert Bolt, from *A Man for All Seasons,* copyright © 1960, 1962 by Robert Bolt. Reprinted by permission of Random House, Inc.

Kevin Bowen, "Playing Basketball with the Vietcong" from *Playing Basketball with the Vietcong,* copyright © 1994 by Kevin Bowen. Published by Curbstone Press. Distributed by Consortium.

Bertolt Brecht, "About the Way to Construct Enduring Works" from *Brecht's Poems 1913–1956,* Methuen Inc., 1987.

Young and Dana Habova. Field Translation Series 16, © 1990. Reprinted by permission of Oberlin College Press.

bell hooks, *Bone Black, Memories of Girlhood*, copyright © 1996 by Gloria Watkins. Reprinted by permission of Henry Holt & Co., Inc.

Myles Horton, with Judith Kohl and Herbert Kohl, *The Long Haul: An Autobiography*, Simon & Schuster, 1990. Copyright © Judith Kohl, Herbert Kohl, and the Estate of Myles Horton. Reprinted by permission of the authors.

Johann Huizinga, from *Homo Ludens*, Beacon Press, © 1955 reprinted by permission of the publisher.

Erica Hunt, from *Correspondance Theory*, Roof Books/Segue Foundation. Copyright © Erica Hunt, 1993.

Lawson Fusao Inada, "Instructions to All Persons" from *Legends from Camp*, Coffee House Press, 1993. Used by permission of the publisher. Copyright © 1993 by Lawson Fusao Inada.

Edmond Jabès, from *The Book of Resemblances*, © 1990 by Wesleyan University Press by permission of University Press of New England, 1976. University Press of New England. Translation by Rosemarie Waldrop, 1990.

Louis Jenkins, "Green Tomato" from *All Tangled up with the Living*, poems by Louis Jenkins, The Nineties Press, St. Paul, Minn., © 1991 by Louis Jenkins.

Charles Johnson, reprinted with permission of Scribners, a Division of Simon & Schuster, from *The Middle Passage*, © 1990 by Charles Johnson.

Hettie Jones, "Lottie and Oscar" originally appeared in Hanging Loose Press, reprinted by permission of the author.

June Jordan, "1977: Poem for Mrs. Fannie Lou Hamer" from *Naming Our Destiny*, copyright © 1989, used by permission of the publisher, Thunder's Mouth Press.

C. G. Jung, from *Psychological Types*, Bollingen Series XX, *Collected Works of C.G. Jung*, Vol. 6, 1971. Reprinted by permission of Princeton University Press.

Franz Kafka, "Before the Law" from *The Complete Stories*, Schocken, 1971.

Si Kahn, "What You Do with What You've Got," © Si Kahn, reprinted by permission of the author.

Bob Kaufman, "I Have Folded My Sorrows" from *Solitudes Crowded with Loneliness*, copyright © 1965 by Bob Kaufman. Reprinted by permission of New Directions Publishing Corp.

Herbert Kohl, "The Story of Rosa Parks and the Montgomery Bus Boycott," © Herbert Kohl, 1996.

Amitava Kumar, "Primary Lessons in Political Economy" from *Premonitions: The Kaya Anthology of New Asian North American Poetry*, edited by Walter K. Lew (New York: Kaya Production, 1995). Reprinted by permission of the author.

Vol. 17, No. 4. Copyright © by Quincy Troupe. Reprinted by permission of the author.

Aida Tsunao, "Wild Duck" from *Like Underground Water*, edited and translated by Edward Lueders and Naoshi Koriyama, © 1995. Reprinted by permission of Copper Canyon Press, Post Office Box 271, Port Townsend, Wash., 98368.

Georgiana Valoyce-Sanchez, "The Eye of the Flute" from *The Sound of Rattles and Clappers*, edited by Greg Sarris, copyright © 1994, The University of Arizona Press.

Gerald Vizenor, from *Interior Landscapes: Autobiographical Myths and Metaphors*, University of Minnesota Press, 1990. Reprinted by permission of the author.

Kurt Vonnegut, from *Jailbird*, copyright © 1979 by Kurt Vonnegut. Used by permission of Delacorte Press, a division of Bantam Doubleday Dell Publishing Group, Inc.

Derek Walcott, from *Another Life*, copyright © 1972, 1973 by Derek Walcott. Reprinted by permission of Farrar, Straus & Giroux, Inc.

William Wantling, "Rune for the Disenchanted," © William Wantling, from *Small Zone*, Nov. 1984.

Simone Weil, "Draft for a Statement of Human Obligations, Profession of Faith" from *Selected Essays 1934–1943*, Oxford University Press, 1962. Reprinted by permission of Peters Fraser and Dunlop Group Ltd. on behalf of the author.

Nathanael West, from *Miss Lonelyhearts & The Day of the Locust*, copyright © 1939 by Estate of Nathanael West. Reprinted by permission of New Directions Publishing Corp.

John Edgar Wideman, copyright © 1994 by John Edgar Wideman. Originally appeared in *The New Yorker* and reprinted by permission of The Wylie Agency, Inc.

William Carlos Williams, "The Yellow Flower" from *Collected Poems: 1909–1939*, Volume I. Copyright © 1938 by New Directions Publishing Corp. Reprinted by permission of New Directions Publishing Corp. "Descent" from *Collected Poems 1939–1962*, Volume II. Copyright © 1951 by William Carlos Williams. Reprinted by permission of New Directions Publishing Corp.

Nellie Wong, "Picnic" from *Dreams in Harrison Railroad Park*, Kelsey Street Press, 1977. Reprinted by permission of the publisher. Copyright © Nellie Wong.

Jay Wright, "Benjamin Banneker Sends His *Almanac* to Thomas Jefferson" from *Selected Poems of Jay Wright*, Princeton University Press, copyright 1987 by Jay Wright. Reprinted by permission of the author.

W. B. Yeats, "Meditations in Time of Civil War" Part VI reprinted with the